RUSSIAN
VOCABULARY

ENGLISH-RUSSIAN

The most useful words
To expand your lexicon and sharpen
your language skills

9000 words

Russian vocabulary for English speakers - 9000 words
By Andrey Taranov

T&P Books vocabularies are intended for helping you learn, memorize, and revise foreign words. The dictionary is divided into themes, covering all major spheres of everyday activities, business, science, culture, etc.

The process of learning words using T&P Books' theme-based dictionaries gives you the following advantages:

- Correctly grouped source information predetermines success at subsequent stages of word memorization
- Availability of words derived from the same root allowing memorization of word units (rather than separate words)
- Small units of words facilitate the process of establishing associative links needed for consolidation of vocabulary
- Level of language knowledge can be estimated by the number of learned words

T&P Books Publishing
www.tpbooks.com

ISBN: 978-1-78071-281-9

This book is also available in E-book formats.
Please visit www.tpbooks.com or the major online bookstores.

RUSSIAN VOCABULARY
for English speakers

T&P Books vocabularies are intended to help you learn, memorize, and review foreign words. The vocabulary contains over 9000 commonly used words arranged thematically.

- Vocabulary contains the most commonly used words
- Recommended as an addition to any language course
- Meets the needs of beginners and advanced learners of foreign languages
- Convenient for daily use, revision sessions, and self-testing activities
- Allows you to assess your vocabulary

Special features of the vocabulary

- Words are organized according to their meaning, not alphabetically
- Words are presented in three columns to facilitate the reviewing and self-testing processes
- Words in groups are divided into small blocks to facilitate the learning process
- The vocabulary offers a convenient and simple transcription of each foreign word

The vocabulary has 256 topics including:

Basic Concepts, Numbers, Colors, Months, Seasons, Units of Measurement, Clothing & Accessories, Food & Nutrition, Restaurant, Family Members, Relatives, Character, Feelings, Emotions, Diseases, City, Town, Sightseeing, Shopping, Money, House, Home, Office, Working in the Office, Import & Export, Marketing, Job Search, Sports, Education, Computer, Internet, Tools, Nature, Countries, Nationalities and more ...

T&P BOOKS' THEME-BASED DICTIONARIES

The Correct System for Memorizing Foreign Words

Acquiring vocabulary is one of the most important elements of learning a foreign language, because words allow us to express our thoughts, ask questions, and provide answers. An inadequate vocabulary can impede communication with a foreigner and make it difficult to understand a book or movie well.

The pace of activity in all spheres of modern life, including the learning of modern languages, has increased. Today, we need to memorize large amounts of information (grammar rules, foreign words, etc.) within a short period. However, this does not need to be difficult. All you need to do is to choose the right training materials, learn a few special techniques, and develop your individual training system.

Having a system is critical to the process of language learning. Many people fail to succeed in this regard; they cannot master a foreign language because they fail to follow a system comprised of selecting materials, organizing lessons, arranging new words to be learned, and so on. The lack of a system causes confusion and eventually, lowers self-confidence.

T&P Books' theme-based dictionaries can be included in the list of elements needed for creating an effective system for learning foreign words. These dictionaries were specially developed for learning purposes and are meant to help students effectively memorize words and expand their vocabulary.

Generally speaking, the process of learning words consists of three main elements:

- Reception (creation or acquisition) of a training material, such as a word list
- Work aimed at memorizing new words
- Work aimed at reviewing the learned words, such as self-testing

All three elements are equally important since they determine the quality of work and the final result. All three processes require certain skills and a well-thought-out approach.

New words are often encountered quite randomly when learning a foreign language and it may be difficult to include them all in a unified list. As a result, these words remain written on scraps of paper, in book margins, textbooks, and so on. In order to systematize such words, we have to create and continually update a "book of new words." A paper notebook, a netbook, or a tablet PC can be used for these purposes.

This "book of new words" will be your personal, unique list of words. However, it will only contain the words that you came across during the learning process. For example, you might have written down the words "Sunday," "Tuesday," and "Friday." However, there are additional words for days of the week, for example, "Saturday," that are missing, and your list of words would be incomplete. Using a theme dictionary, in addition to the "book of new words," is a reasonable solution to this problem.

The theme-based dictionary may serve as the basis for expanding your vocabulary.

It will be your big "book of new words" containing the most frequently used words of a foreign language already included. There are quite a few theme-based dictionaries available, and you should ensure that you make the right choice in order to get the maximum benefit from your purchase.

Therefore, we suggest using theme-based dictionaries from T&P Books Publishing as an aid to learning foreign words. Our books are specially developed for effective use in the sphere of vocabulary systematization, expansion and review.

Theme-based dictionaries are not a magical solution to learning new words. However, they can serve as your main database to aid foreign-language acquisition. Apart from theme dictionaries, you can have copybooks for writing down new words, flash cards, glossaries for various texts, as well as other resources; however, a good theme dictionary will always remain your primary collection of words.

T&P Books' theme-based dictionaries are specialty books that contain the most frequently used words in a language.

The main characteristic of such dictionaries is the division of words into themes. For example, the *City* theme contains the words "street," "crossroads," "square," "fountain," and so on. The *Talking* theme might contain words like "to talk," "to ask," "question," and "answer".

All the words in a theme are divided into smaller units, each comprising 3–5 words. Such an arrangement improves the perception of words and makes the learning process less tiresome. Each unit contains a selection of words with similar meanings or identical roots. This allows you to learn words in small groups and establish other associative links that have a positive effect on memorization.

The words on each page are placed in three columns: a word in your native language, its translation, and its transcription. Such positioning allows for the use of techniques for effective memorization. After closing the translation column, you can flip through and review foreign words, and vice versa. "This is an easy and convenient method of review – one that we recommend you do often."

Our theme-based dictionaries contain transcriptions for all the foreign words. Unfortunately, none of the existing transcriptions are able to convey the exact nuances of foreign pronunciation. That is why we recommend using the transcriptions only as a supplementary learning aid. Correct pronunciation can only be acquired with the help of sound. Therefore our collection includes audio theme-based dictionaries.

The process of learning words using T&P Books' theme-based dictionaries gives you the following advantages:

- You have correctly grouped source information, which predetermines your success at subsequent stages of word memorization

- Availability of words derived from the same root (lazy, lazily, lazybones), allowing you to memorize word units instead of separate words

- Small units of words facilitate the process of establishing associative links needed for consolidation of vocabulary

- You can estimate the number of learned words and hence your level of language knowledge

- The dictionary allows for the creation of an effective and high-quality revision process

- You can revise certain themes several times, modifying the revision methods and techniques

- Audio versions of the dictionaries help you to work out the pronunciation of words and develop your skills of auditory word perception

The T&P Books' theme-based dictionaries are offered in several variants differing in the number of words: 1.500, 3.000, 5.000, 7.000, and 9.000 words. There are also dictionaries containing 15,000 words for some language combinations. Your choice of dictionary will depend on your knowledge level and goals.

We sincerely believe that our dictionaries will become your trusty assistant in learning foreign languages and will allow you to easily acquire the necessary vocabulary.

TABLE OF CONTENTS

PRONUNCIATION GUIDE

Letter	Russian sample	T&P phonetics alphabet	English sample
А, а	трава	[ɑ], [a]	bath, to pass
Е, е	перерыв	[e]	elm, medal
Ё, ё	ёлка	[jo:], [ɜ:]	yourself, girl
И, и	филин	[i], [i:]	feet, Peter
О, о	корова	[o], [o:]	floor, doctor
У, у	Тулуза	[u], [u:]	book, shoe
Э, э	эволюция	[ɛ]	man, bad
Ю, ю	трюм	[ju:], [ju]	cued, cute
Я, я	яблоко	[ja:], [æ:]	royal
Б, б	баобаб	[b]	baby, book
В, в	врач, вино	[v]	very, river
Г, г	глагол	[g]	game, gold
Д, д	дом, труд	[d]	day, doctor
Ж, ж	живот	[ʒ]	forge, pleasure
З, з	зоопарк	[z]	zebra, please
Й, й	йога	[j]	yes, New York
ой	стройка	[ɔi]	oil, boy, point
ай	край	[aj]	time, white
К, к	кино, сок	[k]	clock, kiss
Л, л	лопата	[l]	lace, people
М, м	март, сом	[m]	magic, milk
Н, н	небо	[n]	name, normal
П, п	папа	[p]	pencil, private
Р, р	урок, робот	[r]	rice, radio
С, с	собака	[s]	city, boss
Т, т	ток, стая	[t]	tourist, trip
Ф, ф	фарфор	[f]	face, food
Х, х	хобот, страх	[h]	home, have
Ц, ц	цапля	[ts]	cats, tsetse fly
Ч, ч	чемодан	[ʧ]	church, French
Ш, ш	шум, шашки	[ʃ]	machine, shark
Щ, щ	щенок	[ɕ]	sheep, shop
Ы, ы	рыба	[ɪ]	big, America
Ь, ь	дверь	[ʲ]	soft sign - no sound

Letter	Russian sample	T&P phonetics alphabet	English sample
нь	конь	[ɲ]	canyon, new
ль	соль	[ʎ]	daily, million
ть	статья	soft [t]	tune, student
Ъ, ъ	подъезд	[ˈ]	hard sign - no sound

ABBREVIATIONS
used in the vocabulary

ab.	-	about
adj	-	adjectif
adv	-	adverb
attr	-	attributive noun
e.g.	-	for example
etc.	-	et cetera
fem.	-	feminine
masc.	-	masculine
noun	-	noun
pl	-	plural
pron.	-	pronoun
sb	-	somebody
sing.	-	singular
sth	-	something
vi	-	intransitive verb
vi, vt	-	intransitive, transitive verb
vt	-	transitive verb
m	-	masculine
m pl	-	masculine plural
f	-	feminine
f pl	-	feminine plural
n	-	neuter
n pl	-	neuter plural
m, f	-	masculine, feminine

BASIC CONCEPTS

Basic concepts. Part 1

1. Pronouns

I, me	я	[ja]
you	ты	[tı]
he	он	[ɔn]
she	она	[a'na]
it	оно	[a'nɔ]
we	мы	[mı]
you	вы	[vı]
they	они	[a'ni]

2. Greetings. Salutations. Farewells

Hello! (familiar)	Здравствуй!	['zdrafstvuj]
Hello! (formal)	Здравствуйте!	['zdrafstvujte]
Good morning!	Доброе утро!	['dɔbrae 'utra]
Good afternoon!	Добрый день!	['dɔbrıj deɲ]
Good evening!	Добрый вечер!	['dɔbrıj 'wetʃer]
to say hello	здороваться	[zda'rovatse]
Hi! (hello)	Привет!	[pri'wet]
greeting (noun)	привет (m)	[pri'wet]
to greet (vt)	приветствовать	[pri'wetstvavat']
How are you?	Как дела?	[kak de'la]
What's new?	Что нового?	[ʃta 'novava]
Bye-Bye! Goodbye!	До свидания!	[da swi'danija]
See you soon!	До скорой встречи!	[da 'skɔraj 'fstretʃi]
Farewell! (to a friend)	Прощай!	[pra'ɕaj]
Farewell (formal)	Прощайте!	[pra'ɕajte]
to say goodbye	прощаться	[pra'ɕatse]
So long!	Пока!	[pa'ka]
Thank you!	Спасибо!	[spa'siba]
Thank you very much!	Большое спасибо!	[baʌ'ʃoe spa'siba]
You're welcome	Пожалуйста.	[pa'ʒalujste]
Don't mention it!	Не стоит благодарности.	[ne 'stɔit blagadarnasti]

It was nothing	Не за что.	[ˈne za ʃtə]
Excuse me! (familiar)	Извини!	[izwiˈni]
Excuse me! (formal)	Извините!	[izwiˈnite]
to excuse (forgive)	извинять	[izwiˈɲatʲ]

to apologize (vi)	извиняться	[izwiˈɲatsə]
My apologies	Мои извинения	[maˈi izwiˈneniə]
I'm sorry!	Простите!	[prasˈtite]
to forgive (vt)	прощать	[praˈɕatʲ]
It's OK	Ничего страшного	[nitʃiˈvo ˈstraʃnavə]

| please (adv) | пожалуйста | [paˈʒalujstə] |
| Don't forget! | Не забудьте! | [ne zaˈbutʲte] |

Certainly!	Конечно!	[kaˈneʃna]
Of course not!	Конечно нет!	[kaˈneʃna ˈnet]
OK! (I agree)	Согласен!	[sagˈlasen]
That's enough!	Хватит!	[ˈhvatit]

3. How to address

Excuse me!	Извините!	[izwiˈnite]
Mister, Sir	Господин!	[gaspaˈdin]
Ma'am	Госпожа!	[gaspaˈʒa]
Miss	Девушка!	[ˈdevuʃka]
Young man	Молодой человек!	[malaˈdoj tʃilaˈwek]
Young man (little boy)	Мальчик!	[ˈmaʎtʃik]
Miss (little girl)	Девочка!	[ˈdevatʃka]

4. Cardinal numbers. Part 1

0 zero	ноль	[nɔʎ]
1 one	один	[aˈdin]
2 two	два	[dvə]
3 three	три	[tri]
4 four	четыре	[tʃiˈtıre]

5 five	пять	[pʲatʲ]
6 six	шесть	[ʃestʲ]
7 seven	семь	[semʲ]
8 eight	восемь	[ˈvɔsemʲ]
9 nine	девять	[ˈdewitʲ]

10 ten	десять	[ˈdesitʲ]
11 eleven	одиннадцать	[aˈdinatsatʲ]
12 twelve	двенадцать	[dwiˈnatsatʲ]
13 thirteen	тринадцать	[triˈnatsatʲ]
14 fourteen	четырнадцать	[tʃiˈtırnatsatʲ]

15 fifteen	**пятнадцать**	[pit'natsatʲ]
16 sixteen	**шестнадцать**	[ʃɛs'natsatʲ]
17 seventeen	**семнадцать**	[sim'natsatʲ]
18 eighteen	**восемнадцать**	[vasem'natsatʲ]
19 nineteen	**девятнадцать**	[diwit'natsatʲ]
20 twenty	**двадцать**	['dvatsatʲ]
21 twenty-one	**двадцать один**	['dvatsatʲ a'din]
22 twenty-two	**двадцать два**	['dvatsatʲ 'dva]
23 twenty-three	**двадцать три**	['dvatsatʲ 'tri]
30 thirty	**тридцать**	['tritsatʲ]
31 thirty-one	**тридцать один**	['tritsatʲ a'din]
32 thirty-two	**тридцать два**	['tritsatʲ 'dva]
33 thirty-three	**тридцать три**	['tritsatʲ 'tri]
40 forty	**сорок**	['sɔrak]
41 forty-one	**сорок один**	['sɔrak a'din]
42 forty-two	**сорок два**	['sɔrak 'dva]
43 forty-three	**сорок три**	['sɔrak 'tri]
50 fifty	**пятьдесят**	[pitʲdi'sʲat]
51 fifty-one	**пятьдесят один**	[pitʲdi'sʲat a'din]
52 fifty-two	**пятьдесят два**	[pitʲdi'sʲat 'dva]
53 fifty-three	**пятьдесят три**	[pitʲdi'sʲat 'tri]
60 sixty	**шестьдесят**	[ʃistʲdi'sʲat]
61 sixty-one	**шестьдесят один**	[ʃestʲdi'sʲat a'din]
62 sixty-two	**шестьдесят два**	[ʃestʲdi'sʲat 'dva]
63 sixty-three	**шестьдесят три**	[ʃestʲdi'sʲat 'tri]
70 seventy	**семьдесят**	['semʲdisit]
71 seventy-one	**семьдесят один**	['semʲdisit a'din]
72 seventy-two	**семьдесят два**	['semʲdisit 'dva]
73 seventy-three	**семьдесят три**	['semʲdisit 'tri]
80 eighty	**восемьдесят**	['vɔsemʲdisit]
81 eighty-one	**восемьдесят один**	['vɔsemʲdisit a'din]
82 eighty-two	**восемьдесят два**	['vɔsemʲdisit 'dva]
83 eighty-three	**восемьдесят три**	['vɔsemʲdisit 'tri]
90 ninety	**девяносто**	[diwi'nɔstə]
91 ninety-one	**девяносто один**	[diwi'nɔsta a'din]
92 ninety-two	**девяносто два**	[diwi'nɔsta 'dva]
93 ninety-three	**девяносто три**	[diwi'nɔsta 'tri]

5. Cardinal numbers. Part 2

100 one hundred	**сто**	[stɔ]
200 two hundred	**двести**	['dwesti]

300 three hundred	триста	['tristə]
400 four hundred	четыреста	[tʃi'tɪrestə]
500 five hundred	пятьсот	[pi'tsɔt]

600 six hundred	шестьсот	[ʃɛs'sɔt]
700 seven hundred	семьсот	[simʲ'sɔt]
800 eight hundred	восемьсот	[vasemʲ'sɔt]
900 nine hundred	девятьсот	[diwi'tsɔt]

1000 one thousand	тысяча	['tɪsitʃə]
2000 two thousand	две тысячи	[dwe 'tɪsitʃi]
3000 three thousand	три тысячи	[tri 'tɪsitʃi]
10000 ten thousand	десять тысяч	['desitʲ 'tɪsitʃ]
one hundred thousand	сто тысяч	[stɔ 'tɪsitʃ]
million	миллион (m)	[mili'ɔn]
billion	миллиард (m)	[mili'art]

6. Ordinal numbers

first	первый	['pervɪj]
second	второй	[fta'rɔj]
third	третий	['tretij]
fourth	четвёртый	[tʃit'wɜrtɪj]
fifth	пятый	['pʲatɪj]

sixth	шестой	[ʃɛs'tɔj]
seventh	седьмой	[sidʲ'mɔj]
eighth	восьмой	[vasʲ'mɔj]
ninth	девятый	[di'vʲatɪj]
tenth	десятый	[di'sʲatɪj]

7. Numbers. Fractions

fraction	дробь (f)	[drɔpʲ]
one half	одна вторая	[ad'na fta'raja]
one third	одна третья	[ad'na 'tretja]
one quarter	одна четвертая	[ad'na tʃet'wɜrtaja]
one eighth	одна восьмая	[ad'na vasʲ'maja]
one tenth	одна десятая	[ad'na de'sʲataja]
two thirds	две третьих	[dwe 'tretʲih]
three quarters	три четвёртых	[tri tʃet'wɜrtɪh]

8. Numbers. Basic operations

| subtraction | вычитание (n) | [vɪtʃi'tanie] |
| to subtract (vi, vt) | вычитать | [vɪtʃi'tatʲ] |

| division | деление (n) | [di'lenie] |
| to divide (vt) | делить | [di'lit'] |

addition	сложение (n)	[sla'ʒenie]
to add up (vt)	сложить	[sla'ʒit']
to add (vi)	прибавлять	[pribav'ʎat']
multiplication	умножение (n)	[umna'ʒenie]
to multiply (vi, vt)	умножать	[umna'ʒat']

9. Numbers. Miscellaneous

digit, figure	цифра (f)	['tsifrə]
number	число (n)	[tʃis'lɔ]
numeral	числительное (n)	[tʃis'liteʎnae]
minus	минус (m)	['minʊs]
plus	плюс (m)	[plys]
formula	формула (f)	['fɔrmʊlə]

calculation	вычисление (n)	[vɪtʃis'lɛnie]
to count (vi, vt)	считать	[ɕi'tat']
to count up	подсчитывать	[pa'tɕitivat']
to compare (vt)	сравнивать	['sravnivat']

How much? How many?	Сколько?	['skɔʎkə]
sum, total	сумма (f)	['sʊmmə]
result	результат (m)	[rizuʎ'tat]
remainder	остаток (m)	[as'tatak]

a few …	несколько	['neskaʎkə]
the rest	остальное (n)	[astaʎ'nɔe]
one and a half	полтора	[palta'ra]
dozen	дюжина (f)	['dyʒinə]

in half	пополам	[papa'lam]
equally (evenly)	поровну	['pɔravnʊ]
half	половина (f)	[pala'winə]
time (instance)	раз (m)	[ras]

10. The most important verbs. Part 1

to advise (vt)	советовать	[sa'wetavat']
to agree (say yes)	соглашаться	[sagla'ʃʌtsə]
to answer (vi, vt)	отвечать	[atwe'tʃat']
to apologize (vi)	извиняться	[izwi'ɲatsə]
to arrive (vi)	приезжать	[prii'zat']

| to ask (~ sb to do sth) | просить | [pra'sit'] |
| to ask (e.g., ~ oneself) | спрашивать | ['spraʃivat'] |

to be (e.g., ~ a teacher)	**быть**	[bɨtʲ]
to be afraid	**бояться**	[baˈjatsə]
to be hungry	**хотеть есть**	[haˈtetʲ ˈestʲ]
to be interested in …	**интересоваться**	[intirisaˈvatsə]
to be necessary	**требоваться**	[ˈtrebavatsə]
to be surprised	**удивляться**	[udivˈʎatsə]
to be thirsty	**хотеть пить**	[haˈtetʲ ˈpitʲ]
to begin (vi, vt)	**начинать**	[natʃiˈnatʲ]
to belong to …	**принадлежать …**	[prinadleˈʒatʲ]
to boast (vi)	**хвастаться**	[ˈhvastatsə]
to break (split into pieces)	**ломать**	[laˈmatʲ]
to call (for help)	**звать**	[zvatʲ]
can (modal verb)	**мочь**	[mɔtʃ]
to catch (vt)	**ловить**	[laˈwitʲ]
to change (vt)	**изменить**	[izmeˈnitʲ]
to choose (select)	**выбирать**	[vɨbiˈratʲ]
to come down	**спускаться**	[spusˈkatsə]
to come in (enter)	**входить**	[fhaˈditʲ]
to compare (vt)	**сравнивать**	[ˈsravnivatʲ]
to complain (vi, vt)	**жаловаться**	[ˈʒalavatsə]
to continue (vi, vt)	**продолжать**	[pradaˈlʒatʲ]
to control (vt)	**контролировать**	[kantraˈliravatʲ]
to cook (dinner)	**готовить**	[gaˈtowitʲ]
to cost (vt)	**стоить**	[ˈstɔitʲ]
to count (add up)	**считать**	[ɕiˈtatʲ]
to count on …	**рассчитывать на …**	[raˈɕitɪvatʲ na]
to create (vt)	**создать**	[sazˈdatʲ]
to cry (weep)	**плакать**	[ˈplakatʲ]

11. The most important verbs. Part 2

to deceive (vi, vt)	**обманывать**	[abˈmanɪvatʲ]
to decorate (tree, street)	**украшать**	[ukraˈʃʌtʲ]
to defend (a country etc.)	**защищать**	[zaɕiˈɕatʲ]
to demand (request firmly)	**требовать**	[ˈtrebavatʲ]
to dig (vi, vt)	**рыть**	[rɪtʲ]
to direct (supervise)	**руководить**	[rʊkavaˈditʲ]
to discuss (talk about)	**обсуждать**	[apsʊʒˈdatʲ]
to do (vt)	**делать**	[ˈdelatʲ]
to doubt (have doubts)	**сомневаться**	[samneˈvatsə]
to drop (let fall)	**ронять**	[raˈɲatʲ]
to excuse (forgive)	**извинять**	[izwiˈɲatʲ]
to exist (vi)	**существовать**	[sʊɕestvaˈvatʲ]

to expect (foresee)	предвидеть	[prid'widetⁱ]
to explain (vi, vt)	объяснять	[abʰes'ɲatⁱ]
to fall (vi)	падать	['padatⁱ]
to find (vt)	находить	[naha'ditⁱ]
to finish (vt)	заканчивать	[za'kantʃivatⁱ]
to fly (vi)	лететь	[li'tetⁱ]
to follow … (come after)	следовать за …	['sledavatⁱ za]
to forget (vi, vt)	забывать	[zabı'vatⁱ]
to forgive (vt)	прощать	[pra'ɕatⁱ]
to give (vt)	давать	[da'vatⁱ]
to go (to walk)	идти	[it'ti]
to go for a swim	купаться	[kʊ'patsə]
to go out	выходить	[vıha'ditⁱ]
to guess right	отгадать	[atga'datⁱ]
to have (vt)	иметь	[i'metⁱ]
to have breakfast	завтракать	['zaftrakatⁱ]
to have dinner	ужинать	['uʒınatⁱ]
to have lunch	обедать	[a'bedatⁱ]
to hear (vi, vt)	слышать	['slıʃʌtⁱ]
to help (assist, aid)	помогать	[pama'gatⁱ]
to hide (vt)	прятать	['prⁱatatⁱ]
to hint (vi)	намекать	[name'katⁱ]
to hope (vi, vt)	надеяться	[na'deitsə]
to hunt (vi, vt)	охотиться	[a'hɔtitsə]
to hurry (vi)	торопиться	[tara'pitsə]

12. The most important verbs. Part 3

to inform (vi, vt)	информировать	[infar'miravatⁱ]
to insist (vi, vt)	настаивать	[nas'taivatⁱ]
to insult (vt)	оскорблять	[askarb'ʎatⁱ]
to invite (vt)	приглашать	[prigla'ʃʌtⁱ]
to joke (vi)	шутить	[ʃʊ'titⁱ]
to keep (vt)	сохранять	[sahra'ɲatⁱ]
to keep silence	молчать	[mal'tʃatⁱ]
to kill (vt)	убивать	[ubi'vatⁱ]
to know (sb)	знать	[znatⁱ]
to laugh (vi)	смеяться	[smi'jatsə]
to liberate (vt)	освобождать	[asvabaʒ'datⁱ]
to like (I like …)	нравиться	['nrawitsə]
to look for … (search)	искать …	[is'katⁱ]
to love sb	любить	[ly'bitⁱ]
to make a mistake	ошибаться	[aʃi'batsə]
to mean (signify)	означать	[azna'tʃatⁱ]

to mention (talk about)	упоминать	[upɐmi'nat']
to miss (school etc.)	пропускать	[prɐpʊs'kat']
to mix up (confuse)	путать	['pʊtat']
to notice (see)	замечать	[zame'ʧat']
to object (vi, vt)	возражать	[vazrɐ'ʒat']
to observe (see)	наблюдать	[nɐblʲ'dat']
to open (vt)	открывать	[atkrɪ'vat']
to order (meal etc.)	заказывать	[zɐ'kazɪvat']
to order (military)	приказывать	[pri'kazɪvat']
to own (possess)	владеть	[vlɐ'det']
to participate (vi)	участвовать	[u'ʧastvavat']
to pay (vi, vt)	платить	[plɐ'tit']
to permit (allow)	разрешать	[razre'ʃʌt']
to plan (vi, vt)	планировать	[plɐ'niravat']
to play (vi, vt)	играть	[ig'rat']
to pray (vi, vt)	молиться	[mɐ'litsə]
to prefer (vt)	предпочитать	[pritpɐʧi'tat']
to promise (vt)	обещать	[abi'ɕat']
to pronounce (say)	произносить	[praiznɐ'sit']
to propose (vt)	предлагать	[pridlɐ'gat']
to punish (vt)	наказывать	[nɐ'kazɪvat']
to read (vi, vt)	читать	[ʧi'tat']
to recommend (vt)	рекомендовать	[rikamendɐ'vat']
to refuse (vi, vt)	отказываться	[at'kazɪvatsə]
to regret (be sorry)	сожалеть	[saʒi'let']
to rent (of a tenant)	снимать	[sni'mat']
to repeat (say again)	повторять	[pɐftɐ'rʲat']
to reserve, to book	резервировать	[rezir'wiravat']
to run (vi)	бежать	[bi'ʒat']

13. The most important verbs. Part 4

to save (rescue)	спасать	[spɐ'sat']
to say (e.g., ~ thank you)	сказать	[skɐ'zat']
to scold (vt)	ругать	[rʊ'gat']
to see (vi, vt)	видеть	['widet']
to sell (goods)	продавать	[prɐdɐ'vat']
to send (vt)	отправлять	[atprɐv'ʎat']
to shoot (vi)	стрелять	[stri'ʎat']
to shout (vi)	кричать	[kri'ʧat']
to show (vi, vt)	показывать	[pɐ'kazɪvat']
to sign (document)	подписывать	[pat'pisɪvat']
to sit down (vi)	садиться	[sɐ'ditsə]

| to smile (vi) | улыбаться | [ulɪ'batsə] |
| to speak (vi, vt) | говорить | [gava'ritʲ] |

to steal (money, etc.)	красть	[krastʲ]
to stop (cease)	прекращать	[prikra'ɕatʲ]
to stop (vi)	останавливаться	[asta'navlivatsə]
to study (vt)	изучать	[izu'tʃatʲ]
to swim (vi)	плавать	['plavatʲ]

to take (vt)	брать	[bratʲ]
to think (vi, vt)	думать	['dumatʲ]
to threaten (vt)	угрожать	[ugra'ʒatʲ]
to touch (by hands)	трогать	['trogatʲ]
to translate (word, text)	переводить	[pireva'ditʲ]
to trust (vt)	доверять	[dawe'rʲatʲ]
to try (attempt)	пробовать	['probavatʲ]
to turn (change direction)	поворачивать	[pava'ratʃivatʲ]

to underestimate (vt)	недооценивать	[nidaa'tsenivatʲ]
to understand (vi, vt)	понимать	[pani'matʲ]
to unite (join)	объединять	[abʰedi'ɲatʲ]

to wait (vi, vt)	ждать	[ʒdatʲ]
to want (wish, desire)	хотеть	[ha'tetʲ]
to warn (of the danger)	предупреждать	[pridupreʒ'datʲ]

to work (vi)	работать	[ra'botatʲ]
to write (vi, vt)	писать	[pi'satʲ]
to write down	записывать	[za'pisɪvatʲ]

14. Colors

color	цвет (m)	[tswet]
shade (nuance)	оттенок (m)	[at'tenak]
tone	тон (m)	[ton]
rainbow	радуга (f)	['radugə]

white	белый	['belɪj]
black	чёрный	['tʃornɪj]
gray	серый	['serɪj]

green	зелёный	[ze'lɜnɪj]
yellow	жёлтый	['ʒɜltɪj]
red	красный	['krasnɪj]

blue	синий	['sinɪj]
light blue	голубой	[galu'bɔj]
pink	розовый	['rɔzavɪj]
orange	оранжевый	[a'ranʒɪvɪj]
violet	фиолетовый	[fia'letavɪj]

brown	коричневый	[ka'ritʃnevɪj]
golden	золотой	[zala'tɔj]
silvery	серебристый	[sireb'ristɪj]

beige	бежевый	['beʒɪvɪj]
cream	кремовый	['kremavɪj]
turquoise	бирюзовый	[biry'zovɪj]
cherry	вишнёвый	[wiʃ'nɜvɪj]
lilac	лиловый	[li'lovɪj]
raspberry	малиновый	[ma'linavɪj]

light	светлый	['swetlɪj]
dark	тёмный	['tɜmnɪj]
bright	яркий	['jarkij]

colored (pencils)	цветной	[tswit'nɔj]
color (e.g., ~ film)	цветной	[tswit'nɔj]
black-and-white	чёрно-белый	['tʃɔrna 'belɪj]
plain (one color)	одноцветный	[adnats'wetnɪj]
multicolored	разноцветный	[raznats'wetnɪj]

15. Questions

Who?	Кто?	[ktɔ]
What?	Что?	[ʃtɔ]
Where? (at, in)	Где?	[gde]
Where (to)?	Куда?	[ku'da]
Where … from?	Откуда?	[at'kuda]
When?	Когда?	[kag'da]

| Why? (aim) | Зачем? | [za'tʃem] |
| Why? (reason) | Почему? | [patʃe'mu] |

| What for? | Для чего? | [dʎa tʃe'vɔ] |
| How? (in what way) | Как? | [kak] |

| What? (which?) | Какой? | [ka'kɔj] |
| Which? | Который? | [ka'torɪj] |

| To whom? | Кому? | [ka'mu] |
| About whom? | О ком? | [a 'kɔm] |

| About what? | О чём? | [a 'tʃɔm] |
| With whom? | С кем? | [s kem] |

| How many? How much? | Сколько? | ['skoʎka] |
| Whose? | Чей? | [tʃej] |

| Whose? (fem.) | Чья? | [tʃja] |
| Whose? (pl) | Чьи? | [tʃʲi] |

16. Prepositions

with (accompanied by)	с	[s]
without	без	[bes]
to (indicating direction)	в	[v]
about (e.g., talking ~ ...)	о	[ɔ]
before (in time)	перед	['peret]
in front of ...	перед	['peret]
under (beneath, below)	под	[pɔt]
above (in a higher position)	над	[nɑt]
on (e.g., ~ the table)	на	[nə]
from (off, out of)	из	[is]
of (made from)	из	[is]
in (e.g., ~ ten minutes)	через	['tʃeres]
over (across the top of)	через	['tʃeres]

17. Function words. Adverbs. Part 1

Where? (at, in)	Где?	[gde]
here	здесь	[zdesʲ]
there (in a particular place)	там	[tɑm]
somewhere	где-то	['gde tə]
nowhere (not anywhere)	нигде	[nig'de]
by (near, beside)	у, около	[u], ['ɔkɑlə]
by the window	у окна	[u ak'na]
Where (to)?	Куда?	[ku'da]
here (e.g., come ~!)	сюда	[sy'da]
there (e.g., to go ~)	туда	[tu'da]
from here	отсюда	[a'tsydə]
from there	оттуда	[at'tudə]
near (in space)	близко	['bliskə]
far (distant in space)	далеко	[dali'kɔ]
near (e.g., ~ Paris)	около	['ɔkɑlə]
nearby	рядом	['rʲadam]
not far	недалеко	[nidali'kɔ]
left	левый	['levɪj]
on the left	слева	['slevə]
to the left	налево	[na'levə]
right	правый	['pravɪj]
on the right	справа	['spravə]

to the right	направо	[nap'ravə]
in front	спереди	['speredi]
front (attr)	передний	[pi'rednij]
ahead (in space)	вперёд	[fpi'rʒt]
behind	сзади	['zzadi]
from behind	сзади	['zzadi]
back (towards the rear)	назад	[na'zat]
middle	середина (f)	[sire'dinə]
in the middle	посередине	[pasere'dine]
at the side	сбоку	['zbɔkʊ]
everywhere	везде	[wez'de]
around (in all directions)	вокруг	[vak'rʊk]
from inside	изнутри	[iznʊt'ri]
somewhere (to go)	куда-то	[kʊ'da tə]
straight (directly)	напрямик	[napri'mik]
back (e.g., come ~)	обратно	[ab'ratnə]
from anywhere	откуда-нибудь	[at'kʊda ni'bʊtʲ]
from somewhere	откуда-то	[at'kʊda tə]
firstly	во-первых	[va'pervɪh]
secondly	во-вторых	[vafta'rɪh]
thirdly	в-третьих	['ftretih]
suddenly	вдруг	[vdrʊk]
at first	вначале	[vna'tʃale]
for the first time	впервые	[fpir'vɪe]
long before ...	задолго до ...	[za'dɔlga da]
anew (over again)	заново	['zanavə]
for good	насовсем	[nasaf'sem]
never	никогда	[nikag'da]
again	опять	[a'pʲatʲ]
now	теперь	[ti'perʲ]
often	часто	['tʃastə]
then	тогда	[tag'da]
urgently (quickly)	срочно	['srɔtʃnə]
usually	обычно	[a'bɪtʃnə]
by the way, ...	кстати, ...	['kstati]
possible (e.g., that is ~)	возможно	[vaz'mɔʒnə]
probably	вероятно	[wira'jatnə]
maybe	может быть	['mɔʒɛt 'bɪtʲ]
besides ...	кроме того, ...	['krome ta'vɔ]
that's why ...	поэтому ...	[pa'ɛtamʊ]
in spite of ...	несмотря на ...	[nismat'rʲa na]
thanks to ...	благодаря ...	[blagada'rʲa]
what (pron.)	что	[ʃtɔ]

that	что	[ʃtɔ]
something	что-то	[ˈʃtɔ tə]
anything (something)	что-нибудь	[ʃtɔ niˈbutʲ]
nothing	ничего	[nitʃiˈvɔ]

who (pron.)	кто	[ktɔ]
someone	кто-то	[ˈktɔ tə]
somebody	кто-нибудь	[ˈktɔ niˈbutʲ]

nobody	никто	[nikˈtɔ]
nowhere (not to any place)	никуда	[nikʊˈda]
nobody's	ничей	[niˈtʃej]
somebody's	чей-нибудь	[tʃej niˈbutʲ]

so (e.g., I'm ~ glad)	так	[tak]
also (as well)	также	[ˈtakʒɛ]
too (as well)	тоже	[ˈtɔʒɛ]

18. Function words. Adverbs. Part 2

Why?	Почему?	[patʃeˈmʊ]
for some reason	почему-то	[patʃeˈmʊ tə]
because …	потому, что …	[pataˈmuʃta]
for some purpose	зачем-то	[zaˈtʃemtə]

and	и	[i]
or	или	[ˈili]
but	но	[nɔ]
for (e.g., ~ me)	для	[dʌa]

too (excessively)	слишком	[ˈsliʃkam]
only (exclusively)	только	[ˈtɔʌkə]
exactly	точно	[ˈtɔtʃnə]
about (more or less)	около	[ˈɔkalə]

approximately	приблизительно	[pribliˈziteʌnə]
approximate	приблизительный	[pribliˈziteʌnɪj]
almost	почти	[patʃˈti]
the rest	остальное (n)	[astaʌˈnɔe]

other, another	другой	[drʊˈgɔj]
each	каждый	[ˈkaʒdɪj]
any (no matter which)	любой	[lyˈbɔj]
many, much (a lot of)	много	[ˈmnɔgə]
many people	многие	[ˈmnɔgie]
all (everyone)	все	[fse]

in exchange for …	в обмен на …	[v abˈmen na]
in exchange	взамен	[vzaˈmen]
by hand (made)	вручную	[vrʊtʃˈnuju]

hardly (negative opinion)	вряд ли	['vrʲatli]
probably	наверное	[nɑ'wernɑe]
on purpose	нарочно	[nɑ'rɔʃnə]
by accident	случайно	[slu'ʧajnə]

very	очень	['ɔʧeɲ]
for example	например	[nɑpri'mer]
between	между	['meʒdʊ]
among	среди	[sre'di]
so much (such a lot)	столько	['stoʌkə]
especially	особенно	[ɑ'sɔbennə]

Basic concepts. Part 2

19. Weekdays

Monday	понедельник (m)	[pɑniˈdeʎnik]
Tuesday	вторник (m)	[ˈftornik]
Wednesday	среда (f)	[sreˈdɑ]
Thursday	четверг (m)	[ʧitˈwerk]
Friday	пятница (f)	[ˈpʲatnitsə]
Saturday	суббота (f)	[suˈbotə]
Sunday	воскресенье (n)	[vɑskriˈseɲje]
today	сегодня	[siˈvodnɑ]
tomorrow	завтра	[ˈzɑftrə]
the day after tomorrow	послезавтра	[pɑsleˈzɑftrə]
yesterday	вчера	[fʧiˈrɑ]
the day before yesterday	позавчера	[pɑzɑfʧeˈrɑ]
day	день (m)	[deɲ]
workday	рабочий день (m)	[rɑˈbotʃij deɲ]
holiday	празник (m)	[ˈprɑznik]
day off	выходной день (m)	[vɪhɑdˈnoj deɲ]
weekend	выходные (pl)	[vɪhɑdˈnɪe]
all day long	весь день	[wesʲ ˈdeɲ]
next day	на следующий день	[nɑ sleˈduɕij deɲ]
two days ago	2 дня назад	[dvɑ dnɑ nɑˈzɑt]
the day before	накануне	[nɑkɑˈnune]
daily	ежедневный	[eʒɪdˈnevnɪj]
every day	ежедневно	[eʒɪdˈnevnə]
week	неделя (f)	[niˈdeʎɑ]
last week	на прошлой неделе	[nɑ ˈproʃlɑj niˈdele]
next week	на следующей неделе	[nɑ sleˈduɕej niˈdele]
weekly (adj)	еженедельный	[eʒɪniˈdeʎnɪj]
every week	еженедельно	[eʒɪniˈdeʎnə]
twice a week	2 раза в неделю	[dvɑ ˈrɑzɑ v niˈdely]
every Tuesday	каждый вторник	[ˈkɑʒdɪj ˈftornik]

20. Hours. Day and night

morning	утро (n)	[ˈutrə]
in the morning	утром	[ˈutrɑm]
noon, midday	полдень (m)	[ˈpoldeɲ]

in the afternoon	после обеда	['pɔsle a'bedə]
evening	вечер (m)	['wetʃer]
in the evening	вечером	['wetʃeram]
night	ночь (f)	[nɔtʃ]
at night	ночью	['nɔtʃjy]
midnight	полночь (f)	['pɔlnatʃ]
second	секунда (f)	[si'kundə]
minute	минута (f)	[mi'nutə]
hour	час (m)	[tʃas]
half an hour	полчаса (pl)	[paltʃe'sa]
quarter of an hour	четверть (f) часа	['tʃetwertⁱ 'tʃasə]
fifteen minutes	15 минут	[pit'natsatⁱ mi'nut]
24 hours	сутки (pl)	['sutki]
sunrise	восход (m) солнца	[vas'hɔt 'sɔntsə]
dawn	рассвет (m)	[ras'wet]
early morning	раннее утро (n)	['rannee 'utrə]
sunset	закат (m)	[za'kat]
early in the morning	рано утром	['rana 'utram]
this morning	сегодня утром	[si'vɔdɲa 'utram]
tomorrow morning	завтра утром	['zaftra 'utram]
this afternoon	сегодня днём	[si'vɔdɲa 'dnɜm]
in the afternoon	после обеда	['pɔsle a'bedə]
tomorrow afternoon	завтра после обеда	['zaftra 'pɔsle a'bedə]
tonight (this evening)	сегодня вечером	[si'vɔdɲa 'wetʃeram]
tomorrow evening	завтра вечером	['zaftra 'wetʃeram]
at 3 o'clock sharp	ровно в 3 часа	['rɔvna ftri tʃe'sa]
about 4 o'clock	около 4-х часов	['ɔkala tʃetⁱ'rɜh tʃe'sɔf]
by 12 o'clock	к 12-ти часам	[k dwi'natsati tʃi'sam]
in 20 minutes	через 20 минут	['tʃeres 'dvatsatⁱ mi'nut]
in an hour	через час	['tʃeres 'tʃas]
on time	вовремя	['vɔvremⁱa]
term (end of period)	срок (m)	[srɔk]
a quarter of …	без четверти …	[bes 'tʃetwerti]
within an hour	в течение часа	[f ti'tʃenii 'tʃasə]
every 15 minutes	каждые 15 минут	['kaʒdⁱe pit'natsatⁱ mi'nut]
round the clock	круглые сутки	['kruglⁱe 'sutki]

21. Months. Seasons

January	январь (m)	[en'varⁱ]
February	февраль (m)	[fiv'raʎ]
March	март (m)	[mart]

April	**апрель** (m)	[ap'rexʌ]
May	**май** (m)	[maj]
June	**июнь** (m)	[iˈjuɲ]
July	**июль** (m)	[iˈjuʌ]
August	**август** (m)	[ˈavgʊst]
September	**сентябрь** (m)	[sinˈtʲabrʲ]
October	**октябрь** (m)	[akˈtʲabrʲ]
November	**ноябрь** (m)	[naˈjabrʲ]
December	**декабрь** (m)	[diˈkabrʲ]
spring	**весна** (f)	[wisˈna]
in spring	**весной**	[wisˈnɔj]
spring (attr)	**весенний**	[wiˈsennij]
summer	**лето** (n)	[ˈletə]
in summer	**летом**	[ˈletam]
summer (attr)	**летний**	[ˈletnij]
fall	**осень** (f)	[ˈɔseɲ]
in the fall	**осенью**	[ˈɔseɲy]
fall (attr)	**осенний**	[aˈsennij]
winter	**зима** (f)	[ziˈma]
in winter	**зимой**	[ziˈmɔj]
winter (attr)	**зимний**	[ˈzimnij]
month	**месяц** (m)	[ˈmesits]
this month	**в этом месяце**	[v ˈɛtam ˈmesitsə]
next month	**в следующем месяце**	[f ˈsleduɕem ˈmesitsə]
last month	**в прошлом месяце**	[f ˈprɔʃlam ˈmesitsə]
a month ago	**месяц назад**	[ˈmesits naˈzat]
in a month	**через месяц**	[ˈtʃeres ˈmesits]
in two months	**через 2 месяца**	[ˈtʃeres dva ˈmesitsə]
a whole month	**весь месяц**	[wesʲ ˈmesits]
all month long	**целый месяц**	[ˈtselij ˈmesits]
monthly (~ magazine)	**ежемесячный**	[eʒɪˈmesitʃnij]
monthly (adv)	**ежемесячно**	[eʒɪˈmesitʃnə]
every month	**каждый месяц**	[ˈkaʒdij ˈmesits]
twice a month	**2 раза в месяц**	[dva ˈraza v ˈmesits]
year	**год** (m)	[gɔt]
this year	**в этом году**	[v ˈɛtam gaˈdu]
next year	**в следующем году**	[f ˈsleduɕem gaˈdu]
last year	**в прошлом году**	[f ˈprɔʃlam gaˈdu]
a year ago	**год назад**	[gɔt naˈzat]
in a year	**через год**	[ˈtʃerez ˈgɔt]
in two years	**через 2 года**	[ˈtʃeres dva ˈgɔdə]
a whole year	**весь год**	[wesʲ ˈgɔt]

all year long	**целый год**	['tselɪj 'gɔt]
every year	**каждый год**	['kaʒdɪj gɔt]
annual (adj)	**ежегодный**	[eʒɪ'gɔdnɪj]
annually	**ежегодно**	[eʒɪ'gɔdnɔ]
4 times a year	**4 раза в год**	[tʃɪ'tɪre 'raza v gɔt]

date (e.g., today's ~)	**число** (n)	[tʃɪs'lɔ]
date (e.g., ~ of birth)	**дата** (f)	['datə]
calendar (of dates)	**календарь** (m)	[kalın'darʲ]

half a year	**полгода**	[pal'gɔdə]
six months	**полугодие** (n)	[palu'gɔdie]
season (summer etc.)	**сезон** (m)	[si'zɔn]
century	**век** (m)	[wek]

22. Time. Miscellaneous

time	**время** (n)	['vremʲa]
instant (noun)	**миг** (m)	[mik]
moment	**мгновение** (n)	[mgna'wenie]
instant (adj)	**мгновенный**	[mgna'wennɪj]
period (length of time)	**отрезок** (m)	[at'rezak]
life	**жизнь** (f)	[ʒɪzn]
eternity	**вечность** (f)	['wetʃnastʲ]

epoch	**эпоха** (f)	[ɛ'pohə]
era	**эра** (f)	['ɛrə]
cycle	**цикл** (m)	[tsɪkl]
period	**период** (m)	[pi'riat]
term (period)	**срок** (m)	[srɔk]

the future	**будущее** (n)	['buduɕee]
future (attr)	**будущий**	['buduɕij]
next time	**в следующий раз**	[f 'sleduɕij ras]
the past	**прошлое** (n)	['prɔʃlae]
past (recent)	**прошлый**	['prɔʃlɪj]
last time	**в прошлый раз**	[f 'prɔʃlɪj ras]

later	**позже**	['pɔʒɛ]
after	**после**	['pɔsle]
nowadays	**теперь**	[ti'perʲ]
now	**сейчас**	[si'tʃas]
immediately	**немедленно**	[ni'medlenə]
soon	**скоро**	['skɔrə]
in advance (beforehand)	**заранее**	[za'ranie]

a long time ago	**давно**	[dav'nɔ]
recently	**недавно**	[ni'davnə]
destiny	**судьба** (f)	[sud'ʲba]
memories (recollection)	**память** (f)	['pamitʲ]

archives	**архив** (m)	[ar'hif]
during …	**во время …**	[va 'vremʲa]
long, a long time	**долго**	['dolgə]
not long	**недолго**	[ni'dolgə]
early (in the morning)	**рано**	['ranə]
late (not early)	**поздно**	['poznə]

forever (for good)	**навсегда**	[nafseg'da]
to start (begin)	**начинать**	[natʃi'natʲ]
to postpone (vt)	**перенести**	[pirenes'ti]

at the same time	**одновременно**	[adnavre'mennə]
permanently	**постоянно**	[pasta'jannə]
constant (noise, pain)	**постоянный**	[pasta'jannɪj]
temporary	**временный**	['vremennɪj]

sometimes	**иногда**	[inag'da]
rarely	**редко**	['retkə]
often	**часто**	['tʃastə]

23. Opposites

| rich | **богатый** | [ba'gatɪj] |
| poor | **бедный** | ['bednɪj] |

| ill, sick | **больной** | [baʎ'nɔj] |
| healthy | **здоровый** | [zda'rovɪj] |

| big | **большой** | [baʎ'ʃɔj] |
| small | **маленький** | ['maliɲkij] |

| quickly | **быстро** | ['bɪstrə] |
| slowly | **медленно** | ['medlenə] |

| fast | **быстрый** | ['bɪstrɪj] |
| slow | **медленный** | ['medlenɪj] |

| cheerful | **весёлый** | [wi'sзlɪj] |
| sad | **грустный** | ['grʊsnɪj] |

| together | **вместе** | ['vmeste] |
| separately | **отдельно** | [ad'deʎnə] |

| aloud (read) | **вслух** | [vsluh] |
| silently | **про себя** | [pra se'bʲa] |

tall	**высокий**	[vɪ'sɔkij]
low	**низкий**	['niskij]
deep	**глубокий**	[glu'bɔkij]
shallow	**мелкий**	['melkij]

yes	да	[də]
no	нет	[net]
distant	далёкий	[dɑ'lɔkij]
nearby (adj)	близкий	['bliskij]
far	далеко	[dɑli'kɔ]
nearby (adv)	рядом	['rʲadɑm]
long	длинный	['dlinnɪj]
short	короткий	[kɑ'rɔtkij]
kind	добрый	['dɔbrɪj]
evil	злой	[zlɔj]
married	женатый	[ʒɪ'nɑtɪj]
single	холостой	[hɑlɑs'tɔj]
to forbid (vt)	запретить	[zɑpri'titʲ]
to permit (vi, vt)	разрешить	[rɑzri'ʃitʲ]
end	конец (m)	[kɑ'nets]
beginning	начало (n)	[nɑ'tʃalə]
left	левый	['levɪj]
right	правый	['prɑvɪj]
first	первый	['pervɪj]
last	последний	[pɑs'lednij]
crime	преступление (n)	[pristʊp'lenie]
punishment	наказание (n)	[nɑkɑ'zɑnie]
to order (vi, vt)	приказать	[prikɑ'zɑtʲ]
to obey (vi, vt)	подчиниться	[pɑtʃi'nitsə]
straight	прямой	[pri'mɔj]
curved	кривой	[kri'vɔj]
Paradise	рай (m)	[rɑj]
Hell	ад (m)	[ɑt]
to be born	родиться	[rɑ'ditsə]
to die (vi, vt)	умереть	[umi'retʲ]
strong	сильный	['silʌnɪj]
weak	слабый	['slɑbɪj]
old	старый	['stɑrɪj]
young	молодой	[mɑlɑ'dɔj]
old	старый	['stɑrɪj]
new	новый	['nɔvɪj]

hard	твёрдый	['twɜrdɪj]
soft	мягкий	['mʲaⁿkij]
warm	тёплый	['tɜplɪj]
cold	холодный	[hɑ'lɔdnɪj]
fat	толстый	['tɔlstɪj]
slim	худой	[hʊ'dɔj]
narrow	узкий	['uskij]
wide	широкий	[ʃɪ'rɔkij]
good	хороший	[hɑ'rɔʃɪj]
bad	плохой	[plɑ'hɔj]
brave	храбрый	['hrabrɪj]
cowardly	трусливый	[trʊs'livɪj]

24. Lines and shapes

square	квадрат (m)	[kvad'rat]
square (attr)	квадратный	[kvad'ratnɪj]
circle	круг (m)	[krʊk]
round	круглый	['krʊglɪj]
triangle	треугольник (m)	[triu'gɔʎnik]
triangular	треугольный	[triu'gɔʎnɪj]
oval	овал (m)	[ɑ'val]
oval (attr)	овальный	[ɑ'vaʎnɪj]
rectangle	прямоугольник (m)	[primau'gɔʎnik]
rectangular	прямоугольный	[primau'gɔʎnɪj]
pyramid	пирамида (f)	[pira'midə]
rhombus	ромб (m)	[rɔmp]
trapezoid	трапеция (f)	[tra'petsija]
cube	куб (m)	[kʊp]
prism	призма (f)	['prizmə]
circumference	окружность (f)	[ɑk'rʊʒnastʲ]
sphere	сфера (f)	['sferə]
sphere (ball)	шар (m)	[ʃʌr]
diameter	диаметр (m)	[di'ametr]
radius	радиус (m)	['radius]
perimeter	периметр (m)	[pi'rimetr]
center	центр (m)	[tsentr]
horizontal	горизонтальный	[garizan'taʎnɪj]
vertical	вертикальный	[wirti'kaʎnɪj]
parallel (noun)	параллель (f)	[para'leʎ]
parallel (adj)	параллельный	[para'leʎnɪj]

line	ли́ния (f)	['linija]
stroke	черта́ (f)	[tʃir'ta]
straight line	пряма́я (f)	[pri'majə]
curve	крива́я (f)	[kri'vaja]
thin (layer)	то́нкий	['tɔnkij]
contour (outline)	ко́нтур (m)	['kɔntʊr]

intersection	пересече́ние (n)	[pirise'tʃenie]
right angle (angle of 90°)	прямо́й у́гол (m)	[pri'mɔj 'ugal]
segment	сегме́нт (m)	[sig'ment]
sector	се́ктор (m)	['sektar]
side (of triangle)	сторона́ (f)	[stara'na]
angle	у́гол (m)	['ugal]

25. Units of measurement

weight	вес (m)	[wes]
length	длина́ (f)	[dli'na]
width	ширина́ (f)	[ʃiri'na]
height	высота́ (f)	[vɪsa'ta]
depth	глубина́ (f)	[glubi'na]
volume	объём (m)	[abʰзm]
area	пло́щадь (f)	['plɔçatⁱ]

gram	грамм (m)	[gram]
milligram	миллигра́мм (m)	[milig'ram]
kilogram	килогра́мм (m)	[kilag'ram]
ton	то́нна (f)	['tɔnnə]
pound (unit of weight)	фунт (m)	[fʊnt]
ounce	у́нция (f)	['untsija]

meter	метр (m)	[metr]
millimeter	миллиме́тр (m)	[mili'metr]
centimeter	сантиме́тр (m)	[santi'metr]
kilometer	киломе́тр (m)	[kila'metr]
mile	ми́ля (f)	['miʎa]

inch	дюйм (m)	[dyjm]
foot	фут (m)	[fʊt]
yard	ярд (m)	['jart]

| square meter | квадра́тный метр (m) | [kvad'ratnɪj metr] |
| hectare | гекта́р (m) | [gik'tar] |

liter	литр (m)	[litr]
degree	гра́дус (m)	['gradʊs]
volt	вольт (m)	[vɔʎt]
ampere	ампе́р (m)	[am'per]
horsepower	лошади́ная си́ла (f)	[laʃʌ'dinaja 'silə]
quantity	коли́чество (n)	[ka'litʃestvə]

a little bit of …	немного … (f)	[nem'nɔgə]
half	половина (f)	[pɑlɑ'winə]
dozen	дюжина (f)	['dyʒɪnə]
piece (item)	штука (f)	['ʃtʊkə]
size	размер (m)	[raz'mer]
scale (of model, drawing)	масштаб (m)	[mɑʃ'tɑp]
minimum	минимальный	[mini'mɑʎnɪj]
the smallest	наименьший	[nɑi'menʃɪj]
medium	средний	['srednij]
maximum	максимальный	[mɑksi'mɑʎnɪj]
the largest	наибольший	[nɑi'bɔʎʃɪj]

26. Containers

jar (glass)	банка (f)	['bɑnkə]
can	банка (f)	['bɑnkə]
bucket	ведро (n)	[wid'rɔ]
barrel	бочка (f)	['bɔʧkə]
basin (for washing)	таз (m)	[tɑs]
tank (for liquid, gas)	бак (m)	[bɑk]
flask (for water, wine)	фляжка (f)	['fʎɑʃkə]
jerrycan	канистра (f)	[kɑ'nistrə]
cistern (tank)	цистерна (f)	[tsɪs'ternə]
mug	кружка (f)	['krʊʃkə]
cup (of coffee etc.)	чашка (f)	['ʧaʃkə]
saucer	блюдце (n)	['blytse]
glass (~ of water)	стакан (m)	[stɑ'kɑn]
glass (~ of vine)	бокал (m)	[bɑ'kɑl]
stew pot	кастрюля (f)	[kɑst'ryʎɑ]
bottle (e.g., ~ of wine)	бутылка (f)	[bʊ'tɪlkə]
neck (of the bottle)	горлышко (n)	['gɔrlɪʃkə]
carafe	графин (m)	[grɑ'fin]
pitcher (earthenware)	кувшин (m)	[kʊf'ʃin]
vessel (container)	сосуд (m)	[sɑ'sʊt]
pot (crock)	горшок (m)	[gɑr'ʃɔk]
vase	ваза (f)	['vɑzə]
bottle (e.g., ~ of perfume)	флакон (m)	[flɑ'kɔn]
vial, small bottle	пузырёк (m)	[pʊzɪ'rɜk]
tube (of toothpaste)	тюбик (m)	['tybik]
sack (bag)	мешок (m)	[mi'ʃɔk]
bag (paper, plastic)	пакет (m)	[pɑ'ket]
package (small parcel)	пакет (m)	[pɑ'ket]

| pack (of cigarettes etc.) | пачка (f) | ['patʃkə] |
| pack | упаковка (f) | [upɑ'kɔfkə] |

box (e.g., shoebox)	коробка (f)	[kɑ'rɔpkə]
box (for transportation)	ящик (m)	['jaɕik]
basket (for carrying)	корзина (f)	[kar'zinə]

27. Materials

material	материал (m)	[materi'al]
wood	дерево (n)	['derevə]
wooden	деревянный	[diri'vʲannɪj]

| glass (noun) | стекло (n) | [stik'lɔ] |
| glass (attr) | стеклянный | [stik'ʎannɪj] |

| stone (noun) | камень (m) | ['kameɲ] |
| stone (attr) | каменный | ['kamennɪj] |

plastic (noun)	пластик (m)	['plastik]
plastic (attr)	пластмассовый	[plas'masavɪj]
rubber (noun)	резина (f)	[ri'zinə]
rubber (attr)	резиновый	[ri'zinavɪj]

| material, fabric (noun) | ткань (f) | [tkaɲ] |
| fabric (attr) | из ткани | [is 'tkani] |

paper (noun)	бумага (f)	[bʊ'magə]
paper (attr)	бумажный	[bʊ'maʒnɪj]
cardboard (noun)	картон (m)	[kar'tɔn]
cardboard (attr)	картонный	[kar'tɔnnɪj]

polythene	полиэтилен (m)	[paliɛti'len]
cellophane	целлофан (m)	[tsila'fan]
linoleum	линолеум (m)	[li'nɔleum]
plywood	фанера (f)	[fɑ'nerə]

porcelain (noun)	фарфор (m)	[far'fɔr]
porcelain (attr)	фарфоровый	[far'fɔravɪj]
clay (noun)	глина (f)	['glinə]
clay (attr)	глиняный	['glininɪj]
ceramics (noun)	керамика (f)	[ki'ramikə]
ceramic (attr)	керамический	[kira'mitʃeskij]

28. Metals

| metal (noun) | металл (m) | [mi'tal] |
| metal (attr) | металлический | [mita'litʃeskij] |

alloy (noun)	**сплав** (m)	[splaf]
gold (noun)	**золото** (n)	['zɔlatə]
gold, golden	**золотой**	[zala'tɔj]
silver (noun)	**серебро** (n)	[sirib'rɔ]
silver (attr)	**серебряный**	[si'rebrinɪj]
iron (noun)	**железо** (n)	[ʒɪ'lezə]
iron, made of iron	**железный**	[ʒɪ'leznɪj]
steel (noun)	**сталь** (f)	[staʎ]
steel (attr)	**стальной**	[staʎ'nɔj]
copper (noun)	**медь** (f)	[metʲ]
copper (attr)	**медный**	['mednɪj]
aluminum (noun)	**алюминий** (m)	[aly'minij]
aluminum (attr)	**алюминиевый**	[aly'minivɪj]
bronze (noun)	**бронза** (f)	['brɔnzə]
bronze (attr)	**бронзовый**	['brɔnzavɪj]
brass	**латунь** (f)	[la'tuʃ]
nickel	**никель** (m)	['nikeʎ]
platinum	**платина** (f)	['platinə]
mercury	**ртуть** (f)	[rtutʲ]
tin	**олово** (n)	['ɔlavə]
lead	**свинец** (m)	[swi'nets]
zinc	**цинк** (m)	[tsɪnk]

HUMAN BEING

Human being. The body

29. Humans. Basic concepts

human, human being	человек (m)	[tʃila'wek]
man (adult male)	мужчина (m)	[mu'ɕinə]
woman	женщина (f)	['ʒɛɲɕinə]
child	ребёнок (m)	[ri'bɜnɑk]
girl	девочка (f)	['devatʃkə]
boy	мальчик (m)	['maʎtʃik]
teenager	подросток (m)	[pad'rostak]
old man	старик (m)	[sta'rik]
old woman	старая женщина (f)	['staraja 'ʒɛɲɕinə]

30. Human anatomy

organism	организм (m)	[arga'nizm]
heart	сердце (n)	['sertse]
blood	кровь (f)	[krɔfʲ]
artery	артерия (f)	[ar'tɛrija]
vein	вена (f)	['wenə]
brain	мозг (m)	[mɔsk]
nerve	нерв (m)	[nerf]
nerves	нервы (pl)	['nervı]
vertebra	позвонок (m)	[pazva'nɔk]
spine	позвоночник (m)	[pazva'notʃnik]
stomach (organ)	желудок (m)	[ʒı'ludak]
intestines	кишечник (m)	[ki'ʃetʃnik]
intestine	кишка (f)	[kiʃ'ka]
liver	печень (f)	['petʃeɲ]
kidney	почка (f)	['potʃkə]
bone	кость (f)	[kɔstʲ]
skeleton	скелет (m)	[ski'let]
rib	ребро (n)	[rib'rɔ]
skull	череп (m)	['tʃerep]
muscle	мышца (f)	['mıʃtsə]
biceps	бицепс (m)	['bitsıps]

triceps	**трицепс** (m)	['tritsɪps]
tendon	**сухожилие** (n)	[sʊhaˈʒɪlie]
joint	**сустав** (m)	[sʊsˈtaf]
lungs	**лёгкие** (pl)	[ˈlɔħkie]
genitals	**половые органы** (pl)	[palaˈvie ˈɔrganɪ]
skin	**кожа** (f)	[ˈkɔʒə]

31. Head

head	**голова** (f)	[galaˈva]
face	**лицо** (n)	[liˈtsɔ]
nose	**нос** (m)	[nɔs]
mouth	**рот** (m)	[rɔt]

eye	**глаз** (m)	[glas]
eyes	**глаза** (pl)	[glaˈza]
pupil	**зрачок** (m)	[zraˈtʃɔk]
eyebrow	**бровь** (f)	[brɔfʲ]
eyelash	**ресница** (f)	[risˈnitsə]
eyelid	**веко** (n)	[ˈwekə]

tongue	**язык** (m)	[jaˈzɪk]
tooth	**зуб** (m)	[zup]
lips	**губы** (pl)	[ˈgʊbɪ]
cheekbones	**скулы** (pl)	[ˈskʊlɪ]
gum	**десна** (f)	[disˈna]
palate	**нёбо** (n)	[ˈnɔbə]

nostrils	**ноздри** (pl)	[ˈnɔzdri]
chin	**подбородок** (m)	[padbaˈrɔdak]
jaw	**челюсть** (f)	[ˈtʃelystʲ]
cheek	**щека** (f)	[ɕiˈka]

forehead	**лоб** (m)	[lɔp]
temple	**висок** (m)	[wiˈsɔk]
ear	**ухо** (n)	[ˈuhə]
back of the head	**затылок** (m)	[zaˈtɪlak]
neck	**шея** (f)	[ˈʃəja]
throat	**горло** (n)	[ˈgɔrlə]

hair	**волосы** (pl)	[ˈvɔlasɪ]
hairstyle	**причёска** (f)	[priˈtʃɔskə]
haircut	**стрижка** (f)	[ˈstriʃkə]
wig	**парик** (m)	[paˈrik]

mustache	**усы** (pl)	[uˈsɪ]
beard	**борода** (f)	[baraˈda]
to have (a beard etc.)	**носить**	[naˈsitʲ]
braid	**коса** (f)	[kaˈsa]
sideburns	**бакенбарды** (pl)	[bakinˈbardɪ]

red-haired	**рыжий**	[ˈrɪʒɪj]
gray (hair)	**седой**	[siˈdɔj]
bald	**лысый**	[ˈlɪsɪj]
bald patch	**лысина** (f)	[ˈlɪsinə]

| ponytail | **хвост** (m) | [hvɔst] |
| bangs | **чёлка** (f) | [ˈʧɔlkə] |

32. Human body

| hand | **кисть** (f) | [kistʲ] |
| arm | **рука** (f) | [rʊˈka] |

finger, toe	**палец** (m)	[ˈpalets]
thumb	**большой палец** (m)	[baʎˈʃɔj ˈpalets]
little finger	**мизинец** (m)	[miˈzinets]
nail	**ноготь** (m)	[ˈnɔgatʲ]

fist	**кулак** (m)	[kʊˈlak]
palm	**ладонь** (f)	[laˈdɔɲ]
wrist	**запястье** (n)	[zaˈpʲasʲtje]
forearm	**предплечье** (n)	[pritpˈletʃje]
elbow	**локоть** (m)	[ˈlɔkatʲ]
shoulder	**плечо** (n)	[pliˈʧɔ]

leg	**нога** (f)	[naˈga]
foot	**ступня** (f)	[stʊpˈɲa]
knee	**колено** (n)	[kaˈlenə]
calf (part of leg)	**икра** (f)	[ikˈra]
hip	**бедро** (n)	[bidˈrɔ]
heel	**пятка** (f)	[ˈpʲatkə]

body	**тело** (n)	[ˈtelə]
stomach (abdomen)	**живот** (m)	[ʒɪˈvɔt]
chest	**грудь** (f)	[grʊtʲ]
breast	**грудь** (f)	[grʊtʲ]
side (of the body)	**бок** (m)	[bɔk]
back	**спина** (f)	[spiˈna]

| lower back | **поясница** (f) | [pais'nitsə] |
| waist | **талия** (f) | [ˈtalija] |

navel	**пупок** (m)	[pʊˈpɔk]
buttocks	**ягодицы** (pl)	[jagaˈditsɪ]
behind	**зад** (m)	[zat]

beauty mark	**родинка** (f)	[ˈrɔdinkə]
birthmark	**родимое пятно** (n)	[raˈdimae pitˈnɔ]
tattoo	**татуировка** (f)	[tatʊiˈrɔfkə]
scar	**шрам** (m)	[ʃram]

Clothing & Accessories

33. Outerwear. Coats

clothes	**одежда** (f)	[a'deʒdə]
outer clothing	**верхняя одежда** (f)	['werhnija a'deʒdə]
winter clothing	**зимняя одежда** (f)	['zimɲaja a'deʒdə]
overcoat	**пальто** (n)	[paʎ'tɔ]
fur coat	**шуба** (f)	['ʃubə]
fur jacket	**полушубок** (m)	[palu'ʃubak]
down coat	**пуховик** (m)	[puha'wik]
jacket (e.g., leather ~)	**куртка** (f)	['kurtkə]
raincoat	**плащ** (m)	[plaɕ]
waterproof	**непромокаемый**	[niprama'kaemɪj]

34. Men's & women's clothing

shirt	**рубашка** (f)	[ru'baʃkə]
pants	**брюки** (pl)	['bryki]
jeans	**джинсы** (pl)	['dʒinsɪ]
jacket (of man's suit)	**пиджак** (m)	[pi'dʒak]
suit	**костюм** (m)	[kas'tym]
dress (frock)	**платье** (n)	['platje]
skirt (garment)	**юбка** (f)	['jupkə]
blouse	**блузка** (f)	['bluskə]
knitted jacket	**кофта** (f)	['kɔftə]
jacket (of woman's suit)	**жакет** (m)	[ʒe'ket]
shawl	**платок** (m)	[pla'tɔk]
T-shirt	**футболка** (f)	[fud'bɔlkə]
shorts (short trousers)	**шорты** (pl)	['ʃɔrtɪ]
tracksuit	**спортивный костюм** (m)	[spar'tivnɪj kas'tym]
bathrobe	**халат** (m)	[ha'lat]
pajamas	**пижама** (f)	[pi'ʒamə]
sweater	**свитер** (m)	['switer]
pullover	**пуловер** (m)	[pu'lɔwer]
vest	**жилет** (m)	[ʒɪ'let]
tailcoat	**фрак** (m)	[frak]
tuxedo	**смокинг** (m)	['smɔkink]

uniform	форма (f)	['formə]
workwear	рабочая одежда (f)	[ra'botʃija a'deʒdə]
overalls	комбинезон (m)	[kambini'zɔn]
coat (e.g., doctor's ~)	халат (m)	[ha'lat]

35. Clothing. Underwear

underwear	бельё (n)	[bi'ʎjo]
boxers	трусы (m)	[tru'sɪ]
panties	бельё (n)	[bi'ʎjo]
undershirt (underwear)	майка (f)	['majkə]
socks	носки (pl)	[nas'ki]
nightgown	ночная рубашка (f)	[natʃ'naja ru'baʃkə]
bra	бюстгальтер (m)	[bys'gaʎtɛr]
knee highs	гольфы (pl)	['gɔʎfɪ]
pantyhose	колготки (pl)	[kal'gotki]
stockings	чулки (pl)	[tʃul'ki]
bathing suit	купальник (m)	[ku'paʎnik]

36. Headwear

hat	шапка (f)	['ʃʌpkə]
fedora	шляпа (f)	['ʃʎapə]
baseball cap	бейсболка (f)	[bijz'bolkə]
flatcap	кепка (f)	['kepkə]
beret	берет (m)	[bi'ret]
hood	капюшон (m)	[kapy'ʃɔn]
panama	панамка (f)	[pa'namkə]
knitted hat	вязаная шапочка (f)	['vʲazanaja 'ʃʌpatʃkə]
headscarf	платок (m)	[pla'tɔk]
women's hat	шляпка (f)	['ʃʎapkə]
scarf (headscarf)	косынка (f)	[ka'sɪnkə]
hard hat	каска (f)	['kaskə]
garrison cap	пилотка (f)	[pi'lɔtkə]
helmet	шлем (m)	[ʃlem]
derby	котелок (m)	[kate'lɔk]
top hat	цилиндр (m)	[tsɪ'lindr]

37. Footwear

| footwear | обувь (f) | ['ɔbʊfʲ] |
| ankle boots | ботинки (pl) | [ba'tinki] |

shoes (wingtip shoes)	туфли (pl)	['tʊfli]
boots (e.g., cowboy ~)	сапоги (pl)	[sapa'gi]
slippers	тапочки (pl)	['tapatʃki]
tennis shoes	кроссовки (pl)	[kra'sɔfki]
sneakers	кеды (pl)	['kedɪ]
sandals	сандалии (pl)	[san'dali]
cobbler	сапожник (m)	[sa'pɔʒnik]
heel (of shoe)	каблук (m)	[kab'luk]
pair (of shoes)	пара (f)	['parə]
shoestring	шнурок (m)	[ʃnʊ'rɔk]
to lace (vt)	шнуровать	[ʃnʊra'vatʲ]
shoehorn	рожок (m)	[ra'ʒɔk]
shoe polish	крем (m) для обуви	[krem dʌ́a 'ɔbʊwi]

38. Textile. Fabrics

cotton (noun)	хлопок (m)	['hlɔpak]
cotton (attr)	из хлопка	[is 'hlɔpkə]
flax (noun)	лён (m)	['lɔn]
flax (attr)	из льна	[iz 'ʌna]
silk (noun)	шёлк (m)	['ʃɔlk]
silk (attr)	шёлковый	['ʃɔlkavɪj]
wool (noun)	шерсть (f)	[ʃɛrstʲ]
woolen	шерстяной	[ʃɪrsti'nɔj]
velvet	бархат (m)	['barhat]
suede	замша (f)	['zamʃə]
corduroy	вельвет (m)	[wiʌ'wet]
nylon (noun)	нейлон (m)	[nij'lɔn]
nylon (attr)	из нейлона	[iz nij'lɔnə]
polyester (noun)	полиэстер (m)	[pali'ɛstr]
polyester (attr)	полиэстровый	[pali'ɛstravɪj]
leather (noun)	кожа (f)	['kɔʒə]
leather (attr)	из кожи	[is 'kɔʒɪ]
fur (noun)	мех (m)	[meh]
fur (e.g., ~ coat)	меховой	[miha'vɔj]

39. Personal accessories

gloves	перчатки (pl)	[pir'tʃatki]
mittens	варежки (f pl)	['variʃki]
scarf (long)	шарф (m)	[ʃʌrf]

glasses	**очки** (pl)	[aʧ'ki]
frame (for spectacles)	**оправа** (f)	[ap'ravə]
umbrella	**зонт** (m)	[zɔnt]
walking stick	**трость** (f)	[trɔstʲ]
hairbrush	**щётка** (f) **для волос**	['ɕɜtka dʎa va'lɔs]
fan (accessory)	**веер** (m)	['weer]
necktie	**галстук** (m)	['galstʊk]
bow tie	**галстук-бабочка** (m)	[galstʊk 'babaʧkə]
suspenders	**подтяжки** (pl)	[pa'tʲaʃki]
handkerchief	**носовой платок** (m)	[nasa'vɔj pla'tɔk]
comb (for hair)	**расчёска** (f)	[ra'ɕɜskə]
barrette	**заколка** (f)	[za'kɔlkə]
hairpin	**шпилька** (f)	['ʃpiʎkə]
buckle	**пряжка** (f)	['prʲaʃkə]
belt	**пояс** (m)	['pɔis]
shoulder strap	**ремень** (m)	[ri'meɲ]
bag (handbag)	**сумка** (f)	['sʊmkə]
purse	**сумочка** (f)	['sʊmaʧkə]
backpack	**рюкзак** (m)	[ryk'zak]

40. Clothing. Miscellaneous

fashion	**мода** (f)	['mɔdə]
in vogue	**модный**	['mɔdnɪj]
fashion designer	**модельер** (m)	[madɛ'ʎjer]
collar	**воротник** (m)	[varat'nik]
pocket	**карман** (m)	[kar'man]
pocket (e.g., ~ camera)	**карманный**	[kar'mannɪj]
sleeve	**рукав** (m)	[rʊ'kaf]
hanging tab (loop)	**вешалка** (f)	['weʃʌlkə]
fly (on trousers)	**ширинка** (f)	[ʃɪ'rinkə]
zipper (fastener)	**молния** (f)	['mɔlnija]
fastener	**застёжка** (f)	[zas'tɜʃkə]
button	**пуговица** (f)	['pʊgawiʦə]
buttonhole	**петля** (f)	[pit'ʎa]
to come off (ab. button)	**оторваться**	[atar'vaʦə]
to sew (vi, vt)	**шить**	[ʃɪtʲ]
to embroider (vi, vt)	**вышивать**	[vɪʃɪ'vatʲ]
embroidery	**вышивка** (f)	['vɪʃɪfkə]
sewing needle	**игла** (f)	[ig'la]
thread	**нитка** (f)	['nitkə]
seam	**шов** (m)	[ʃɔf]
to get dirty (vi)	**испачкаться**	[is'paʧkaʦə]

stain (mark, spot)	пятно (n)	[pit'nɔ]
to crease, crumple (vi)	помяться	[pɑ'mʲatsə]
to tear (vt)	порвать	[par'vatʲ]
clothes moth	моль (m)	[mɔʎ]

41. Personal care. Cosmetics

toothpaste	зубная паста (f)	[zub'naja 'pastə]
toothbrush	зубная щётка (f)	[zub'naja 'ɕʑtkə]
to brush one's teeth	чистить зубы	['tʃistitʲ 'zubɪ]

razor	бритва (f)	['britvə]
shaving cream	крем (m) для бритья	[krem dʎa bri'tja]
to shave (vi)	бриться	['britsə]

| soap | мыло (n) | ['mɪlə] |
| shampoo | шампунь (m) | [ʃʌm'puɲ] |

scissors	ножницы (pl)	['nɔʒnitsɪ]
nail file	пилочка (f) для ногтей	['pilatʃka dʎa nak'tej]
nail clippers	щипчики (pl)	['ɕiptʃiki]
tweezers	пинцет (m)	[pin'tsət]

cosmetics	косметика (f)	[kas'metikə]
face mask	маска (f)	['maskə]
manicure	маникюр (m)	[mani'kyr]
to have a manicure	делать маникюр	['delatʲ mani'kyr]
pedicure	педикюр (m)	[pidi'kyr]

make-up bag	косметичка (f)	[kasme'titʃkə]
powder (for face)	пудра (f)	['pudrə]
powder compact	пудреница (f)	['pudrinitsə]
blusher	румяна (f)	[rʊ'mʲanə]

perfume (bottled)	духи (pl)	[dʊ'hi]
toilet water	туалетная вода (f)	[tʊa'letnaja va'da]
lotion	лосьон (m)	[la'sjon]
cologne	одеколон (m)	[adika'lon]

eyeshadow	тени (pl) для век	['teni dʎa 'wek]
eyeliner	карандаш (m) для глаз	[karan'daʃ dʎa 'glas]
mascara	тушь (f)	[tʊʃ]

lipstick	губная помада (f)	[gub'naja pa'madə]
nail polish, enamel	лак (m) для ногтей	[lak dʎa nak'tej]
hair spray	лак (m) для волос	[lak dʎa va'los]
deodorant	дезодорант (m)	[dizada'rant]

| cream | крем (m) | [krem] |
| face cream | крем (m) для лица | [krem dʎa li'tsa] |

hand cream	крем (m) для рук	[krem dʌa ˈruk]
anti-wrinkle cream	крем (m) против морщин	[krem ˈprɔtif marˈɕin]
day cream	дневной крем (m)	[dnivˈnɔj krem]
night cream	ночной крем (m)	[natʃˈnɔj krem]
day (attr)	дневной	[dnivˈnɔj]
night (attr)	ночной	[natʃˈnɔj]

tampon	тампон (m)	[tamˈpɔn]
toilet paper	туалетная бумага (f)	[tuaˈletnaja buˈmagə]
hair dryer	фен (m)	[fen]

42. Jewelry

jewelry	драгоценности (pl)	[dragaˈtsenasti]
precious (e.g., ~ stone)	драгоценный	[dragaˈtsennɪj]
hallmark	проба (f)	[ˈprɔbə]

ring	кольцо (n)	[kaʌˈtsɔ]
wedding ring	обручальное кольцо (n)	[abruˈtʃaʌnae kaʌˈtsɔ]
bracelet	браслет (m)	[brasˈlet]

earrings	серьги (pl)	[ˈserʲgi]
necklace (~ of pearls)	ожерелье (n)	[aʒɛˈreʌje]
crown	корона (f)	[kaˈrɔnə]
beads (necklace)	бусы (pl)	[ˈbusɪ]

diamond	бриллиант (m)	[briliˈant]
emerald	изумруд (m)	[izumˈrut]
ruby	рубин (m)	[ruˈbin]
sapphire	сапфир (m)	[sapˈfir]
pearl	жемчуг (m)	[ˈʒɛmtʃuk]
amber	янтарь (m)	[janˈtarʲ]

43. Watches. Clocks

watch (wristwatch)	часы (pl)	[tʃiˈsɪ]
dial	циферблат (m)	[tsɪferbˈlat]
hand (of clock, watch)	стрелка (f)	[ˈstrelkə]
bracelet	браслет (m)	[brasˈlet]
watch strap	ремешок (m)	[rimeˈʃɔk]

battery	батарейка (f)	[bataˈrejkə]
to be dead (battery)	сесть	[sestʲ]
to change a battery	поменять батарейку	[pamiˈnatʲ bataˈrejku]
to run fast	спешить	[spiˈʃitʲ]
to run slow	отставать	[atstaˈvatʲ]
wall clock	настенные часы (pl)	[nasˈtennɪe tʃəˈsɪ]
hourglass	песочные часы (pl)	[peˈsɔtʃnɪe tʃəˈsɪ]

sundial	**солнечные часы** (pl)	['sɔlnetʃnɪe ʧə'sɪ]
alarm clock	**будильник** (m)	[bʊ'diʎnik]
watchmaker	**часовщик** (m)	[ʧisaf'ɕik]
to repair (vt)	**ремонтировать**	[riman'tiravatʲ]

Food. Nutricion

44. Food

meat	мясо (n)	['m'asə]
chicken	курица (f)	['kuritsə]
young chicken	цыплёнок (m)	[tsɪp'lɔnɑk]
duck	утка (f)	['utkə]
goose	гусь (m)	[gusʲ]
game	дичь (f)	[ditʃ]
turkey	индейка (f)	[in'dejkə]
pork	свинина (f)	[swi'ninə]
veal	телятина (f)	[ti'ʎatinə]
lamb	баранина (f)	[ba'raninə]
beef	говядина (f)	[ga'vʲadinə]
rabbit	кролик (m)	['krɔlik]
sausage (salami etc.)	колбаса (f)	[kɑlba'sɑ]
hot dog (frankfurter)	сосиска (f)	[sa'siskə]
bacon	бекон (m)	[bi'kɔn]
ham	ветчина (f)	[witʃi'nɑ]
gammon (ham)	окорок (m)	['ɔkɑrɑk]
pâté	паштет (m)	[paʃ'tet]
liver	печень (f)	['petʃeɲ]
lard	сало (n)	['salə]
ground beef	фарш (m)	[farʃ]
tongue	язык (m)	[ja'zɪk]
egg	яйцо (n)	[jaj'tsɔ]
eggs	яйца (pl)	['jajtsə]
egg white	белок (m)	[bi'lɔk]
egg yolk	желток (m)	[ʒɪl'tɔk]
fish	рыба (f)	['rɪbə]
seafood	морепродукты (pl)	[marepra'duktɪ]
crustaceans	ракообразные (pl)	[rakaab'raznɪe]
caviar	икра (f)	[ik'ra]
crab	краб (m)	[krap]
shrimp	креветка (f)	[kri'wetkə]
oyster	устрица (f)	['ustritsə]
spiny lobster	лангуст (m)	[la'ŋust]
octopus	осьминог (m)	[asʲmi'nɔk]
squid	кальмар (m)	[kaʎ'mar]

sturgeon	**осетрина** (f)	[ɑsit'rinə]
salmon	**лосось** (m)	[la'sɔsʲ]
halibut	**палтус** (m)	['pɑltʊs]
cod	**треска** (f)	[tris'ka]
mackerel	**скумбрия** (f)	['skʊmbrija]
tuna	**тунец** (m)	[tʊ'nets]
eel	**угорь** (m)	['ugɑrʲ]
trout	**форель** (f)	[fɑ'reʎ]
sardine	**сардина** (f)	[sar'dinə]
pike	**щука** (f)	['ɕukə]
herring	**сельдь** (f)	[seʎtʲ]
bread	**хлеб** (m)	[hlep]
cheese	**сыр** (m)	[sɪr]
sugar	**сахар** (m)	['sahɑr]
salt	**соль** (f)	[sɔʎ]
rice	**рис** (m)	[ris]
pasta	**макароны** (pl)	[maka'rɔnɪ]
noodles	**лапша** (f)	[lap'ʃʌ]
butter	**сливочное масло** (n)	['slivatʃnae 'maslə]
vegetable oil	**растительное масло** (n)	[ras'titeʎnae 'maslə]
sunflower oil	**подсолнечное масло** (n)	[pa'tsɔlnetʃnae 'maslə]
margarine	**маргарин** (m)	[marga'rin]
olives	**оливки** (pl)	[a'lifki]
olive oil	**оливковое масло** (n)	[a'lifkavae 'maslə]
milk	**молоко** (n)	[mala'kɔ]
condensed milk	**сгущённое молоко** (n)	[sgʊ'ɕɘnae mala'kɔ]
yogurt	**йогурт** (m)	['jogʊrt]
sour cream	**сметана** (f)	[smi'tanə]
cream (of milk)	**сливки** (pl)	['slifki]
mayonnaise	**майонез** (m)	[mai'nɛs]
cream (filling for biscuits)	**крем** (m)	[krem]
cereal grains	**крупа** (f)	[krʊ'pa]
flour	**мука** (f)	[mʊ'ka]
canned food	**консервы** (pl)	[kan'servɪ]
cornflakes	**кукурузные хлопья** (pl)	[kʊkʊ'rʊznɪe 'hlɔpja]
honey	**мёд** (m)	['mɜt]
jelly (e.g., strawberry ~)	**джем** (m)	[dʒɛm]
chewing gum	**жевательная резинка** (m)	[ʒɪ'vɑteʎnaja re'zinkə]

45. Drinks

water	вода (f)	[va'da]
drinking water	питьевая вода (f)	[pitje'vaja va'da]
mineral water	минеральная вода (f)	[mini'raʎnaja va'da]
still	без газа	[bez 'gazə]
carbonated	газированный	[gazi'rovanıj]
sparkling	с газом	[s gazam]
ice	лёд (m)	['lɔt]
with ice	со льдом	[saʎ'dɔm]
non-alcoholic	безалкогольный	[bizalka'goʎnıj]
soft drink	безалкогольный напиток (m)	[bizalka'goʎnıj na'pitak]
cool soft drink	прохладительный напиток (m)	[prahla'diteʎnıj na'pitak]
lemonade	лимонад (m)	[lima'nat]
liquor	алкогольные напитки (pl)	[alka'goʎnıe na'pitki]
wine	вино (n)	[wi'nɔ]
white wine	белое вино (n)	['belae wi'nɔ]
red wine	красное вино (n)	['krasnae wi'nɔ]
liqueur	ликёр (m)	[li'kɜr]
champagne	шампанское (n)	[ʃʌm'panskae]
vermouth	вермут (m)	['wermʊt]
whisky	виски (n)	['wiski]
vodka	водка (f)	['vɔtkə]
gin	джин (m)	[dʒın]
cognac	коньяк (m)	[ka'njak]
rum	ром (m)	[rɔm]
coffee	кофе (m)	['kɔfe]
black coffee	чёрный кофе (m)	['tʃɔrnıj 'kɔfe]
coffee with milk	кофе (m) с молоком	['kɔfe s mala'kɔm]
cappuccino	кофе (m) со сливками	['kɔfe sa 'slifkami]
instant coffee	растворимый кофе (m)	[rastva'rimıj 'kɔfe]
milk	молоко (n)	[mala'kɔ]
cocktail	коктейль (m)	[kak'tɛjʎ]
milk shake	молочный коктейль (m)	[ma'lɔtʃnıj kak'tɛjʎ]
juice	сок (m)	[sɔk]
tomato juice	томатный сок (m)	[ta'matnıj sɔk]
orange juice	апельсиновый сок (m)	[apiʎ'sinavıj sɔk]
freshly squeezed juice	свежевыжатый сок (m)	[sweʒɛ'vıʒatıj sɔk]
beer	пиво (n)	['pivə]
light beer	светлое пиво (n)	['swetlae 'pivə]

dark beer	тёмное пиво (n)	['tɔmnɑe 'pivə]
tea	чай (m)	[ʧaj]
black tea	чёрный чай (m)	['ʧɔrnɪj ʧaj]
green tea	зелёный чай (m)	[zi'lɜnɪj ʧaj]

46. Vegetables

vegetables	овощи (pl)	['ɔvɑçi]
greens	зелень (f)	['zeleɲ]
tomato	помидор (m)	[pɑmi'dɔr]
cucumber	огурец (m)	[ɑgʊ'reʦ]
carrot	морковь (f)	[mɑr'kɔfʲ]
potato	картофель (m)	[kɑr'tɔfeʎ]
onion	лук (m)	[luk]
garlic	чеснок (m)	[ʧis'nɔk]
cabbage	капуста (f)	[kɑ'pʊstə]
cauliflower	цветная капуста (f)	[ʦwet'nɑjɑ kɑ'pʊstə]
Brussels sprouts	брюссельская капуста (f)	[bry'seʎskɑjɑ kɑ'pʊstə]
broccoli	капуста (f) брокколи	[kɑ'pʊstɑ 'brɔkɑli]
beet	свёкла (f)	['swɜklə]
eggplant	баклажан (m)	[bɑklɑ'ʒɑn]
zucchini	кабачок (m)	[kɑbɑ'ʧɔk]
pumpkin	тыква (f)	['tɪkvə]
turnip	репа (f)	['repə]
parsley	петрушка (f)	[pit'rʊʃkə]
dill	укроп (m)	[uk'rɔp]
lettuce	салат (m)	[sɑ'lɑt]
celery	сельдерей (m)	[siʎde'rej]
asparagus	спаржа (f)	['spɑrʒə]
spinach	шпинат (m)	[ʃpi'nɑt]
pea	горох (m)	[gɑ'rɔh]
beans	бобы (pl)	[bɑ'bɪ]
corn (maize)	кукуруза (f)	[kʊkʊ'rʊzə]
kidney bean	фасоль (f)	[fɑ'sɔʎ]
bell pepper	перец (m)	['pereʦ]
radish	редис (m)	[ri'dis]
artichoke	артишок (m)	[ɑrti'ʃɔk]

47. Fruits. Nuts

| fruit | фрукт (m) | [frʊkt] |
| apple | яблоко (n) | ['jablɑkə] |

pear	груша (f)	['gruʃə]
lemon	лимон (m)	[li'mɔn]
orange	апельсин (m)	[apiʎ'sin]
strawberry	клубника (f)	[klub'nikə]

mandarin	мандарин (m)	[mandɑ'rin]
plum	слива (f)	['slivə]
peach	персик (m)	['persik]
apricot	абрикос (m)	[abri'kɔs]
raspberry	малина (f)	[mɑ'linə]
pineapple	ананас (m)	[anɑ'nɑs]

banana	банан (m)	[bɑ'nɑn]
watermelon	арбуз (m)	[ar'bʊs]
grapes	виноград (m)	[winɑg'rɑt]
cherry (sour cherry)	вишня (f)	['wiʃnə]
cherry (sweet cherry)	черешня (f)	[ʧi'reʃnə]
melon	дыня (f)	['dɪnə]

grapefruit	грейпфрут (m)	[gripf'rʊt]
avocado	авокадо (n)	[avɑ'kadə]
papaya	папайя (f)	[pɑ'pɑjɑ]
mango	манго (n)	['mɑhgə]
pomegranate	гранат (m)	[grɑ'nɑt]

redcurrant	красная смородина (f)	['krasnɑjɑ smɑ'rɔdinə]
blackcurrant	чёрная смородина (f)	['ʧɔrnɑjɑ smɑ'rɔdinə]
gooseberry	крыжовник (m)	[krɪ'ʒɔvnik]
bilberry	черника (f)	[ʧir'nikə]
blackberry	ежевика (f)	[eʒɪ'wikə]

raisin	изюм (m)	[i'zym]
fig	инжир (m)	[in'ʒir]
date	финик (m)	['finik]

peanut	арахис (m)	[ɑ'rɑhis]
almond	миндаль (m)	[min'dɑʎ]
walnut	грецкий орех (m)	['gretskij ɑ'reh]
hazelnut	лесной орех (m)	[lis'nɔj ɑ'reh]
coconut	кокосовый орех (m)	[kɑ'kɔsɑvɪj ɑ'reh]
pistachios	фисташки (pl)	[fis'taʃki]

48. Bread. Candy

confectionery (pastry)	кондитерские изделия (pl)	[kan'diterskie iz'delijɑ]
bread	хлеб (m)	[hlep]
cookies	печенье (n)	[pi'ʧeɲje]
chocolate (noun)	шоколад (m)	[ʃʌkɑ'lɑt]
chocolate (attr)	шоколадный	[ʃʌkɑ'lɑdnɪj]

candy	конфета (f)	[kɑnˈfetə]
cake (e.g., cupcake)	пирожное (n)	[piˈrɔʒnɑe]
cake (e.g., birthday ~)	торт (m)	[tɔrt]

| pie (e.g., apple ~) | пирог (m) | [piˈrɔk] |
| filling (for cake, pie) | начинка (f) | [nɑˈtʃinkə] |

jam	варенье (n)	[vɑˈreɲe]
marmalade	мармелад (m)	[mɑrmeˈlɑt]
wafer	вафли (pl)	[ˈvɑfli]
ice-cream	мороженое (n)	[mɑˈrɔʒnɑe]
pudding	пудинг (m)	[ˈpʊdink]

49. Cooked dishes

course, dish	блюдо (n)	[ˈblydə]
cuisine	кухня (f)	[ˈkʊhɲa]
recipe	рецепт (m)	[riˈtsept]
portion	порция (f)	[ˈpɔrtsija]

| salad | салат (m) | [sɑˈlɑt] |
| soup | суп (m) | [sʊp] |

clear soup (broth)	бульон (m)	[bʊˈʎjon]
sandwich (bread)	бутерброд (m)	[bʊterbˈrɔt]
fried eggs	яичница (f)	[iˈiʃnitsə]

cutlet	котлета (f)	[kɑtˈletə]
hamburger (beefburger)	гамбургер (m)	[ˈgɑmbʊrger]
beefsteak	бифштекс (m)	[bifʃˈtɛks]
roast meat	жаркое (n)	[ʒɑrˈkɔe]

side dish	гарнир (m)	[gɑrˈnir]
spaghetti	спагетти (pl)	[spɑˈgetti]
mashed potatoes	картофельное пюре (n)	[kɑrˈtɔfeʎnɑe pyˈrɛ]
pizza	пицца (f)	[ˈpitsə]
porridge (oatmeal, etc)	каша (f)	[ˈkɑʃə]
omelet	омлет (m)	[ɑmˈlet]

boiled (e.g., ~ beef)	варёный	[vɑˈrɜnij]
smoked	копчёный	[kɑpˈtʃonij]
fried	жареный	[ˈʒɑrenij]
dried	сушёный	[sʊˈʃonij]
frozen	замороженный	[zamɑˈrɔʒinij]
pickled	маринованный	[mɑriˈnɔvanij]

sweet (in taste)	сладкий	[ˈslɑtkij]
salty	солёный	[sɑˈlɜnij]
cold	холодный	[hɑˈlɔdnij]
hot	горячий	[gɑˈrʲatʃij]

bitter	**горький**	[ˈgorʲkij]
tasty	**вкусный**	[ˈfkusnɪj]
to cook (vt)	**варить**	[vaˈritʲ]
to cook (vi)	**готовить**	[gaˈtowitʲ]
to fry (vt)	**жарить**	[ˈʒaritʲ]
to heat up (food)	**разогревать**	[razagreˈvatʲ]
to salt (vt)	**солить**	[saˈlitʲ]
to pepper (vt)	**перчить**	[pirˈtʃitʲ]
to grate (vt)	**тереть**	[tiˈretʲ]
peel (noun)	**кожура** (f)	[kaʒuˈra]
to peel (vt)	**чистить**	[ˈtʃistitʲ]

50. Spices

salt	**соль** (f)	[sɔʎ]
salty	**солёный**	[saˈlɜnɪj]
to salt (vt)	**солить**	[saˈlitʲ]
black pepper	**чёрный перец** (m)	[ˈtʃornɪj ˈperets]
red pepper	**красный перец** (m)	[ˈkrasnɪj ˈperets]
mustard	**горчица** (f)	[garˈtʃitsə]
horseradish	**хрен** (m)	[hren]
seasoning (condiment)	**приправа** (f)	[pripˈravə]
spice	**пряность** (f)	[ˈprʲanəstʲ]
sauce	**соус** (m)	[ˈsɔus]
vinegar	**уксус** (m)	[ˈuksus]
anise	**анис** (m)	[aˈnis]
basil	**базилик** (m)	[baziˈlik]
cloves	**гвоздика** (f)	[gvazˈdikə]
ginger	**имбирь** (m)	[imˈbirʲ]
coriander	**кориандр** (m)	[kariˈandr]
cinnamon	**корица** (f)	[kaˈritsə]
sesame	**кунжут** (m)	[kunˈʒut]
bay leaf	**лавровый лист** (m)	[lavˈrovɪj list]
paprika	**паприка** (f)	[ˈpaprikə]
caraway	**тмин** (m)	[tmin]
saffron	**шафран** (m)	[ʃʌfˈran]

51. Meals

food (noun)	**еда** (f)	[eˈda]
to eat (vi, vt)	**есть**	[estʲ]
breakfast	**завтрак** (m)	[ˈzaftrak]

to have breakfast	**завтракать**	[ˈzaftrakatʲ]
lunch	**обед** (m)	[aˈbet]
to have lunch	**обедать**	[aˈbedatʲ]
dinner (evening meal)	**ужин** (m)	[ˈuʒɪn]
to have dinner	**ужинать**	[ˈuʒɪnatʲ]
appetite	**аппетит** (m)	[apiˈtit]
Enjoy your meal!	**Приятного аппетита!**	[priˈjatnəvə apeˈtita]
to open (e.g., ~ a bottle)	**открывать**	[atkrɪˈvatʲ]
to spill (liquid)	**пролить**	[praˈlitʲ]
to spill out (vi)	**пролиться**	[praˈlitsə]
to boil (vi)	**кипеть**	[kiˈpetʲ]
to boil (vt)	**кипятить**	[kipiˈtitʲ]
boiled	**кипячёный**	[kipiˈtʃɔnɪj]
to cool (vt)	**охладить**	[ahlaˈditʲ]
to cool down (vi)	**охлаждаться**	[ahlaʒˈdatsə]
taste, flavor	**вкус** (m)	[fkʊs]
aftertaste	**привкус** (m)	[ˈprifkʊs]
to be on a diet	**худеть**	[hʊˈdetʲ]
diet	**диета** (f)	[diˈetə]
vitamin	**витамин** (m)	[witaˈmin]
calorie	**калория** (f)	[kaˈlɔrija]
vegetarian (noun)	**вегетарианец** (m)	[wigitariˈanets]
vegetarian (adj)	**вегетарианский**	[wigitariˈanskij]
fats (nutrient)	**жиры** (pl)	[ʒɪˈrɪ]
proteins	**белки** (pl)	[bilˈki]
carbohydrates	**углеводы** (pl)	[ugleˈvɔdɪ]
slice (of lemon, ham)	**ломтик** (m)	[ˈlɔmtik]
piece (of cake, pie)	**кусок** (m)	[kʊˈsɔk]
crumb (of bread)	**крошка** (f)	[ˈkrɔʃkə]

52. Table setting

spoon	**ложка** (f)	[ˈlɔʃkə]
knife	**нож** (m)	[nɔʃ]
fork	**вилка** (f)	[ˈwilkə]
cup (of coffee)	**чашка** (f)	[ˈtʃaʃkə]
dinner plate	**тарелка** (f)	[taˈrelkə]
saucer	**блюдце** (n)	[ˈblytsə]
napkin (on table)	**салфетка** (f)	[salˈfetkə]
toothpick	**зубочистка** (f)	[zubaˈtʃistkə]

53. Restaurant

restaurant	ресторан (m)	[rista'ran]
café	кафе (n)	[ka'fɛ]
coffee house	кофейня (f)	[ka'fejna]
pub, bar	бар (m)	[bar]
tearoom	чайный салон (m)	['tʃajnɪj sa'lɔn]

waiter	официант (m)	[afɪtsɪ'ant]
waitress	официантка (f)	[afɪtsɪ'antkə]
bartender	бармен (m)	[bar'men]

menu	меню (n)	[mi'ny]
wine list	карта (f) вин	['karta win]
to book a table	забронировать столик	[zabra'niravatʲ 'stɔlik]

course, dish	блюдо (n)	['blydə]
to order (meal)	заказать	[zaka'zatʲ]
to make an order	сделать заказ	['sdelatʲ za'kas]
aperitif	аперитив (m)	[apiri'tif]
appetizer	закуска (f)	[za'kuskə]
dessert	десерт (m)	[di'sert]

check	счёт (m)	['ɕɔt]
to pay the check	оплатить счёт	[apla'titʲ 'ɕɔt]
to give change	дать сдачу	[datʲ 'sdatʃu]
tip	чаевые (pl)	[tʃii'vɪe]

Family, relatives and friends

54. Personal information. Forms

name, first name	**имя** (n)	['im'a]
family name	**фамилия** (f)	[fɑ'milijɑ]
date of birth	**дата** (f) **рождения**	['dɑtɑ rɑʒ'denijɑ]
place of birth	**место** (n) **рождения**	['mestɑ rɑʒ'denijɑ]
nationality	**национальность** (f)	[nɑtsiɑ'nɑʌnɑsti]
place of residence	**место** (n) **жительства**	['mestɑ 'ʒiteʌstvɑ]
country	**страна** (f)	[strɑ'nɑ]
profession (occupation)	**профессия** (f)	[prɑ'fesijɑ]
gender, sex	**пол** (m)	[pɔl]
height	**рост** (m)	[rɔst]
weight	**вес** (m)	[wes]

55. Family members. Relatives

mother	**мать** (f)	[mɑti]
father	**отец** (m)	[ɑ'teʦ]
son	**сын** (m)	[sɪn]
daughter	**дочь** (f)	[dɔtʃ]
younger daughter	**младшая дочь** (f)	['mlɑtʃʌjɑ dɔtʃ]
younger son	**младший сын** (m)	['mlɑtʃij sɪn]
elder daughter	**старшая дочь** (f)	['stɑrʃʌjɑ dɔtʃ]
elder son	**старший сын** (m)	['stɑrʃij sɪn]
brother	**брат** (m)	[brɑt]
sister	**сестра** (f)	[sist'rɑ]
cousin (masc.)	**двоюродный брат** (m)	[dvɑ'jurɑdnɪj brɑt]
cousin (fem.)	**двоюродная сестра** (f)	[dvɑ'jurɑdnɑjɑ sist'rɑ]
mom	**мама** (f)	['mɑmɑ]
dad, daddy	**папа** (m)	['pɑpɑ]
parents	**родители** (pl)	[rɑ'diteli]
child (boy or girl)	**ребёнок** (m)	[ri'bɔnɑk]
children	**дети** (pl)	['deti]
grandmother	**бабушка** (f)	['bɑbuʃkɑ]
grandfather	**дедушка** (m)	['deduʃkɑ]
grandson	**внук** (m)	[vnʊk]
granddaughter	**внучка** (f)	['vnʊtʃkɑ]

grandchildren	внуки (pl)	['vnʊki]
uncle	дядя (m)	['dʲadʲa]
aunt	тётя (f)	['tɜtʲa]
nephew	племянник (m)	[plʲi'mʲanik]
niece	племянница (f)	[plʲi'mʲanitsə]
mother-in-law	тёща (f)	['tɜɕə]
father-in-law	свёкор (m)	['swɜkɑr]
son-in-law	зять (m)	[zʲatʲ]
stepmother	мачеха (f)	['matʃehə]
stepfather	отчим (m)	['ɔtʃim]
baby (infant)	грудной ребенок (m)	[grʊd'nɔj rʲi'bɜnɑk]
infant	младенец (m)	[mlɑ'denets]
little boy, kid	малыш (m)	[mɑ'lɪʃ]
wife	жена (f)	[ʒɪ'nɑ]
husband	муж (m)	[mʊʃ]
spouse (husband)	супруг (m)	[sʊp'rʊk]
spouse (wife)	супруга (f)	[sʊp'rʊgə]
married (man)	женатый	[ʒɪ'nɑtɪj]
married (woman)	замужняя	[za'mʊʒnija]
single (unmarried)	холостой	[hɑlɑs'tɔj]
bachelor	холостяк (m)	[hɑlɑs'tʲak]
divorced (man)	разведённый	[razwe'dɜnɪj]
widow	вдова (f)	[vdɑ'vɑ]
widower	вдовец (m)	[vdɑ'wets]
relative	родственник (m)	['rɔtstwenik]
close relative	близкий родственник (m)	['blizkij 'rɔtstwenik]
distant relative	дальний родственник (m)	['dɑʎnij 'rɔtstwenik]
relatives	родные (pl)	[rɑd'nɪe]
orphan (boy or girl)	сирота (m, f)	[sira'ta]
orphan (boy)	сирота (m)	[sira'ta]
orphan (girl)	сирота (f)	[sira'ta]
guardian (of minor)	опекун (m)	[api'kʊn]
to adopt (a boy)	усыновить	[usɪnɑ'witʲ]
to adopt (a girl)	удочерить	[udatʃe'ritʲ]

56. Friends. Coworkers

friend (man)	друг (m)	[drʊk]
friend (girlfriend)	подруга (f)	[pɑd'rʊgə]
friendship	дружба (f)	['drʊʒbə]
to be friends	дружить	[drʊ'ʒitʲ]
buddy (man)	приятель (m)	[pri'jateʎ]
buddy (woman)	приятельница (f)	[pri'jateʎnitsə]

comrade (politics)	товарищ (m)	[ta'variɕ]
partner	партнёр (m)	[part'nɜr]
business partner	деловой партнёр (m)	[dila'vɔj part'nɜr]

chief (boss)	шеф (m)	[ʃəf]
boss, superior	начальник (m)	[na'tʃaʎnik]
owner	владелец (m)	[vla'delets]
subordinate	подчинённый (m)	[patʃi'nɜnnij]
colleague	коллега (m)	[ka'legə]

acquaintance (person)	знакомый (m)	[zna'kɔmij]
fellow traveler	попутчик (m)	[pa'pʊtʃik]
classmate	одноклассник (m)	[adnak'lasnik]

neighbor (man)	сосед (m)	[sa'set]
neighbor (woman)	соседка (f)	[sa'setkə]
neighbors	соседи (pl)	[sa'sedi]

57. Man. Woman

woman	женщина (f)	['ʒɛɲɕinə]
girl (young woman)	девушка (f)	['devʊʃkə]
bride	невеста (f)	[ni'westə]

beautiful	красивая	[kra'sivaja]
tall	высокая	[vɪ'sɔkaja]
slender	стройная	['strɔjnaja]
short	невысокого роста	[nevɪ'sɔkava 'rɔstə]

| blonde (noun) | блондинка (f) | [blan'dinkə] |
| brunette (noun) | брюнетка (f) | [bry'netkə] |

ladies'	дамский	['damskij]
virgin (girl)	девственница (f)	['defstwenitsə]
pregnant	беременная	[bi'remenaja]

man (adult male)	мужчина (m)	[mʊ'ɕinə]
blond (noun)	блондин (m)	[blan'din]
brunet (noun)	брюнет (m)	[bry'net]
tall	высокий	[vɪ'sɔkij]
short	невысокого роста	[nevɪ'sɔkava 'rɔstə]

rude (rough)	грубый	['grʊbɪj]
stocky	коренастый	[kari'nastɪj]
robust	крепкий	['krepkij]
strong	сильный	['siʎnɪj]
strength (physical power)	сила (f)	['silə]

| stout, fat | полный | ['pɔlnɪj] |
| swarthy | смуглый | ['smʊglɪj] |

| well-built | **стройный** | [ˈstrɔjnɪj] |
| elegant | **элегантный** | [ɛliˈɡantnɪj] |

58. Age

age	**возраст** (m)	[ˈvɔzrast]
youth (young age)	**юность** (f)	[ˈjunastʲ]
young	**молодой**	[malaˈdɔj]

| younger | **младше** | [ˈmlatʃə] |
| older | **старше** | [ˈstarʃə] |

young man	**юноша** (m)	[ˈjunaʃə]
teenager	**подросток** (m)	[padˈrostak]
guy, fellow	**парень** (m)	[ˈpareɲ]

| old man | **старик** (m) | [staˈrik] |
| old woman | **старая женщина** (m) | [ˈstaraja ˈʒɛɲɕinə] |

adult	**взрослый**	[ˈvzrɔslɪj]
middle-aged	**средних лет**	[ˈsrednih let]
elderly	**пожилой**	[paʒɪˈlɔj]
old	**старый**	[ˈstarɪj]

retirement	**пенсия** (f)	[ˈpeɲsija]
to retire (from job)	**уйти на пенсию**	[ujˈti na ˈpeɲsiju]
retiree	**пенсионер** (f)	[piɲsiaˈner]

59. Children

child (boy or girl)	**ребёнок** (m)	[riˈbɜnak]
children	**дети** (pl)	[ˈdeti]
twins	**близнецы** (pl)	[blizneˈtsɪ]

cradle (for baby)	**люлька** (f), **колыбель** (f)	[ˈlyʎka], [kalɪˈbeʎ]
rattle (for baby)	**погремушка** (f)	[pagreˈmuʃkə]
diaper	**подгузник** (m)	[padˈɡuznik]

pacifier	**соска** (f)	[ˈsɔskə]
baby carriage	**коляска** (f)	[kaˈʎaskə]
kindergarten	**детский сад** (m)	[ˈdetskij sat]
babysitter	**няня** (f)	[ˈɲaɲa]

childhood	**детство** (n)	[ˈdetstvə]
doll	**кукла** (f)	[ˈkuklə]
toy	**игрушка** (f)	[igˈruʃkə]
construction set	**конструктор** (m)	[kanstˈruktar]
well-bred	**воспитанный**	[vasˈpitanɪj]

ill-bred	**невоспитанный**	[nivas'pitanɪj]
spoiled	**избалованный**	[izba'lovanɪj]
to be naughty	**шалить**	[ʃʌ'litʲ]
naughty	**шаловливый**	[ʃʌlav'livɪj]
naughtiness	**шалость** (f)	['ʃʌlastʲ]
naughty boy	**шалун** (m)	[ʃʌ'lun]
obedient	**послушный**	[pas'luʃnɪj]
disobedient	**непослушный**	[nipas'luʃnɪj]
docile	**умный**	['umnɪj]
clever (smart)	**умный**	['umnɪj]
child prodigy	**вундеркинд** (m)	[vʊndɛr'kint]

60. Married couples. Family life

to kiss (vt)	**целовать**	[tsɪla'vatʲ]
to kiss (vi)	**целоваться**	[tsɪla'vatsə]
family (noun)	**семья** (f)	[si'mja]
family (attr)	**семейный**	[si'mejnɪj]
couple	**пара** (f), **чета** (f)	['para], [tɕe'ta]
marriage (state)	**брак** (m)	[brak]
hearth (home)	**домашний очаг** (m)	[da'maʃnij a'tɕak]
dynasty	**династия** (f)	[di'nastija]
date	**свидание** (n)	[swi'danie]
kiss	**поцелуй** (m)	[patsɪ'luj]
love (for sb)	**любовь** (f)	[ly'bofʲ]
to love (sb)	**любить**	[ly'bitʲ]
beloved	**любимый**	[ly'bimɪj]
tenderness	**нежность** (f)	['neʒnastʲ]
tender (affectionate)	**нежный**	['neʒnɪj]
faithfulness	**верность** (f)	['wernastʲ]
faithful	**верный**	['wernɪj]
care (attention)	**забота** (f)	[za'botə]
caring (thoughtful)	**заботливый**	[za'botlivɪj]
newlyweds	**молодожёны** (pl)	[malada'ʒɜnɪ]
honeymoon	**медовый месяц** (m)	[me'dovɪj 'mesits]
to get married (woman)	**выйти замуж**	['vɪjti 'zamuʃ]
to get married (man)	**жениться**	[ʒɪ'nitsə]
wedding	**свадьба** (f)	['svadʲbə]
golden wedding	**золотая свадьба** (f)	[zala'taja 'svadʲbə]
anniversary	**годовщина** (f)	[gadaf'ɕinə]
lover (man)	**любовник** (m)	[ly'bovnik]
mistress	**любовница** (f)	[ly'bovnitsə]

adultery	**измена** (f)	[iz'menə]
to commit adultery	**изменить**	[izme'nitʲ]
jealous (fearful of rivals)	**ревнивый**	[riv'nivɪj]
to be jealous	**ревновать**	[rivnɑ'vɑtʲ]
divorce	**развод** (m)	[rɑz'vot]
to divorce (vi)	**развестись**	[rɑzwes'tisʲ]
to quarrel (vi)	**ссориться**	['sɔritsə]
to become reconciled	**мириться**	[mi'ritsə]
together	**вместе**	['vmeste]
sex (sexual activity)	**секс** (m)	[sɛks]
happiness	**счастье** (n)	['ɕastje]
happy	**счастливый**	[ɕis'livɪj]
misfortune (accident)	**несчастье** (n)	[ni'ɕastje]
unhappy	**несчастный**	[ni'ɕasnɪj]

Character. Feelings. Emotions

61. Feelings. Emotions

feeling (emotion)	чувство (n)	['ʧustvə]
feelings	чувства (pl)	['ʧustvə]
to feel (vt)	чувствовать	['ʧustvavatʲ]
hunger	голод (m)	['gɔlat]
to be hungry	хотеть есть	[ha'tetʲ 'estʲ]
thirst	жажда (f)	['ʒaʒdə]
to be thirsty	хотеть пить	[ha'tetʲ 'pitʲ]
sleepiness	сонливость (f)	[san'livastʲ]
to feel sleepy	хотеть спать	[ha'tetʲ 'spatʲ]
tiredness	усталость (f)	[us'talastʲ]
tired	усталый	[us'talɪj]
to get tired	устать	[us'tatʲ]
mood (humor)	настроение (n)	[nastra'enie]
boredom	скука (f)	['skukə]
to be bored	скучать	[sku'ʧatʲ]
seclusion	уединение (n)	[uidi'nenie]
to seclude oneself	уединиться	[uidi'nitsə]
to worry (make anxious)	беспокоить	[bispa'kɔitʲ]
to be worried	беспокоиться	[bispa'kɔitsə]
anxiety	беспокойство (n)	[bispa'kɔjstvə]
worrying (noun)	тревога (f)	[tri'vɔgə]
preoccupied	озабоченный	[aza'bɔʧenɪj]
to be nervous	нервничать	['nervniʧatʲ]
to panic (vi)	паниковать	[panika'vatʲ]
hope	надежда (f)	[na'deʒdə]
to hope (vi, vt)	надеяться	[na'deitsə]
certainty	уверенность (f)	[u'werenastʲ]
certain, sure	уверенный	[u'werenɪj]
uncertainty	неуверенность (f)	[niu'werenastʲ]
uncertain	неуверенный	[niu'werenɪj]
drunk	пьяный	['pjanɪj]
sober	трезвый	['trezvɪj]
weak	слабый	['slabɪj]
to scare (vt)	испугать	[ispu'gatʲ]
fury (madness)	бешенство (n)	['beʃenstvə]

rage (fury)	**ярость** (f)	['jarəstʲ]
depression	**депрессия** (f)	[dip'resijə]
discomfort (unease)	**дискомфорт** (m)	[diskam'fort]
comfort	**комфорт** (m)	[kam'fort]
to regret (be sorry)	**сожалеть**	[saʒi'letʲ]
regret	**сожаление** (n)	[saʒi'lenie]
bad luck	**невезение** (n)	[niwe'zenie]
sadness	**огорчение** (n)	[agar'ʧenie]

shame (feeling)	**стыд** (m)	[stɪt]
merriment	**веселье** (n)	[wi'seʎje]
enthusiasm	**энтузиазм** (m)	[ɛntʊzi'azm]
enthusiast	**энтузиаст** (m)	[ɛntʊzi'ast]
to show enthusiasm	**проявить энтузиазм**	[prai'witʲ ɛntʊzi'azm]

62. Character. Personality

character	**характер** (m)	[ha'rakter]
character flaw	**недостаток** (m)	[nidas'tatak]
mind (intellect)	**разум** (m)	['razum]

conscience	**совесть** (f)	['sɔwestʲ]
habit (custom)	**привычка** (f)	[pri'vɪʧkə]
ability	**способность** (f)	[spa'sɔbnastʲ]
can (e.g., ~ swim)	**уметь**	[u'metʲ]

patient	**терпеливый**	[terpe'livɪj]
impatient	**нетерпеливый**	[niterpe'livɪj]
curious (inquisitive)	**любопытный**	[lyba'pɪtnɪj]
curiosity	**любопытство** (n)	[lyba'pɪʦtvə]

modesty	**скромность** (f)	['skrɔmnastʲ]
modest	**скромный**	['skrɔmnɪj]
immodest	**нескромный**	[nisk'rɔmnɪj]

laziness	**лень** (f)	[leɲ]
lazy	**ленивый**	[li'nivɪj]
lazy person (masc.)	**лентяй** (m)	[lin'tʲaj]

cunning (noun)	**хитрость** (f)	['hitrastʲ]
cunning (attr)	**хитрый**	['hitrɪj]
distrust	**недоверие** (n)	[nida'werie]
distrustful	**недоверчивый**	[nida'werʧivɪj]

generosity	**щедрость** (f)	['ɕedrastʲ]
generous	**щедрый**	['ɕedrɪj]
talented	**талантливый**	[ta'lantlivɪj]
talent	**талант** (m)	[ta'lant]
courageous	**смелый**	['smelɪj]
courage	**смелость** (f)	['smelastʲ]

| honest | честный | ['ʧesnıj] |
| honesty | честность (f) | ['ʧesnɑstʲ] |

careful (cautious)	осторожный	[ɑstaˈrɔʒnıj]
brave	отважный	[atˈvaʒnıj]
serious	серьёзный	[siˈrjoznıj]
strict (severe, stern)	строгий	['strɔgij]

determined (resolute)	решительный	[reˈʃiteʎnıj]
indecisive	нерешительный	[nireˈʃiteʎnıj]
shy, timid	робкий	['rɔpkij]
shyness, timidity	робость (f)	['rɔbɑstʲ]

trust (confidence)	доверие (n)	[daˈwerie]
to trust (vt)	верить	['weritʲ]
trusting (naïve)	доверчивый	[daˈwerʧivıj]

sincerely	искренне	['iskrene]
sincere	искренний	['iskrenij]
sincerity	искренность (f)	['iskrenɑstʲ]
open (person)	открытый	[atkˈrıtıj]

calm	тихий	['tihij]
frank, sincere	откровенный	[atkraˈwennıj]
naive	наивный	[naˈivnıj]
absent-minded	рассеянный	[raˈseinıj]
funny (amusing)	смешной	[smiʃˈnɔj]

greed	жадность (f)	['ʒadnɑstʲ]
greedy	жадный	['ʒadnıj]
stingy	скупой	[skʊˈpɔj]
evil	злой	[zlɔj]
stubborn	упрямый	[upˈrʲamıj]
unpleasant (person)	неприятный	[nipriˈjatnıj]

selfish person (masc.)	эгоист (m)	[ɛgaˈist]
selfish	эгоистичный	[ɛgaisˈtiʧnıj]
coward	трус (m)	[trʊs]
cowardly	трусливый	[trʊsˈlivıj]

63. Sleep. Dreams

to sleep (vi)	спать	[spatʲ]
sleep, sleeping	сон (m)	[sɔn]
dream	сон (m)	[sɔn]
to dream (in sleep)	видеть сны	['widetʲ snı]
sleepy (person)	сонный	['sɔnnıj]

| bed | кровать (f) | [kraˈvatʲ] |
| mattress | матрас (m) | [matˈras] |

blanket (e.g., comforter)	одеяло (n)	[adi'jalə]
pillow	подушка (f)	[pa'duʃkə]
sheet (for bed)	простыня (f)	[prasti'ɲa]

insomnia	бессонница (f)	[bi'sɔnitsə]
sleepless	бессонный	[bis'sɔnnɪj]
sleeping pill	снотворное (n)	[snat'vɔrnae]
to take a sleeping pill	принять снотворное	[pri'ɲatʲ snat'vɔrnae]

to feel sleepy	хотеть спать	[ha'tetʲ 'spatʲ]
to yawn (vi)	зевать	[ze'vatʲ]
to go to bed	идти спать	[it'ti 'spatʲ]
to make up the bed	стелить постель	[ste'litʲ pas'teʌ]
to fall asleep	заснуть	[zas'nutʲ]

nightmare	кошмар (m)	[kaʃ'mar]
snoring	храп (m)	[hrap]
to snore (vi)	храпеть	[hra'petʲ]

alarm clock	будильник (m)	[bu'diʌnik]
to wake (vt)	разбудить	[razbu'ditʲ]
to wake up (vi)	просыпаться	[prasɪ'patsə]
to get up (vi)	подниматься	[padni'matsə]
to wash up (vi)	умываться	[umɪ'vatsə]

64. Humour. Laughter. Gladness

humor (wit, fun)	юмор (m)	['jumar]
sense (of humor)	чувство (n)	['ʧustvə]
to have fun	веселиться	[wise'litsə]

| merry, cheerful | весёлый | [wi'sɜlɪj] |
| merriment | веселье (n) | [wi'seʌje] |

smile	улыбка (f)	[u'lɪpkə]
to smile (vi)	улыбаться	[ulɪ'batsə]
to start laughing	засмеяться	[zasme'jatsə]

| to laugh (vi) | смеяться | [smi'jatsə] |
| laugh, laughter | смех (m) | [smeh] |

anecdote	анекдот (m)	[anik'dɔt]
funny (amusing)	смешной	[smiʃ'nɔj]
funny (odd)	смешной	[smiʃ'nɔj]

to joke (vi)	шутить	[ʃu'titʲ]
joke (verbal)	шутка (f)	['ʃutkə]
joy (such a ~)	радость (f)	['radastʲ]
to be glad	радоваться	['radavatsə]
glad, cheerful	радостный	['radasnɪj]

65. Discussion, conversation. Part 1

communication	общение (n)	[ap'ɕenie]
to communicate	общаться	[ap'ɕatsə]
conversation	разговор (m)	[razga'vɔr]
dialog	диалог (m)	[dia'lɔk]
discussion (debate)	дискуссия (f)	[dis'kusija]
debate	спор (m)	[spɔr]
to debate (vi)	спорить	['sporitʲ]
interlocutor	собеседник (m)	[sabe'sednik]
topic (theme)	тема (f)	['temə]
point of view	точка (f) зрения	['totʃka 'zrenija]
opinion (viewpoint)	мнение (n)	['mnenie]
speech (talk)	речь (f)	[retʃ]
discussion (of report etc.)	обсуждение (n)	[apsuʒ'denie]
to discuss (proposal etc.)	обсуждать	[apsuʒ'datʲ]
talk (conversation)	беседа (f)	[bi'sedə]
to talk (vi)	беседовать	[bi'sedavatʲ]
meeting	встреча (f)	['fstretʃə]
to meet (vi, vt)	встречаться	[fstre'tʃatsə]
proverb	пословица (f)	[pas'lɔwitsə]
saying	поговорка (f)	[paga'vorkə]
riddle (poser)	загадка (f)	[za'gatkə]
to ask a riddle	загадывать загадку	[za'gadıvatʲ za'gatku]
password	пароль (m)	[pa'rɔʎ]
secret	секрет (m)	[sik'ret]
oath (vow)	клятва (f)	['kʎatvə]
to swear (an oath)	клясться	['kʎastsə]
promise	обещание (n)	[abi'ɕanie]
to promise (vt)	обещать	[abi'ɕatʲ]
advice (counsel)	совет (m)	[sa'wet]
to advise (vt)	советовать	[sa'wetavatʲ]
to follow one's advice	следовать совету	['sledavatʲ sa'wetu]
to listen (vi)	слушаться	['sluʃʌtsə]
news	новость (f)	['nɔvastʲ]
sensation (news)	сенсация (f)	[sin'satsija]
information (facts)	сведения (pl)	['swedenija]
conclusion (decision)	вывод (m)	['vıvat]
voice	голос (f)	['gɔlas]
compliment	комплимент (m)	[kampli'ment]
kind (nice)	любезный	[ly'beznıj]
word	слово (n)	['slɔvə]
phrase	фраза (f)	['frazə]

answer	**ответ** (m)	[at'wet]
response	**ответ** (m)	[at'wet]
truth (true facts)	**правда** (f)	['pravdə]
lie (untruth)	**ложь** (f)	[loʃ]
thought	**мысль** (f)	[mɪsʎ]
fantasy	**фантазия** (f)	[fan'tazija]

66. Discussion, conversation. Part 2

respected	**уважаемый**	[uva'ʒaemɪj]
to respect (vt)	**уважать**	[uva'ʒatʲ]
respect	**уважение** (n)	[u'vaʒɛnie]
Dear …	**Уважаемый …**	[uva'ʒaemɪj]
to introduce (present)	**познакомить**	[pazna'komitʲ]
to make acquaintance	**познакомиться**	[pazna'komitsə]
intention	**намерение** (n)	[na'merenie]
to intend (have in mind)	**намереваться**	[namere'vatsə]
wish	**пожелание** (n)	[paʒɪ'lanie]
to wish (~ good luck)	**пожелать**	[paʒɪ'latʲ]
surprise (astonishment)	**удивление** (n)	[udiv'lenie]
to surprise (amaze)	**удивлять**	[udiv'ʎatʲ]
to be surprised	**удивляться**	[udiv'ʎatsə]
to give (vt)	**дать**	[datʲ]
to take (get hold of)	**взять**	[vzʲatʲ]
to give back (vt)	**вернуть**	[wir'nutʲ]
to return (give back)	**отдать**	[ad'datʲ]
to apologize (vi)	**извиняться**	[izwi'ɲatsə]
apology	**извинение** (n)	[izwi'nenie]
to forgive (vt)	**прощать**	[pra'ɕatʲ]
to talk (speak)	**разговаривать**	[razga'varivatʲ]
to listen (vi)	**слушать**	['sluʃʌtʲ]
to hear sb out	**выслушать**	['vɪsluʃʌtʲ]
to understand (vt)	**понять**	[pa'ɲatʲ]
to show (display)	**показать**	[paka'zatʲ]
to look at …	**глядеть на …**	[gli'detʲ na]
to call (with one's voice)	**позвать**	[paz'vatʲ]
to bother (vt)	**беспокоить**	[bispa'koitʲ]
to disturb (vt)	**мешать**	[mi'ʃʌtʲ]
to pass (to hand sth)	**передать**	[piri'datʲ]
request (demand)	**просьба** (f)	['prozʲbə]
to request (ask)	**просить**	[pra'sitʲ]

| demand (firm request) | **требование** (n) | ['trebavanie] |
| to demand (request firmly) | **требовать** | ['trebavatʲ] |

to tease sb	**дразнить**	[draz'nitʲ]
to mock (deride)	**насмехаться**	[nasme'hatsə]
mockery, derision	**насмешка** (f)	[nas'meʃkə]
nickname	**прозвище** (n)	['prɔzwiɕe]

hint (indirect suggestion)	**намёк** (m)	[na'mɜk]
to hint (vi)	**намекать**	[name'katʲ]
to mean (what do you ~ ?)	**подразумевать**	[padrazume'vatʲ]

description	**описание** (n)	[api'sanie]
to describe (vt)	**описать**	[api'satʲ]
praise (compliments)	**похвала** (f)	[pahva'la]
to praise (vt)	**похвалить**	[pahva'litʲ]

disappointment	**разочарование** (n)	[razatʃira'vanie]
to disappoint (vt)	**разочаровать**	[razatʃira'vatʲ]
to be disappointed	**разочароваться**	[razatʃera'vatsə]

supposition	**предположение** (n)	[pritpala'ʒenie]
to suppose (assume)	**предполагать**	[pritpala'gatʲ]
warning (caution)	**предостережение** (n)	[pridastire'ʒenie]
to warn	**предостеречь**	[pridastere'ʒɛnie]

67. Discussion, conversation. Part 3

| to talk into (persuade) | **уговорить** | [pridaste'retʃ] |
| to calm down (vt) | **успокаивать** | [uspa'kaivatʲ] |

silence (~ is golden)	**молчание** (n)	[uspa'kaivatʲ]
to keep silent	**молчать**	[mal'tʃatʲ]
to whisper (vt)	**шепнуть**	[ʃɛp'nʊtʲ]
whisper	**шёпот** (m)	['ʃopat]

| frankly, sincerely | **откровенно** | [atkra'wennə] |
| in my opinion … | **по моему мнению …** | [pa mae'mʊ 'mneniju] |

detail (of the story)	**подробность** (f)	[pad'rɔbnastʲ]
detailed	**подробный**	[pad'rɔbnɪj]
in detail	**подробно**	[pad'rɔbnə]

| hint, clue | **подсказка** (f) | [pats'kaskə] |
| to give a hint | **подсказать** | [patska'zatʲ] |

look (glance)	**взгляд** (m)	[vzgʎat]
to have a look	**взглянуть**	[vzgli'nʊtʲ]
fixed (look)	**неподвижный**	[nipad'wiʒnɪj]
to blink (vi)	**моргать**	[mar'gatʲ]

| to wink (vi) | **мигнуть** | [mig'nutʲ] |
| to nod (in assent) | **кивнуть** | [kiv'nutʲ] |

sigh	**вздох** (m)	[vzdɔh]
to sigh (vi)	**вздохнуть**	[vzdah'nutʲ]
to shudder (vi)	**вздрагивать**	['vzdragivatʲ]
gesture	**жест** (m)	[ʒɛst]
to touch (one's arm etc.)	**прикоснуться**	[prikas'nutsə]
to seize (by the arm)	**хватать**	[hva'tatʲ]
to tap (on the shoulder)	**хлопать**	['hlɔpatʲ]

Look out!	**Осторожно!**	[asta'rɔʒna]
Really?	**Неужели?**	[niu'ʒɛli]
Are you sure?	**Ты уверен?**	[tɪ u'weren]
Good luck!	**Удачи!**	[u'datʃi]
I see!	**Ясно!**	['jasna]
It's a pity!	**Жаль!**	[ʒaʎ]

68. Agreement. Refusal

agreement	**согласие** (n)	[sag'lasie]
to agree (say yes)	**соглашаться**	[sagla'ʃʌtsə]
approval	**одобрение** (n)	[adab'renie]
to approve (vt)	**одобрить**	[a'dɔbritʲ]
refusal	**отказ** (m)	[at'kas]
to refuse (vi, vt)	**отказываться**	[at'kazıvatsə]

Great!	**Отлично!**	[at'litʃna]
All right!	**Хорошо!**	[hara'ʃɔ]
OK! (I agree)	**Ладно!**	['ladna]
That's wrong!	**Это неправильно!**	['ɛta nip'rawiʎna]

forbidden	**запрещённый**	[zapre'ɕɛnnıj]
it's forbidden	**нельзя**	[niʎ'zʲa]
it's impossible	**невозможно**	[nivaz'mɔʒnə]
incorrect (adj)	**неправильный**	[nip'rawiʎnıj]

to reject (~ a demand)	**отклонить**	[atkla'nitʲ]
to support (cause, idea)	**поддержать**	[padder'ʒatʲ]
to accept (~ an apology)	**принять**	[pri'natʲ]

to confirm (vt)	**подтвердить**	[patwer'ditʲ]
confirmation	**подтверждение** (n)	[patwerʒ'denie]
permission	**разрешение** (n)	[razre'ʃenie]
to permit (allow)	**разрешить**	[razri'ʃitʲ]
decision	**решение** (n)	[ri'ʃenie]
to say nothing	**промолчать**	[pramal'tʃatʲ]

| condition (term) | **условие** (n) | [us'lɔwie] |
| excuse (pretext) | **отговорка** (f) | [atga'vɔrkə] |

| praise (compliments) | похвала (f) | [pɑhvɑ'lɑ] |
| to praise (vt) | похвалить | [pɑhvɑ'litʲ] |

69. Success. Good luck. Failure

success	успех (m)	[us'peh]
successfully	успешно	[us'peʃnə]
successful	успешный	[us'peʃnɪj]

good luck	удача (f)	[u'dɑtʃə]
Good luck!	Удачи!	[u'dɑtʃi]
lucky (e.g., ~ day)	удачный	[u'dɑtʃnɪj]
lucky (fortunate)	удачливый	[u'dɑtʃlivɪj]

failure (lack of success)	неудача (f)	[niu'dɑtʃə]
bad luck (failure)	неудача (f)	[niu'dɑtʃə]
misfortune (bad luck)	невезение (n)	[niwe'zenie]
unsuccessful (attempt)	неудачный	[niu'dɑtʃnɪj]
catastrophe	катастрофа (f)	[kɑtɑst'rɔfə]

pride	гордость (f)	['gɔrdɑstʲ]
proud	гордый	['gɔrdɪj]
to be proud	гордиться	[gɑr'ditsə]

winner (of competition)	победитель (m)	[pɑbe'diteʎ]
to win (vi)	победить	[pɑbe'ditʲ]
to lose (not win)	проиграть	[prɑig'rɑtʲ]
try	попытка (f)	[pɑ'pɪtkə]
to try (vi)	пытаться	[pɪ'tɑtsə]
chance (opportunity)	шанс (m)	[ʃʌns]

70. Quarrels. Negative emotions

shout (scream)	крик (m)	[krik]
to shout (vi)	кричать	[kri'tʃatʲ]
to cry out (yell)	закричать	[zɑkri'tʃatʲ]

quarrel	ссора (f)	['ssɔrə]
to quarrel (vi)	ссориться	['sɔritsə]
fight (argument)	скандал (m)	[skɑn'dɑl]
to have a fight	скандалить	[skɑn'dɑlitʲ]
conflict	конфликт (m)	[kɑnf'likt]
misunderstanding	недоразумение (n)	[nidɑrɑzu'menie]

insult	оскорбление (n)	[ɑskɑrb'lenie]
to insult (vt)	оскорблять	[ɑskɑrb'ʎatʲ]
insulted	оскорбленный	[ɑskɑrb'lɜnnɪj]
offense (e.g., to take ~)	обида (f)	[ɑ'bidə]

| to offend (sb) | **обидеть** | [a'bidet^j] |
| to take offense | **обидеться** | [a'bidetsə] |

indignation	**возмущение** (n)	[vazmʊ'ɕenie]
to be indignant	**возмущаться**	[vazmʊ'ɕatsə]
complaint	**жалоба** (f)	['ʒalabə]
to complain (vi, vt)	**жаловаться**	['ʒalavatsə]

apology	**извинение** (n)	[izwi'nenie]
to apologize (vi)	**извиняться**	[izwi'ɲatsə]
to beg pardon	**просить прощения**	[pra'sit^j pra'ɕenija]

criticism	**критика** (f)	['kritikə]
to criticize (vt)	**критиковать**	[kritika'vat^j]
accusation	**обвинение** (n)	[abwi'nenie]
to accuse (vt)	**обвинять**	[abwi'ɲat^j]

revenge	**месть** (f)	[mest^j]
to avenge (vt)	**мстить**	[mstit^j]
to pay back	**отплатить**	[atpla'tit^j]

disdain	**презрение** (n)	[priz'renie]
to despise (vt)	**презирать**	[prizi'rat^j]
hatred, hate	**ненависть** (f)	['nenawist^j]
to hate (vt)	**ненавидеть**	[nina'widet^j]

nervous	**нервный**	['nervnɪj]
to be nervous	**нервничать**	['nervnitʃat^j]
angry (mad)	**сердитый**	[sir'ditɪj]
to make angry	**рассердить**	[raser'dit^j]

humiliation	**унижение** (n)	[uni'ʒenie]
to humiliate (vt)	**унижать**	[uni'ʒat^j]
to humiliate oneself	**унижаться**	[uni'ʒatsə]

| shock | **шок** (m) | [ʃɔk] |
| to shock (vt) | **шокировать** | [ʃʌ'kiravat^j] |

| trouble (e.g., to be in ~) | **неприятность** (f) | [nipri'jatnast^j] |
| unpleasant | **неприятный** | [nipri'jatnɪj] |

fear (dread)	**страх** (m)	[strah]
terrible (storm, heat)	**страшный**	['straʃnɪj]
scary (e.g., ~ story)	**страшный**	['straʃnɪj]
horror	**ужас** (m)	['uʒas]
awful (crime, news)	**ужасный**	[u'ʒasnɪj]

to begin to tremble	**задрожать**	[zadra'ʒat^j]
to cry (weep)	**плакать**	['plakat^j]
to start crying	**заплакать**	[zap'lakat^j]
tear	**слеза** (pl)	[sli'za]
fault	**вина** (f)	[wi'na]

guilt (feeling)	**вина** (f)	[wi'na]
disgrace (dishonor)	**позор** (m)	[pa'zɔr]
protest	**протест** (m)	[pra'test]
stress (nervous tension)	**стресс** (m)	[strɛs]
to disturb (vt)	**беспокоить**	[bispa'kɔitʲ]
to be angry (with …)	**злиться**	['zlitsə]
mad, angry	**злой**	[zlɔj]
to end (e.g., relationship)	**прекращать**	[prikra'ɕatʲ]
to scold sb	**ругаться**	[ru'gatsə]
to be scared	**пугаться**	[pu'gatsə]
to hit (strike with hand)	**ударить**	[u'daritʲ]
to fight (vi)	**драться**	['dratsə]
to settle (a conflict)	**урегулировать**	[urigu'liravatʲ]
discontented	**недовольный**	[nida'vɔʎnɪj]
furious (look)	**яростный**	['jarasnɪj]
It's not good!	**Это нехорошо!**	['ɛta nehara'ʃɔ]
It's bad!	**Это плохо!**	['ɛta 'plɔha]

Medicine

71. Diseases

sickness	**болезнь** (f)	[bɑ'lezn]
to be sick	**болеть**	[bɑ'letʲ]
health	**здоровье** (n)	[zdɑ'rɔvje]
runny nose	**насморк** (m)	['nɑsmɑrk]
tonsillitis	**ангина** (f)	[a'ŋinə]
cold	**простуда** (f)	[prɑs'tʊdə]
to catch a cold	**простудиться**	[prɑstʊ'ditsə]
bronchitis	**бронхит** (m)	[brɑn'hit]
pneumonia	**воспаление** (n) **лёгких**	[vɑspɑ'lenie 'lɜŋkih]
flu, influenza	**грипп** (m)	[grip]
near-sighted	**близорукий**	[blizɑ'rʊkij]
far-sighted	**дальнозоркий**	[daʎnɑ'zɔrkij]
strabismus	**косоглазие** (n)	[kasɑg'lazie]
cross-eyed	**косоглазый**	[kasɑg'lazɪj]
cataract	**катаракта** (f)	[kata'raktə]
glaucoma	**глаукома** (f)	[glɑu'kɔmə]
stroke	**инсульт** (m)	[in'sʊʌt]
heart attack	**инфаркт** (m)	[in'farkt]
myocardial infarction	**инфаркт** (m) **миокарда**	[in'farkt miɑ'kardə]
paralysis	**паралич** (m)	[parɑ'litʃ]
to paralyze (vt)	**парализовать**	[paraliza'vatʲ]
allergy	**аллергия** (f)	[alir'gija]
asthma	**астма** (f)	['astmə]
diabetes	**диабет** (m)	[diɑ'bet]
toothache	**зубная боль** (f)	[zub'naja bɔʎ]
caries	**кариес** (m)	['karies]
diarrhea	**диарея** (f)	[diɑ'reja]
constipation	**запор** (m)	[za'pɔr]
stomach upset	**расстройство** (n) **желудка**	[rast'rɔjstvɑ ʒɛ'lutkə]
food poisoning	**отравление** (n)	[atrav'lenie]
to have a food poisoning	**отравиться**	[atra'witsə]
arthritis	**артрит** (m)	[art'rit]
rickets	**рахит** (m)	[ra'hit]

rheumatism	ревматизм (m)	[rivma'tizm]
atherosclerosis	атеросклероз (m)	[ateraskle'rɔs]
gastritis	гастрит (m)	[gast'rit]
appendicitis	аппендицит (m)	[apindi'tsɪt]
cholecystitis	холецистит (m)	[haletsɪs'tit]
ulcer	язва (f)	['jazvə]
measles	корь (f)	[kɔrʲ]
German measles	краснуха (f)	[kras'nʊhə]
jaundice	желтуха (f)	[ʒɛl'tʊhə]
hepatitis	гепатит (m)	[gipa'tit]
schizophrenia	шизофрения (f)	[ʃɪzafre'nija]
hydrophobia, rabies	бешенство (n)	['beʃənstvə]
neurosis	невроз (m)	[niv'rɔs]
concussion	сотрясение (n) мозга	[satri'senie 'mɔzgə]
cancer	рак (m)	[rak]
sclerosis	склероз (m)	[skle'rɔs]
multiple sclerosis	рассеянный склероз (m)	[ra'seinɪj skle'rɔs]
alcoholism	алкоголизм (m)	[alkaga'lizm]
alcoholic (noun)	алкоголик (m)	[alka'gɔlik]
syphilis	сифилис (m)	['sifilis]
AIDS	СПИД (m)	[spit]
tumor	опухоль (f)	['ɔpʊhaʎ]
malignant	злокачественная	[zla'katʃestwenaja]
benign	доброкачественная	[dabra'katʃestwenaja]
fever	лихорадка (f)	[liha'ratkə]
malaria	малярия (f)	[mali'rija]
gangrene	гангрена (f)	[gahg'renə]
seasickness	морская болезнь (f)	[mars'kaja ba'lezɲ]
epilepsy	эпилепсия (f)	[ɛpi'lepsija]
epidemic	эпидемия (f)	[ɛpi'demija]
typhus	тиф (m)	[tif]
tuberculosis	туберкулёз (m)	[tʊberkʊ'lɔs]
cholera	холера (f)	[ha'lerə]
plague (bubonic ~)	чума (f)	['tʃumə]

72. Symptoms. Treatments. Part 1

symptom	симптом (m)	[simp'tɔm]
temperature	температура (f)	[timpera'tʊrə]
high temperature	высокая температура (f)	[vɪ'sɔkaja timpera'tʊrə]
pulse	пульс (m)	[pʊʎs]
giddiness	головокружение (n)	[galavakrʊ'ʒenie]

hot	горячий	[ga'rʲatʃij]
shivering	озноб (m)	[az'nɔp]
pale (e.g., ~ face)	бледный	['blednɨj]

cough	кашель (m)	['kaʃəʎ]
to cough (vi)	кашлять	['kaʃlitʲ]
to sneeze (vi)	чихать	[tʃi'hatʲ]
faint	обморок (m)	['ɔbmarak]
to faint (vi)	упасть в обморок	[u'pastʲ v 'ɔbmarak]

bruise	синяк (m)	[si'ɲak]
bump (lump)	шишка (f)	['ʃiʃkə]
to bruise oneself	удариться	[u'daritsə]
bruise	ушиб (m)	[u'ʃip]
to get bruised	ударить ...	[u'daritʲ]

to limp (vi)	хромать	[hra'matʲ]
dislocation	вывих (m)	['vɨwih]
to dislocate (vt)	вывихнуть	['vɨwihnutʲ]
fracture	перелом (m)	[pere'lɔm]
to get a fracture	получить перелом	[palu'tʃitʲ pere'lɔm]

cut (e.g., on the finger)	порез (m)	[pa'res]
to cut oneself	порезаться	[pa'rezatsə]
bleeding	кровотечение (n)	[kravate'tʃenie]

| burn (injury) | ожог (m) | [a'ʒɔk] |
| to burn oneself | обжечься | [ab'ʒetʃsʲa] |

to prick (vt)	уколоть	[uka'lɔtʲ]
to prick oneself	уколоться	[uka'lɔtsə]
to injure (vt)	повредить	[pavre'ditʲ]
injury	повреждение (n)	[pavreʒ'denie]
wound	рана (f)	['ranə]
trauma	травма (f)	['travmə]

to be delirious	бредить	['breditʲ]
to stutter (vi)	заикаться	[zai'katsə]
sunstroke	солнечный удар (m)	['sɔlnitʃnɨj u'dar]

73. Symptoms. Treatments. Part 2

| pain (physical) | боль (f) | [bɔʎ] |
| splinter (in foot, finger) | заноза (f) | [za'nɔzə] |

sweat (perspiration)	пот (m)	[pɔt]
to sweat (perspire)	потеть	[pa'tetʲ]
vomiting	рвота (f)	['rvɔtə]
convulsions	судороги (f pl)	['sudaragi]
pregnant	беременная	[bi'remenaja]

to be born	родиться	[rɑ'ditsə]
delivery, labor	роды (pl)	['rɔdɪ]
to be in labor	рожать	[rɑ'ʒatʲ]
abortion	аборт (m)	[a'bɔrt]

respiration	дыхание (n)	[dɪ'hanie]
inhalation	вдох (m)	[vdɔh]
exhalation	выдох (m)	['vɪdah]
to breathe out	выдохнуть	['vɪdahnutʲ]
to breathe in	сделать вдох	['sdelatʲ vdɔh]

disabled person	инвалид (m)	[inva'lit]
cripple	калека (n)	[ka'lekə]
drug addict	наркоман (m)	[narka'man]

deaf	глухой	[glu'hɔj]
dumb	немой	[ni'mɔj]
deaf-and-dumb	глухонемой	[gluhane'mɔj]

mad, insane	сумасшедший	[sʊma'ʃɛtʃɪj]
madman	сумасшедший (m)	[sʊma'ʃɛtʃɪj]
madwoman	сумасшедшая (f)	[sʊma'ʃɛtʃʌja]
to go insane	сойти с ума	[saj'ti sʊ'ma]

gene	ген (m)	[gen]
immunity	иммунитет (m)	[imʊni'tet]
hereditary	наследственный	[nas'letstwennɪj]
congenital	врождённый	[vraʒ'dɔnnɪj]

virus	вирус (m)	['wirʊs]
microbe	микроб (m)	[mik'rɔp]
bacterium	бактерия (f)	[bak'tɛrija]
infection	инфекция (f)	[in'fektsɪja]

74. Symptoms. Treatments. Part 3

| hospital | больница (f) | [baʎ'nitsə] |
| patient | пациент (m) | [patsɪ'ɛnt] |

diagnosis	диагноз (m)	[di'agnas]
cure, treatment	лечение (n)	[li'tʃenie]
treatment	лечение (n)	[li'tʃenie]
to get treatment	лечиться	[li'tʃitsə]
to treat (vt)	лечить	[li'tʃitʲ]
to nurse (look after)	ухаживать	[u'haʒɪvatʲ]
care (treatment)	уход (m)	[u'hɔt]

operation, surgery	операция (f)	[api'ratsɪja]
to bandage (head, limb)	перевязать	[pirewi'zatʲ]
bandaging	перевязка (f)	[pire'vʲaskə]

vaccination	прививка (f)	[pri'wifkə]
to vaccinate (vt)	делать прививку	['delatʲ pri'wifkʊ]
injection, shot	укол (m)	[u'kɔl]
to give an injection	делать укол	['delatʲ u'kɔl]

amputation	ампутация (f)	[ampʊ'tatsɪja]
to amputate (vt)	ампутировать	[ampʊ'tiravatʲ]
coma	кома (f)	['kɔmə]
to be in a coma	быть в коме	[bɪtʲ f 'kɔme]
intensive care	реанимация (f)	[riani'matsɪja]

to recover (~ from flu)	выздоравливать	[vɪzda'ravlivatʲ]
state (patient's ~)	состояние (n)	[sasta'janie]
consciousness	сознание (n)	[saz'nanie]
memory (faculty)	память (f)	['pamitʲ]

to extract (tooth)	удалять	[uda'ʎatʲ]
filling (in tooth)	пломба (f)	['plɔmbə]
to fill (a tooth)	пломбировать	[plambira'vatʲ]

| hypnosis | гипноз (m) | [gip'nɔs] |
| to hypnotize (vt) | гипнотизировать | [gipnati'ziravatʲ] |

75. Doctors

doctor	врач (m)	[vratʃ]
nurse (in hospital)	медсестра (f)	[mitsest'ra]
private physician	личный врач (m)	['litʃnij vratʃ]
children's doctor	детский врач (m)	['detskij vratʃ]

dentist	дантист (m)	[dan'tist]
ophthalmologist	окулист (m)	[akʊ'list]
internist	терапевт (m)	[tira'peft]
surgeon	хирург (m)	[hi'rʊrk]

psychiatrist	психиатр (m)	[psihi'atr]
pediatrician	педиатр (m)	[pidi'atr]
psychologist	психолог (m)	[psi'hɔlak]
gynecologist	гинеколог (m)	[gine'kɔlak]
cardiologist	кардиолог (m)	[kardi'ɔlak]

76. Medicine. Drugs. Accessories

medicine, drug	лекарство (n)	[li'karstvə]
remedy	средство (n)	['sretstvə]
to prescribe (vt)	прописать	[prapi'satʲ]
prescription	рецепт (m)	[ri'tsəpt]
tablet, pill	таблетка (f)	[tab'letkə]

ointment	мазь (f)	[masʲ]
ampule	ампула (f)	[ˈampʊlə]
mixture	микстура (f)	[miksˈtʊrə]
syrup	сироп (m)	[siˈrɔp]
pill	пилюля (f)	[piˈlyʎa]
powder	порошок (m)	[paraˈʃɔk]

bandage	бинт (m)	[bint]
cotton wool	вата (f)	[ˈvatə]
iodine	йод (m)	[jot]

Band-Aid	лейкопластырь (m)	[lejkapˈlastɪrʲ]
eyedropper	пипетка (f)	[piˈpetkə]
thermometer	градусник (m)	[ˈgradʊsnik]
syringe	шприц (m)	[ʃprits]

| wheelchair | коляска (f) | [kaˈʎaskə] |
| crutches | костыли (m pl) | [kastɪˈli] |

painkiller	обезболивающее (n)	[abizˈbɔlivajuɕeeə]
laxative	слабительное (n)	[slaˈbiteʎnae]
spirit	спирт (m)	[spirt]
medicinal herbs	трава (f)	[traˈva]
herbal	травяной	[trawiˈnɔj]

77. Smoking. Tobacco products

tobacco	табак (m)	[taˈbak]
cigarette	сигарета (f)	[sigaˈretə]
cigar	сигара (f)	[siˈgarə]
pipe	трубка (f)	[ˈtrʊpkə]
pack (of cigarettes)	пачка (f)	[ˈpatʃkə]

matches	спички (f pl)	[ˈspitʃki]
matchbox	спичечный коробок (m)	[ˈspitʃitʃnɪj karaˈbɔk]
lighter	зажигалка (f)	[zaʒɪˈgalkə]
ashtray	пепельница (f)	[ˈpepeʎnitsə]
cigarette case	портсигар (m)	[partsiˈgar]

| cigarette holder | мундштук (m) | [mʊntʃˈtʊk] |
| filter | фильтр (m) | [fiʎtr] |

to smoke (vi, vt)	курить	[kʊˈritʲ]
to light a cigarette	закурить	[zakʊˈritʲ]
smoking	курение (n)	[kʊˈrenie]
smoker	курильщик (m)	[kʊˈriʎɕik]

stub, butt (of cigarette)	окурок (m)	[aˈkʊrak]
smoke	дым (m)	[dɪm]
ash	пепел (m)	[ˈpepel]

HUMAN HABITAT

City

78. City. Life in the city

city, town	**город** (m)	['gorat]
capital	**столица** (f)	[sta'litsə]
village (e.g., fishing ~)	**деревня** (f)	[di'revɲa]
small town	**посёлок** (m)	[pa'sɜlak]
city map	**план** (m) **города**	[plan 'goradə]
downtown	**центр** (m) **города**	[tsɛntr 'goradə]
suburb	**пригород** (m)	['prigarat]
suburban	**пригородный**	['prigaradnɪj]
outskirts	**окраина** (f)	[ak'rainə]
environs (suburbs)	**окрестности** (f pl)	[ak'resnasti]
district (of city)	**район** (m)	[raɜn]
block	**квартал** (m)	[kvar'tal]
residential block	**жилой квартал** (m)	[ʒɪ'loj kvar'tal]
traffic	**движение** (n)	[dwi'ʒɛnie]
traffic lights	**светофор** (m)	[swita'for]
public transportation	**городской транспорт** (m)	[garats'koj 'transpart]
intersection	**перекрёсток** (m)	[pirek'rɜstak]
crosswalk	**переход** (m)	[pere'hot]
pedestrian underpass	**подземный переход** (m)	[pa'dzemnɪj pere'hot]
to cross (vt)	**переходить**	[pereha'ditʲ]
pedestrian	**пешеход** (m)	[piʃe'hot]
sidewalk	**тротуар** (m)	[tratu'ar]
bridge	**мост** (m)	[most]
bank, quay	**набережная** (f)	['nabereʒnaja]
fountain	**фонтан** (m)	[fan'tan]
alley (in park, garden)	**аллея** (f)	[a'leja]
park	**парк** (m)	[park]
boulevard	**бульвар** (m)	[buʎ'var]
square	**площадь** (f)	['plɔcatʲ]
avenue (wide street)	**проспект** (m)	[pras'pekt]
street	**улица** (f)	['ulitsə]
lane	**переулок** (m)	[pire'ulak]
dead end	**тупик** (m)	[tu'pik]

house	**дом** (m)	[dɔm]
building	**здание** (n)	['zdanie]
skyscraper	**небоскрёб** (m)	[nibask'rɜp]
facade	**фасад** (m)	[fa'sat]
roof	**крыша** (f)	['krɪʃə]
window	**окно** (n)	[ak'nɔ]
arch	**арка** (f)	['arkə]
column	**колонна** (f)	[ka'lɔnnə]
corner	**угол** (m)	['ugal]
store window	**витрина** (f)	[wit'rinə]
sign (on shop, bar etc.)	**вывеска** (f)	['vɪwiskə]
poster	**афиша** (f)	[a'fiʃə]
advertising poster	**рекламный плакат** (m)	[rek'lamnɪj pla'kat]
billboard	**рекламный щит** (m)	[rek'lamnɪj ɕit]
garbage, trash	**мусор** (m)	['musar]
garbage can	**урна** (f)	['urnə]
to litter (vi)	**сорить**	[sa'ritʲ]
garbage dump	**свалка** (f)	['svalkə]
phone booth	**телефонная будка** (f)	[tele'fɔnnaja 'butkə]
lightpost	**фонарный столб** (m)	[fa'narnɪj 'stɔlp]
bench (park ~)	**скамейка** (f)	[ska'mejkə]
policeman	**полицейский** (m)	[pali'tsɜjskij]
police	**полиция** (f)	[pa'litsɪja]
beggar	**нищий** (m)	['niɕij]
homeless, bum	**бездомный** (m)	[biz'dɔmnɪj]

79. Urban institutions

store	**магазин** (m)	[maga'zin]
drugstore, pharmacy	**аптека** (f)	[ap'tekə]
optical store	**оптика** (f)	['ɔptikə]
shopping mall	**торговый центр** (m)	[tar'gɔvɪj tsɛntr]
supermarket	**супермаркет** (m)	[super'market]
bakery	**булочная** (f)	['bulatʃnaja]
baker	**пекарь** (m)	['pekarʲ]
confectionery	**кондитерская** (f)	[kan'diterskaja]
grocery store	**бакалея** (f)	[baka'leja]
butcher shop	**мясная лавка** (f)	[mʲas'naja 'lafkə]
produce store	**овощная лавка** (f)	[avaɕ'naja 'lafkə]
market	**рынок** (m)	['rɪnak]
coffee house	**кафе** (n)	[ka'fɛ]
restaurant	**ресторан** (m)	[rista'ran]

pub	**пивная** (f)	[piv'naja]
pizzeria	**пиццерия** (f)	[pitsı'rija]
hair salon	**парикмахерская** (f)	[parih'maherskaja]
post office	**почта** (f)	['potʃtə]
dry cleaners	**химчистка** (f)	[him'tʃistkə]
photo studio	**фотоателье** (n)	[fotaatɛ'ʎje]
shoe store	**обувной магазин** (m)	[abʊv'noj maga'zin]
bookstore	**книжный магазин** (m)	['kniʒnıj maga'zin]
sporting goods store	**спортивный магазин** (m)	[spar'tivnıj maga'zin]
clothes repair	**ремонт** (m) **одежды**	[re'mont a'deʒdı]
formal wear rental	**прокат** (m) **одежды**	[pra'kat a'deʒdı]
movie rental store	**прокат** (m) **фильмов**	[pra'kat 'fiʎmaf]
circus	**цирк** (m)	[tsırk]
zoo	**зоопарк** (m)	[zaa'park]
movie theater	**кинотеатр** (m)	[kinati'atr]
museum	**музей** (m)	[mʊ'zej]
library	**библиотека** (f)	[biblia'tekə]
theater	**театр** (m)	[ti'atr]
opera house	**опера** (f)	['ɔperə]
nightclub	**ночной клуб** (m)	[natʃ'noj klup]
casino	**казино** (n)	[kazi'nɔ]
mosque	**мечеть** (f)	[mi'tʃetʲ]
synagogue	**синагога** (f)	[sina'gɔgə]
cathedral	**собор** (m)	[sa'bɔr]
temple	**храм** (m)	[hram]
church	**церковь** (f)	['tsərkafʲ]
institute	**институт** (m)	[insti'tʊt]
university	**университет** (m)	[uniwersi'tet]
school	**школа** (f)	['ʃkɔlə]
prefecture	**префектура** (f)	[prifek'tʊrə]
city hall	**мэрия** (f)	['mɛrija]
hotel	**гостиница** (f)	[gas'tinitsə]
bank	**банк** (m)	[bank]
embassy	**посольство** (n)	[pa'sɔʎstvə]
travel agency	**турагентство** (n)	[tʊra'genstvə]
information office	**справочное бюро** (n)	['spravatʃnae by'rɔ]
money exchange	**обменный пункт** (m)	[ab'mennıj pʊnkt]
subway	**метро** (n)	[mit'rɔ]
hospital	**больница** (f)	[baʎ'nitsə]
gas station	**бензозаправка** (f)	[binzazap'rafkə]
parking lot	**стоянка** (f)	[sta'jankə]

80. Signs

sign (on shop, bar etc.)	вывеска (f)	['vɪwiskə]
inscription (plaque etc.)	надпись (f)	['natpisʲ]
poster	плакат (m)	[pla'kat]
direction sign	указатель (m)	[uka'zateʎ]
arrow (direction sign)	стрелка (f)	['strelkə]
caution	предостережение (n)	[pridastire'ʒenie]
warning	предупреждение (n)	[pridupriʒ'denie]
to warn (of the danger)	предупредить	[pridupre'ditʲ]
day off	выходной день (m)	[vɪhad'nɔj denʲ]
timetable (schedule)	расписание (n)	[raspi'sanie]
opening hours	часы (pl) работы	[ʧa'sɪ ra'botɪ]
WELCOME!	ДОБРО ПОЖАЛОВАТЬ!	[dab'rɔ pa'ʒalavatʲ]
ENTRANCE	ВХОД	[vhɔt]
EXIT	ВЫХОД	['vɪhat]
PUSH	ОТ СЕБЯ	[at se'bʲa]
PULL	НА СЕБЯ	[na se'bʲa]
OPEN	ОТКРЫТО	[atk'rɪtə]
CLOSED	ЗАКРЫТО	[zak'rɪtə]
WOMEN	ДЛЯ ЖЕНЩИН	[dʎa 'ʒɛɲɕin]
MEN	ДЛЯ МУЖЧИН	[dʎa mu'ɕin]
DISCOUNTS	СКИДКИ	['skitki]
SALE	РАСПРОДАЖА	[raspra'daʒə]
NEW!	НОВИНКА!	[na'winkə]
FREE	БЕСПЛАТНО	[bisp'latnə]
ATTENTION!	ВНИМАНИЕ!	[vni'manie]
NO VACANCIES	МЕСТ НЕТ	[mest 'net]
RESERVED	ЗАРЕЗЕРВИРОВАНО	[zarizir'wiravanə]
ADMINISTRATION	АДМИНИСТРАЦИЯ	[administ'ratsija]
STAFF ONLY	ТОЛЬКО	['toʎka
	ДЛЯ ПЕРСОНАЛА	dʎa persa'nalə]
BEWARE OF THE DOG!	ЗЛАЯ СОБАКА	['zlaja sa'bakə]
NO SMOKING	НЕ КУРИТЬ!	[ne ku'ritʲ]
DO NOT TOUCH!	РУКАМИ НЕ ТРОГАТЬ!	[ru'kami ne 'trogatʲ]
DANGEROUS	ОПАСНО	[a'pasnə]
DANGER	ОПАСНОСТЬ	[a'pasnastʲ]
HIGH TENSION	ВЫСОКОЕ	[vɪ'sokae
	НАПРЯЖЕНИЕ	napri'ʒenie]
NO SWIMMING!	КУПАТЬСЯ	[ku'patsa
	ЗАПРЕЩЕНО	zapreɕe'nɔ]

OUT OF ORDER	НЕ РАБОТАЕТ	[ni ra'botaet]
FLAMMABLE	ОГНЕОПАСНО	[agnea'pasnə]
FORBIDDEN	ЗАПРЕЩЕНО	[zapriçe'nɔ]
NO TRESPASSING!	ПРОХОД ЗАПРЕЩЁН	[pra'hɔd zapri'çзn]
WET PAINT	ОКРАШЕНО	[ak'raʃinə]

81. Urban transport

bus	автобус (m)	[af'tɔbʊs]
streetcar	трамвай (m)	[tram'vaj]
trolley	троллейбус (m)	[tra'lejbʊs]
route (of bus)	маршрут (m)	[marʃ'rʊt]
number (e.g., bus ~)	номер (m)	['nɔmer]

to go by …	ехать на …	['ehatʲ na]
to get on (~ the bus etc.)	сесть на …	[sestʲ na]
to get off …	сойти с …	[saj'ti s]
to get out (vi)	выйти	['vɨjti]

stop (e.g., bus ~)	остановка (f)	[asta'nɔfkə]
next stop	следующая остановка (f)	['sledʊçaja astanɔfkə]
terminus	конечная остановка (f)	[ka'netʃnaja asta'nɔfkə]
schedule	расписание (n)	[raspi'sanie]
to wait (vi, vt)	ждать	[ʒdatʲ]

| ticket | билет (m) | [bi'let] |
| fare (charge for bus etc.) | стоимость (f) билета | ['stɔimastʲ bi'letə] |

cashier	кассир (m)	[kas'sir]
ticket inspection	контроль (m)	[kant'rɔʎ]
conductor	контролёр (m)	[kantra'lзr]

to be late (for …)	опаздывать на …	[a'pazdɨvatʲ na]
to miss … (the train etc.)	опоздать на …	[apaz'datʲ na]
to be in a hurry	спешить	[spi'ʃitʲ]

taxi, cab	такси (n)	[tak'si]
taxi driver	таксист (m)	[tak'sist]
by taxi	на такси	[na tak'si]
taxi stand	стоянка (f) такси	[sta'janka tak'si]
to call a taxi	вызвать такси	['vɨzvatʲ tak'si]
to take a taxi	взять такси	[vzʲatʲ tak'si]

traffic	уличное движение (n)	['ulitʃnae dwi'ʒɛnie]
traffic jam	пробка (f)	['prɔpkə]
rush hour	часы пик (m)	[tʃə'sɨ pik]
to park (vi)	парковаться	[parka'vatsə]
to park (vt)	парковать	[parka'vatʲ]
parking lot	стоянка (f)	[sta'jankə]

subway	**метро** (n)	[mit′rɔ]
station	**станция** (f)	[′stɑntsija]
to take the subway	**ехать на метро**	[′ehatʲ na met′rɔ]
train	**поезд** (m)	[′pɔezt]
train station	**вокзал** (m)	[vak′zal]

82. Sightseeing

monument	**памятник** (m)	[′pamitnik]
fortress	**крепость** (f)	[′krepastʲ]
palace	**дворец** (m)	[dva′rets]
castle	**замок** (m)	[′zamak]
tower	**башня** (f)	[′baʃna]
mausoleum	**мавзолей** (m)	[mavza′lej]

architecture	**архитектура** (f)	[arhitek′tʊrə]
medieval	**средневековый**	[srednewe′kɔvıj]
ancient	**старинный**	[sta′rinnıj]
national	**национальный**	[natsıa′naʎnıj]
famous	**известный**	[iz′wesnıj]

tourist	**турист** (m)	[tʊ′rist]
guide (person)	**гид** (m)	[git]
excursion (organized trip)	**экскурсия** (f)	[ɛks′kʊrsija]
to show (vt)	**показывать**	[pa′kazıvatʲ]
to tell (vi, vt)	**рассказывать**	[ras′kazıvatʲ]

to find (vt)	**найти**	[naj′ti]
to get lost	**потеряться**	[pati′rʲatsə]
map (e.g., subway ~)	**схема** (f)	[′shemə]
map (e.g., city ~)	**план** (m)	[plan]

souvenir, gift	**сувенир** (m)	[sʊwe′nir]
gift shop	**магазин** (m) **сувениров**	[maga′zin sʊwe′niraf]
to take pictures	**фотографировать**	[fatagra′firavatʲ]
to be photographed	**фотографироваться**	[fatagra′firavatsə]

83. Shopping

to buy (purchase)	**покупать**	[pakʊ′patʲ]
purchase	**покупка** (f)	[pa′kʊpkə]
to go shopping	**делать покупки**	[′delatʲ pa′kʊpki]
shopping	**шоппинг** (m)	[′ʃopink]

to be open	**работать**	[ra′botatʲ]
to be closed	**закрыться**	[zak′rɪtsə]
footwear	**обувь** (f)	[′obʊfʲ]
clothes, clothing	**одежда** (f)	[a′deʒdə]

cosmetics	косметика (f)	[kas'metikə]
food	продукты (pl)	[pra'duktɪ]
gift, present	подарок (m)	[pa'darək]
salesman	продавец (m)	[prada'wets]
saleswoman	продавщица (f)	[pradaf'ɕitsə]
check out, cash desk	касса (f)	['kassə]
mirror	зеркало (n)	['zerkalə]
counter (in shop)	прилавок (m)	[pri'lavak]
fitting room	примерочная (f)	[pri'meratʃnaja]
to try on	примерить	[pri'meritʲ]
to fit (about dress etc.)	подходить	[padha'ditʲ]
to like (I like ...)	нравиться	['nrawitsə]
price	цена (f)	[tsɪ'na]
price tag	ценник (m)	['tsɛnnik]
to cost (vt)	стоить	['stoitʲ]
How much?	Сколько?	['skoʎka]
discount	скидка (f)	['skitkə]
inexpensive	недорогой	[nidara'gɔj]
cheap (inexpensive)	дешёвый	[di'ʃovɪj]
expensive	дорогой	[dara'gɔj]
It's expensive	Это дорого.	['ɛta 'dɔragə]
rental (noun)	прокат (m)	[pra'kat]
to rent (~ a tuxedo)	взять напрокат	[vzʲatʲ napra'kat]
credit	кредит (m)	[kri'dit]
on credit	в кредит	[f kre'dit]

84. Money

money	деньги (pl)	['deŋgi]
exchange	обмен (m)	[ab'men]
exchange rate	курс (m)	[kurs]
ATM	банкомат (m)	[banka'mat]
coin	монета (f)	[ma'netə]
dollar	доллар (m)	['dɔllar]
euro	евро (n)	['evrə]
lira (currency)	лира (f)	['lirə]
Deutschmark	марка (f)	['markə]
franc	франк (m)	[frank]
pound sterling	фунт стерлингов (m)	[funt 'sterlihgaf]
yen	йена (f)	['enə]
debt	долг (m)	[dɔlk]
debtor	должник (m)	[daʒ'nik]

| to lend (money) | дать в долг | [datʲ v ˈdɔlk] |
| to borrow (vi, vt) | взять в долг | [vzʲatʲ v ˈdɔlk] |

bank	банк (m)	[bank]
account	счёт (m)	[ˈɕɔt]
to deposit (vt)	положить	[pala'ʒitʲ]
to make a deposit	положить на счёт	[pala'ʒitʲ na ˈɕɔt]
to withdraw (vt)	снять со счёта	[ˈsɲatʲ sa ˈɕɔtə]

credit card	кредитная карта (f)	[kri'ditnaja ˈkartə]
cash	наличные деньги (pl)	[na'litʃnɪe ˈdeŋgi]
check	чек (m)	[tʃek]
to write a check	выписать чек	[ˈvɪpisatʲ tʃek]
checkbook	чековая книжка (f)	[ˈtʃekavaja ˈkniʃkə]

wallet	бумажник (m)	[bʊˈmaʒnik]
change purse	кошелёк (m)	[kaʃiˈlɜk]
billfold	портмоне (n)	[partmaˈnɛ]
safe	сейф (m)	[sɛjf]

heir	наследник (m)	[nasˈlednik]
inheritance	наследство (n)	[nasˈletstvə]
fortune (wealth)	состояние (n)	[sastaˈjanie]

lease, rent	аренда (f)	[aˈrendə]
rent money	квартирная плата (f)	[kvarˈtirnaja ˈplatə]
to rent (of a tenant)	снимать	[sniˈmatʲ]

price	цена (f)	[tsɪˈna]
cost	стоимость (f)	[ˈstɔimastʲ]
sum (amount of money)	сумма (f)	[ˈsʊmmə]

to spend (vi, vt)	тратить	[traˈtitʲ]
expenses	расходы (pl)	[rasˈhɔdɪ]
to economize (vi, vt)	экономить	[ɛkaˈnɔmitʲ]
economical	экономный	[ɛkaˈnɔmnɪj]

to pay (vi, vt)	платить	[plaˈtitʲ]
payment	оплата (f)	[apˈlatə]
change (give the ~)	сдача (f)	[ˈzdatʃə]

tax	налог (m)	[naˈlɔk]
fine	штраф (m)	[ʃtraf]
to fine	штрафовать	[ʃtrafaˈvatʲ]

85. Post. Postal service

post office	почта (f)	[ˈpotʃtə]
mail (letters etc.)	почта (f)	[ˈpotʃtə]
mailman	почтальон (m)	[patʃtaˈʎjon]

working hours	**часы** (pl) **работы**	[tʃa'sɪ ra'botɪ]
letter	**письмо** (n)	[pisʲ'mɔ]
registered letter	**заказное письмо** (n)	[zakaz'nɔe pisʲ'mɔ]
postcard	**открытка** (f)	[atk'rɪtkə]
telegram	**телеграмма** (f)	[tileg'ramə]
parcel	**посылка** (f)	[pa'sɪlkə]
money transfer	**денежный перевод** (m)	['deneʒnɪj pere'vɔt]
to receive (vt)	**получить**	[palu'tʃitʲ]
to send (vt)	**отправить**	[atp'ravitʲ]
sending	**отправка** (f)	[atp'rafkə]
address	**адрес** (m)	['adres]
ZIP code	**индекс** (m)	['indɛks]
addressee	**адресат** (m)	[adre'sat]
sender	**отправитель** (m)	[atpra'witeʌ]
receiver, addressee	**получатель** (m)	[palu'tʃateʌ]
name	**имя** (f)	['imʲa]
family name	**фамилия** (f)	[fa'milija]
rate (of postage)	**тариф** (m)	[ta'rif]
ordinary	**обычный**	[a'bɪtʃnɪj]
standard (adj)	**экономичный**	[ɛkana'mitʃnɪj]
weight	**вес** (m)	[wes]
to weigh up (vt)	**взвешивать**	['vzweʃivatʲ]
envelope	**конверт** (m)	[kan'wert]
postage stamp	**марка** (f)	['markə]
to stamp an envelope	**наклеивать марку**	[nak'leivatʲ 'markʊ]

Dwelling. House. Home

86. House. Dwelling

house	**дом** (m)	[dɔm]
at home	**дома**	[ˈdɔmə]
courtyard	**двор** (m)	[dvɔr]
railings (fence)	**ограда** (f)	[ɑgˈrɑdə]
brick (noun)	**кирпич** (m)	[kirˈpitʃ]
brick (building)	**кирпичный**	[kirˈpitʃnɪj]
stone (noun)	**камень** (m)	[ˈkɑmeɲ]
stone (made of stone)	**каменный**	[ˈkɑmennɪj]
concrete (noun)	**бетон** (m)	[biˈtɔn]
concrete (attr)	**бетонный**	[biˈtɔnnɪj]
new	**новый**	[ˈnɔvɪj]
old	**старый**	[ˈstɑrɪj]
decrepit (house)	**ветхий**	[ˈwethɪj]
modern	**современный**	[sɑvreˈmennɪj]
multistory	**многоэтажный**	[mnɑgɑeˈtɑʒnɪj]
high	**высокий**	[vɪˈsɔkij]
floor, story	**этаж** (m)	[ɛˈtɑʃ]
single-story	**одноэтажный**	[ɑdnɑeˈtɑʒnɪj]
ground floor	**нижний этаж** (m)	[ˈniʒnij ɛˈtɑʃ]
top floor	**верхний этаж** (m)	[ˈwerhnij ɛtɑʃ]
roof (of building)	**крыша** (f)	[ˈkrɪʃə]
chimney	**труба** (f)	[trʊˈbɑ]
tiles (for roof)	**черепица** (f)	[tʃireˈpitsə]
tiled	**черепичный**	[tʃireˈpitʃnɪj]
loft (attic)	**чердак** (m)	[tʃirˈdɑk]
window	**окно** (n)	[ɑkˈnɔ]
glass	**стекло** (n)	[stikˈlɔ]
window ledge	**подоконник** (m)	[pɑdɑˈkɔnnik]
shutters	**ставни** (f pl)	[ˈstɑvni]
wall	**стена** (f)	[stiˈnɑ]
balcony	**балкон** (m)	[bɑlˈkɔn]
downspout	**водосточная труба** (f)	[vɑdɑsˈtɔtʃnaja trʊˈbɑ]
upstairs (to be ~)	**наверху**	[nɑwerˈhʊ]
to go upstairs	**подниматься**	[pɑdniˈmɑtsə]
to come down	**спускаться**	[spʊsˈkɑtsə]
to move (to new premises)	**переезжать**	[piree'zatʲ]

87. House. Entrance. Lift

entrance	подъезд (m)	[pad^h'ezt]
stairs (stairway)	лестница (f)	['lesnitsə]
stairs (steps)	ступени (f pl)	[stʊ'peni]
banisters	перила (pl)	[pi'rilə]
lobby (e.g., hotel ~)	холл (m)	[hɔl]

mailbox	почтовый ящик (m)	[patʃ'tɔvɪj 'jaɕik]
trash can	мусорный бак (m)	['mʊsarnɪj bak]
trash chute	мусоропровод (m)	[mʊsarapra'vɔt]

elevator	лифт (m)	[lift]
freight elevator	грузовой лифт (m)	[grʊza'vɔj lift]
elevator cage	кабина (f)	[ka'binə]
to take the elevator	ехать на лифте	['ehatʲ na 'lifte]

apartment	квартира (f)	[kvar'tirə]
tenants	жильцы (pl)	[ʒiʎ'tsɪ]
neighbor (man)	сосед (m)	[sa'set]
neighbor (woman)	соседка (f)	[sa'setkə]
neighbors	соседи (m pl)	[sa'sedi]

88. House. Electricity

electricity	электричество (n)	[ɛlikt'ritʃestvə]
light bulb	лампочка (f)	['lampatʃkə]
switch (for light)	выключатель (m)	[vɪkly'tʃateʎ]
fuse	пробка (f)	['prɔpkə]

cable, wire (electric ~)	провод (m)	['prɔvat]
wiring	проводка (f)	[pra'vɔtkə]
electricity meter	счётчик (m)	['ɕɵtʃik]
readings	показание (n)	[paka'zanie]

89. House. Doors. Locks

door	дверь (f)	[dwerʲ]
gate (of villa etc.)	ворота (pl)	[va'rɔtə]
handle, doorknob	ручка (f)	['rʊtʃkə]
to unlock (unbolt)	отпереть	[atpe'retʲ]
to open (vi, vt)	открывать	[atkrɪ'vatʲ]
to close (vt)	закрывать	[zakrɪ'vatʲ]

key	ключ (m)	[klytʃ]
bunch (of keys)	связка (f)	['svʲaskə]
to creak (door hinge)	скрипеть	[skri'petʲ]

creak	скрип (m)	[skrip]
hinge (of door)	петля (f)	[pit'ʎa]
doormat	коврик (m)	['kɔvrik]

lock	замок (m)	[zɑ'mɔk]
keyhole	замочная скважина (f)	[zɑ'mɔtʃnaja 'skvaʒɪnə]
bolt (big sliding bar)	засов (m)	[zɑ'sɔf]
bolt (small latch)	задвижка (f)	[zɑd'wiʃkə]
padlock	навесной замок (m)	[nɑwes'nɔj zɑ'mɔk]

to ring (~ the door bell)	звонить	[zvɑ'nitʲ]
ringing (sound)	звонок (m)	[zvɑ'nɔk]
doorbell	звонок (m)	[zvɑ'nɔk]
button	кнопка (f)	['knɔpkə]
knock (at the door)	стук (m)	[stʊk]
to knock (vi)	стучать	[stʊ'tʃatʲ]

code	код (m)	[kɔt]
code lock	кодовый замок (m)	['kɔdavɪj zɑ'mɔk]
door phone	домофон (m)	[dɑmɑ'fɔn]
number (on the door)	номер (m)	['nɔmer]
nameplate	табличка (f)	[tab'litʃkə]
peephole	глазок (m)	[glɑ'zɔk]

90. Country house

village	деревня (f)	[di'revʎa]
vegetable garden	огород (m)	[ɑgɑ'rɔt]
fence	забор (m)	[zɑ'bɔr]

| paling | изгородь (f) | ['izgarɑtʲ] |
| wicket gate | калитка (f) | [kɑ'litkə] |

| granary | амбар (m) | [ɑm'bar] |
| cellar | погреб (m) | ['pɔgrep] |

| shed (in garden) | сарай (m) | [sɑ'raj] |
| well (for water) | колодец (m) | [kɑ'lɔdets] |

| stove (for heating) | печь (f) | [petʃ] |
| to stoke | топить | [tɑ'pitʲ] |

| firewood | дрова (f) | [drɑ'va] |
| log (firewood) | полено (n) | [pɑ'lenə] |

| veranda, stoop | веранда (f) | [wi'randə] |
| terrace (patio) | терраса (f) | [ti'rasə] |

| front steps | крыльцо (n) | [krɪʎ'tsɔ] |
| swing (hanging seat) | качели (pl) | [kɑ'tʃeli] |

91. Villa. Mansion

country house	загородный дом (m)	['zagaradnıj dom]
villa (by sea)	вилла (f)	['willə]
wing (of building)	крыло (n)	[krı'lɔ]
garden	сад (m)	[sat]
park	парк (m)	[park]
greenhouse (tropical ~)	оранжерея (f)	[aranʒı'reja]
to look after (garden etc.)	ухаживать	[u'haʒıvatʲ]
swimming pool	бассейн (m)	[ba'sɛjn]
gym	спортивный зал (m)	[spar'tivnıj zal]
tennis court	теннисный корт (m)	['tɛnisnıj kɔrt]
home theater room	кинотеатр (m)	[kinati'atr]
garage	гараж (m)	[ga'raʃ]
private property	частная собственность (f)	['tʃasnaja 'sɔpstwenastʲ]
private land	частные владения (n pl)	['tʃasnıe vla'denija]
warning (caution)	предупреждение (n)	[pridupriʒ'denie]
warning sign	предупреждающая надпись (f)	[pridupriʒ'dajuɕeja 'natpisʲ]
security	охрана (f)	[ah'ranə]
security guard	охранник (m)	[ah'rannik]
burglar alarm	сигнализация (f)	[signali'zatsıja]

92. Castle. Palace

castle	замок (m)	[za'mɔk]
palace	дворец (m)	[dva'rets]
fortress	крепость (f)	['krepastʲ]
wall (round castle)	стена (f)	[sti'na]
tower	башня (f)	['baʃna]
main tower, donjon	главная башня (f)	['glavnaja 'baʃna]
portcullis	подъёмные ворота (pl)	[padʲ'ɜmnıe va'rotə]
underground passage	подземный ход (m)	[pa'dzemnıj hot]
moat	ров (m)	[rɔf]
chain	цепь (f)	[tsepʲ]
arrow loop	бойница (f)	[baj'nitsə]
magnificent	великолепный	[wilika'lepnıj]
majestic	величественный	[wi'litʃestwenıj]
impregnable	неприступный	[nipris'tupnıj]
knight's	рыцарский	['rıtsarskij]
medieval	средневековый	[srednewe'kɔvıj]

93. Apartment

apartment	квартира (f)	[kvar'tirə]
room	комната (f)	['kɔmnatə]
bedroom	спальня (f)	['spaʎna]
dining room	столовая (f)	[sta'lɔvaja]
living room	гостиная (f)	[gas'tinaja]
study	кабинет (m)	[kabi'net]
entry room	прихожая (f)	[pri'hɔʒaja]
bathroom	ванная комната (f)	['vannaja 'kɔmnatə]
half bath	туалет (m)	[tʊa'let]
ceiling	потолок (m)	[pata'lɔk]
floor	пол (m)	[pɔl]
corner (inside room)	угол (m)	['ugal]

94. Apartment. Cleaning

to clean (vi, vt)	убирать	[ubi'ratʲ]
to put away (vt)	уносить	[una'sitʲ]
dust	пыль (f)	[pɪʎ]
dusty	пыльный	['pɪʎnij]
to dust (vt)	вытирать пыль	[vɪti'ratʲ pɪʎ]
vacuum cleaner	пылесос (m)	[pɪle'sɔs]
to vacuum (vt)	пылесосить	[pɪle'sɔsitʲ]
to sweep (vi, vt)	подметать	[padme'tatʲ]
sweepings	мусор (m)	['mʊsar]
order	порядок (m)	[pa'rʲadak]
disorder, mess	беспорядок (m)	[bispa'rʲadak]
mop	швабра (f)	['ʃvabrə]
dust cloth	тряпка (f)	['trʲapkə]
broom	веник (m)	['wenik]
dustpan	совок (m) для мусора	[sa'vɔk dʎa 'mʊsarə]

95. Furniture. Interior

furniture (for house)	мебель (f)	['mebeʎ]
table	стол (m)	[stɔl]
chair	стул (m)	[stʊl]
bed	кровать (f)	[kra'vatʲ]
couch, sofa	диван (m)	[di'van]
armchair	кресло (n)	['kreslə]
bookcase	книжный шкаф (m)	['knʲʒnij ʃkaf]

shelf	полка (f)	['pɔlkə]
set of shelves	этажерка (f)	[ɛtɑ'ʒɛrkə]
wardrobe	гардероб (m)	[gɑrde'rɔp]
coat rack	вешалка (f)	['weʃʌlkə]
coat stand	вешалка (f)	['weʃʌlkə]
chest of drawers	комод (m)	[kɑ'mɔt]
coffee table	журнальный столик (m)	[ʒur'nɑʎnɪj 'stɔlik]
mirror	зеркало (n)	['zerkɑlə]
carpet	ковёр (m)	[kɑ'wɜr]
rug, small carpet	коврик (m)	['kɔvrik]
fireplace	камин (m)	[kɑ'min]
candle	свеча (f)	[swi'ʧʌ]
candlestick	подсвечник (m)	[pɑts'weʧnik]
kitchen curtains	занавески (f pl)	[zɑnɑ'weski]
drapes	шторы (f pl)	['ʃtɔrɪ]
wallpaper	обои (pl)	[ɑ'bɔi]
blinds (jalousie)	жалюзи (pl)	[ʒɑly'zi]
table lamp	настольная лампа (f)	[nɑs'tɔʎnɑjɑ 'lɑmpə]
wall lamp	светильник (m)	[swi'tiʎnik]
floor lamp	торшер (m)	[tɑr'ʃər]
chandelier	люстра (f)	['lystrə]
leg (of chair, table)	ножка (f)	['nɔʃkə]
armrest	подлокотник (m)	[pɑdlɑ'kɔtnik]
back	спинка (f)	['spinkə]
drawer	ящик (m)	['jaɕik]

96. Bedding

bedclothes	бельё (n)	[bi'ʎjo]
pillow	подушка (f)	[pɑ'duʃkə]
pillowcase	наволочка (f)	['nɑvɑlɑʧkə]
blanket (comforter)	одеяло (n)	[ɑdi'jalə]
sheet	простыня (f)	[prɑstɪ'ɲa]
bedspread	покрывало (n)	[pɑkrɪ'valə]

97. Kitchen

kitchen	кухня (f)	['kuhɲa]
gas	газ (m)	[gɑs]
gas stove	газовая плита (f)	['gɑzɑvɑjɑ pli'tɑ]
electric stove	электроплита (f)	[ɛlektrɑpli'tɑ]

oven	духовка (f)	[duˈhofkə]
microwave oven	микроволновая печь (f)	[mikravalˈnɔvaja petʃ]
fridge	холодильник (m)	[halaˈdiʌnik]
freezer	морозильник (m)	[maraˈziʌnik]
dishwasher	посудомоечная машина (f)	[pasʊdaˈmɔetʃnaja maˈʃinə]
meat grinder	мясорубка (f)	[misaˈrʊpkə]
juicer	соковыжималка (f)	[sɔkavɪʒɪˈmalkə]
toaster	тостер (m)	[ˈtɔster]
mixer	миксер (m)	[ˈmikser]
coffee maker	кофеварка (f)	[kafeˈvarkə]
coffee pot	кофейник (m)	[kaˈfejnik]
coffee grinder	кофемолка (f)	[kafeˈmɔlkə]
kettle	чайник (m)	[ˈtʃajnik]
teapot	чайник (m)	[ˈtʃajnik]
lid	крышка (f)	[ˈkrɪʃkə]
tea strainer	ситечко (n)	[ˈsitetʃkə]
spoon	ложка (f)	[ˈlɔʃkə]
teaspoon	чайная ложка (f)	[ˈtʃajnaja ˈlɔʃkə]
tablespoon	столовая ложка (f)	[staˈlɔvaja ˈlɔʃkə]
fork	вилка (f)	[ˈwilkə]
knife	нож (m)	[nɔʃ]
tableware	посуда (f)	[paˈsʊdə]
plate	тарелка (f)	[taˈrelkə]
saucer	блюдце (n)	[ˈblytsе]
small wineglass	рюмка (f)	[ˈrymkə]
glass (e.g., ~ of water)	стакан (m)	[staˈkan]
cup	чашка (f)	[ˈtʃaʃkə]
sugar bowl	сахарница (f)	[ˈsaharnitsə]
salt shaker	солонка (f)	[saˈlɔnkə]
pepper shaker	перечница (f)	[ˈperetʃnitsə]
butter dish	маслёнка (f)	[masˈlɔnkə]
saucepan	кастрюля (f)	[kastˈryʌa]
frying pan	сковородка (f)	[skavaˈrɔtkə]
ladle	половник (m)	[paˈlɔvnik]
colander	дуршлаг (m)	[dʊrʃˈlak]
tray	поднос (m)	[padˈnɔs]
bottle	бутылка (f)	[bʊˈtɪlkə]
jar (glass)	банка (f)	[ˈbankə]
can	банка (f)	[ˈbankə]
bottle opener	открывалка (f)	[atkrɪˈvalkə]
can opener	открывалка (f)	[atkrɪˈvalkə]

corkscrew	штопор (m)	['ʃtɔpɑr]
filter	фильтр (m)	[fiʌtr]
to filter (vt)	фильтровать	[fiʌtrɑ'vatʲ]

| trash | мусор (m) | ['musɑr] |
| trash can | мусорное ведро (n) | ['musɑrnɑe wid'rɔ] |

98. Bathroom

bathroom	ванная комната (f)	['vannɑjɑ 'kɔmnɑtə]
water	вода (f)	[vɑ'dɑ]
tap, faucet	кран (m)	[krɑn]
hot water	горячая вода (f)	[gɑ'rʲatʃɑjɑ vɑ'dɑ]
cold water	холодная вода (f)	[hɑ'lɔdnɑjɑ vɑ'dɑ]

toothpaste	зубная паста (f)	[zub'nɑjɑ 'pɑstə]
to brush one's teeth	чистить зубы	['tʃistitʲ 'zubɪ]
toothbrush	зубная щётка (f)	[zub'nɑjɑ 'ɕɔtkə]

to shave (vi)	бриться	['britsə]
shaving foam	пена (f) для бритья	['penɑ dʌɑ bri'tjɑ]
razor	бритва (f)	['britvə]
to wash (clean)	мыть	[mɪtʲ]
to take a bath	мыться	['mɪtsə]
shower	душ (m)	[duʃ]
to take a shower	принимать душ	[prini'matʲ duʃ]

bathtub	ванна (f)	['vannə]
toilet	унитаз (m)	[uni'tɑs]
sink	раковина (f)	['rɑkɑwinə]
soap	мыло (n)	['mɪlə]
soap dish	мыльница (f)	['mɪʌnitsə]

sponge	губка (f)	['gupkə]
shampoo	шампунь (m)	[ʃʌm'puɲ]
towel	полотенце (n)	[pɑlɑ'tentsə]
bathrobe	халат (m)	[hɑ'lɑt]

laundry (process)	стирка (f)	['stirkə]
washing machine	стиральная машина (f)	[sti'raʌnɑjɑ mɑ'ʃinə]
to do the laundry	стирать бельё	[sti'ratʲ be'ʌjo]
laundry detergent	стиральный порошок (m)	[sti'raʌnɪj pɑrɑ'ʃɔk]

99. Household appliances

| TV set | телевизор (m) | [tile'wizɑr] |
| tape recorder | магнитофон (m) | [mɑgnitɑ'fɔn] |

video, VCR	видеомагнитофон (m)	['widea magnita'fon]
radio	приёмник (m)	[pri3mnik]
player (CD, MP3 etc.)	плеер (m)	['plɛer]

video projector	видеопроектор (m)	['widea pra'ektar]
home movie theater	домашний кинотеатр (m)	[da'maʃnij kinate'atr]
DVD player	DVD проигрыватель (m)	[diwi'di pra'igrıvateʎ]
amplifier	усилитель (m)	[usi'liteʎ]
video game console	игровая приставка (f)	[igra'vaja pris'tafkə]

video camera	видеокамера (f)	[widea'kamerə]
camera (photo)	фотоаппарат (m)	[fɔtapa'rat]
digital camera	цифровой фотоаппарат (m)	[tsıfra'vɔj fɔtapa'rat]

vacuum cleaner	пылесос (m)	[pıle'sɔs]
iron (e.g., steam ~)	утюг (m)	[u'tyk]
ironing board	гладильная доска (f)	[gla'diʎnaja das'ka]

telephone	телефон (m)	[tile'fɔn]
mobile phone	мобильный телефон (m)	[ma'biʎnıj tele'fɔn]
sewing machine	швейная машинка (f)	['ʃwejnaja ma'ʃinkə]

microphone	микрофон (m)	[mikra'fɔn]
headphones	наушники (m pl)	[na'uʃniki]
remote control (TV)	пульт (m)	[puʎt]

compact disc, CD	компакт-диск (m)	[kam'pakt 'disk]
cassette	кассета (f)	[ka'setə]
record (vinyl LP)	пластинка (f)	[plas'tinkə]

100. Repairs. Renovation

renovations	ремонт (m)	[ri'mɔnt]
to renovate (vt)	делать ремонт	['delatİ re'mɔnt]
to repair (vt)	ремонтировать	[riman'tiravatİ]
to put in order	приводить в порядок	[priva'ditİ f pa'rİadak]
to redo (vt)	переделывать	[pire'delıvatİ]

paint	краска (f)	['kraskə]
to paint (e.g., ~ a wall)	красить	['krasitİ]
house painter	маляр (m)	[ma'ʎar]
brush	кисть (f)	[kistİ]
whitewash	побелка (f)	[pa'belkə]
to whitewash (vt)	белить	[bi'litİ]

wallpaper	обои (pl)	[a'bɔi]
to put up wallpaper	оклеить обоями	[ak'leitİ a'bɔimi]
varnish	лак (m)	[lak]
to varnish (vt)	покрывать лаком	[pakrı'vatİ 'lakam]

101. Plumbing

water	вода (f)	[va'da]
hot water	горячая вода (f)	[ga'rʲatʃaja va'da]
cold water	холодная вода (f)	[ha'lodnaja va'da]
tap, faucet	кран (m)	[kran]

drop (of water)	капля (f)	['kapʎa]
to drip (vi)	капать	['kapatʲ]
to leak (about pipe)	течь	[tetʃ]
leak (in pipe)	течь (f)	[tetʃ]
puddle	лужа (f)	['luʒə]

pipe	труба (f)	[trʊ'ba]
valve	вентиль (m)	['wentiʎ]
to be clogged up	засориться	[zasa'ritsə]

tools	инструменты (m pl)	[instrʊ'mentɪ]
adjustable wrench	разводной ключ (m)	[razvad'noj 'klytʃ]
to unscrew (vt)	открутить	[atkrʊ'titʲ]
to screw (tighten)	закрутить	[zakrʊ'titʲ]

to unclog (vt)	прочищать	[pratʃi'çatʲ]
plumber	сантехник (m)	[san'tehnik]
basement	подвал (m)	[pad'val]
sewerage (system)	канализация (f)	[kanali'zatsɪja]

102. Fire. Conflagration

fire (e.g., to catch ~)	огонь (m)	[a'gɔɲ]
flame	пламя (f)	['plamʲa]
spark	искра (f)	['iskrə]
smoke (from fire)	дым (m)	[dɪm]
torch (flaming stick)	факел (m)	['fakel]
campfire	костёр (m)	[kas'tзr]

gas, gasoline	бензин (m)	[bin'zin]
kerosene (for aircraft)	керосин (m)	[kira'sin]
flammable	горючий	[ga'rytʃij]
explosive	взрывоопасный	[vzrɪvaa'pasnɪj]
NO SMOKING	НЕ КУРИТЬ!	[ne kʊ'ritʲ]

safety	безопасность (f)	[biza'pasnastʲ]
danger	опасность (f)	[a'pasnastʲ]
dangerous	опасный	[a'pasnɪj]

to catch fire	загореться	[zaga'retsə]
explosion	взрыв (m)	[fzrɪf]
to set fire	поджечь	[pa'dʒetʃ]

incendiary (arsonist)	поджигатель (m)	[pɐdʒɪˈgateʎ]
arson	поджог (m)	[pɐˈdʒɔk]
to blaze (vi)	пылать	[pɪˈlatʲ]
to burn (be on fire)	гореть	[gɐˈretʲ]
to burn down	сгореть	[sgɐˈretʲ]
to call the fire department	вызвать пожарных	[ˈvɪzvatʲ pɐˈʒarnɪh]
fireman	пожарный (m)	[pɐˈʒarnɪj]
fire truck	пожарная машина (f)	[pɐˈʒarnaja mɐˈʃɪnə]
fire department	пожарная команда (f)	[pɐˈʒarnaja kɐˈmandə]
fire truck ladder	пожарная лестница (f)	[pɐˈʒarnaja ˈlesnitsə]
fire hose	шланг (m)	[ʃlank]
fire extinguisher	огнетушитель (m)	[ɐgnetʊˈʃiteʎ]
helmet	каска (f)	[ˈkaskə]
siren	сирена (f)	[siˈrenə]
to shout (vi)	кричать	[kriˈʧatʲ]
to call for help	звать на помощь	[zvatʲ na ˈpɔmɑɕ]
rescuer	спасатель (m)	[spɐˈsateʎ]
to rescue (vt)	спасать	[spɐˈsatʲ]
to arrive (vi)	приехать	[priˈehatʲ]
to extinguish (vt)	тушить	[tʊˈʃitʲ]
water	вода (f)	[vɐˈda]
sand	песок (m)	[piˈsɔk]
ruins (destruction)	руины (pl)	[rʊˈinɪ]
to collapse (building, roof)	рухнуть	[ˈrʊhnʊtʲ]
to fall down	обвалиться	[ɐbvɐˈlitsə]
to cave in (ceiling, floor)	обрушиться	[ɐbˈrʊʃitsə]
fragment (piece of wall etc.)	обломок (m)	[ɐbˈlɔmak]
ash	пепел (m)	[ˈpepel]
to suffocate (die)	задохнуться	[zɐdɑhˈnʊtsə]
to be killed (perish)	погибнуть	[pɐˈgibnʊtʲ]

HUMAN ACTIVITIES

Job. Business. Part 1

103. Office. Working in the office

office (of firm)	офис (m)	['ɔfis]
office (of director etc.)	кабинет (m)	[kabi'net]
front desk (in the office)	ресепшн (m)	[ri'sepʃn]
secretary	секретарь (m, f)	[sikre'tarʲ]
secretary (fem.)	секретарша (f)	[sikre'tarʃə]
director	директор (m)	[di'rektar]
manager (employee)	менеджер (m)	['mɛnɛdʒɛr]
accountant	бухгалтер (m)	[bʊ'galter]
employee	сотрудник (m)	[sat'rʊdnik]
furniture	мебель (f)	['mebeʎ]
desk	стол (m)	[stɔl]
desk chair	кресло (n)	['kreslə]
chest of drawers	тумбочка (f)	['tʊmbatʃkə]
coat stand	вешалка (f)	['weʃʌlkə]
computer	компьютер (m)	[kam'pjyter]
printer	принтер (m)	['printer]
fax machine	факс (m)	[faks]
photocopier	копировальный аппарат (m)	[kapira'vaʎnɪj apa'rat]
paper	бумага (f)	[bʊ'magə]
office supplies	канцтовары (f pl)	[kantsta'varɪ]
mouse pad	коврик (m) для мыши	['kɔvrik dʎa 'mɪʃi]
sheet (of paper)	лист (m)	[list]
folder, binder	папка (f)	['papkə]
catalog	каталог (m)	[kata'lɔk]
phone book	справочник (m)	['spravatʃnik]
documentation	документация (f)	[dakʊmen'tatsɪja]
booklet	брошюра (f)	[bra'ʃyrə]
leaflet	листовка (f)	[lis'tɔfkə]
sample	образец (m)	[abra'zets]
training meeting	тренинг (m)	['trenink]
meeting (of managers)	совещание (n)	[sawe'ɕanie]
lunch time	перерыв (m) на обед	[piri'rɪf na a'bet]

to copy (photocopy)	делать копию	['delatʲ 'kɔpiju]
to make copies	размножить	[razm'nɔʒitʲ]
to receive a fax	получать факс	[palu'tʃatʲ faks]
to send a fax	отправлять факс	[atprav'ʎatʲ faks]

to call (telephone)	позвонить	[pazva'nitʲ]
to answer (vi, vt)	ответить	[at'wetitʲ]
to put through	соединить	[saidi'nitʲ]

to arrange (organize, plan)	назначать	[nazna'tʃatʲ]
to show (to display)	демонстрировать	[dimanst'riravatʲ]
to be absent	отсутствовать	[a'tsutstvavatʲ]
absence	пропуск (m)	['prɔpusk]

104. Business processes. Part 1

| business | бизнес (m) | ['biznes] |
| occupation | дело (n) | ['delə] |

firm	фирма (f)	['firmə]
company	компания (f)	[kam'panija]
corporation	корпорация (f)	[karpa'ratsija]
enterprise	предприятие (n)	[pritpri'jatie]
agency	агентство (n)	[a'gentstvə]

agreement (contract)	договор (m)	[daga'vɔr]
contract	контракт (m)	[kant'rakt]
deal	сделка (f)	['sdelkə]
order (to place an ~)	заказ (m)	[za'kas]
term (of contract)	условие (n)	[us'lɔwie]

wholesale (adv)	оптом	['ɔptam]
wholesale (adj)	оптовый	[ap'tɔvij]
wholesale (noun)	продажа (f) оптом	[pra'daʒa 'ɔptam]
retail (adj)	розничный	['rɔznitʃnij]
retail (noun)	продажа (f) в розницу	[pra'daʒa v 'rɔznitsu]

competitor	конкурент (m)	[kanku'rent]
competition	конкуренция (f)	[kanku'rentsija]
to compete (vi)	конкурировать	[kanku'riravatʲ]

| partner (associate) | партнёр (m) | [part'nзr] |
| partnership | партнёрство (n) | [part'nзrstvə] |

crisis	кризис (m)	['krizis]
bankruptcy	банкротство (n)	[bank'rɔtstvə]
to go bankrupt	обанкротиться	[abank'rɔtitsə]
difficulty	трудность (f)	['trudnastʲ]
problem	проблема (f)	[prab'lemə]
catastrophe	катастрофа (f)	[katast'rɔfə]

economy	экономика (f)	[ɛka'nɔmikə]
economic (e.g., ~ growth)	экономический	[ɛkana'mitʃeskij]
economic recession	экономический спад (m)	[ɛkana'mitʃeskij spat]

| goal (aim) | цель (f) | [tseʎ] |
| task | задача (f) | [za'datʃə] |

to trade (vi)	торговать	[targa'vatʲ]
network (distribution ~)	сеть (f)	[setʲ]
stock	склад (m)	[sklat]
assortment	ассортимент (m)	[asarti'ment]

leader	лидер (m)	['lider]
big, large	крупный	['krʊpnɪj]
monopoly	монополия (f)	[mana'pɔlija]

theory	теория (f)	[ti'ɔrija]
practice	практика (f)	['praktikə]
experience (in my ~)	опыт (m)	['ɔpɪt]
trend (tendency)	тенденция (f)	[tɛn'dɛntsɪja]
development	развитие (n)	[raz'witie]

105. Business processes. Part 2

| profit (benefit) | выгода (f) | ['vɪgadə] |
| profitable | выгодный | ['vɪgadnɪj] |

delegation (group)	делегация (f)	[dile'gatsɪja]
salary	заработная плата (f)	['zarabatnaja 'platə]
to correct (vt)	исправлять	[isprav'ʎatʲ]
business trip	командировка (f)	[kamandi'rɔfkə]
commission	комиссия (f)	[ka'misija]

to control (vt)	контролировать	[kantra'liravatʲ]
conference	конференция (f)	[kanfe'rentsɪja]
license	лицензия (f)	[li'tsenzija]
reliable (trustworthy)	надёжный	[na'dɜʒnɪj]

initiative (new project etc.)	начинание (n)	[natʃi'nanie]
norm (standard)	норма (f)	['nɔrmə]
circumstance	обстоятельство (n)	[apsta'jateʎstvə]
duty (of employee)	обязанность (f)	[a'bʲazanastʲ]
enterprise	организация (f)	[argani'zatsɪja]

organization (process)	организация (f)	[argani'zatsɪja]
organized	организованный	[argani'zɔvanɪj]
cancellation (calling off)	отмена (f)	[at'menə]
to cancel (call off)	отменить	[atme'nitʲ]
report (e.g., official ~)	отчёт (m)	[a'tʃɜt]
patent	патент (m)	[pa'tent]

to patent (obtain patent)	патентовать	[patenta'vatʲ]
to plan (vi, vt)	планировать	[pla'niravatʲ]
bonus (money)	премия (f)	['premija]
professional	профессиональный	[prafesʲa'naʎnij]
procedure	процедура (f)	[pratsɪ'durə]
to examine (contract etc.)	рассмотреть	[rassmat'retʲ]
calculation	расчёт (m)	[ra'ɕɜt]
reputation	репутация (f)	[ripʊ'tatsɪja]
risk	риск (m)	[risk]
to manage (business etc.)	руководить	[rʊkava'dʲitʲ]
information	сведения (f)	['swedenija]
property	собственность (f)	['sɔpstwenastʲ]
union (association, group)	союз (m)	[sa'jus]
life insurance	страхование (n) жизни	[straha'vanie 'ʒɪzni]
to insure (vt)	страховать	[straha'vatʲ]
insurance	страховка (f)	[stra'hɔfkə]
auction	торги (pl)	[tar'gi]
to notify (inform)	уведомить	[u'wedamitʲ]
management (process)	управление (n)	[uprav'lenie]
service (in shop, hotel)	услуга (f)	[us'lugə]
forum	форум (m)	['fɔrʊm]
to function (vi)	функционировать	[fʊnktsɪa'niravatʲ]
stage (phase)	этап (m)	[ɛ'tap]
legal	юридический	[juri'dʲitʃeskij]
lawyer (legal expert)	юрист (m)	[ju'rist]

106. Production. Works

plant	завод (m)	[za'vɔt]
factory	фабрика (f)	['fabrikə]
workshop	цех (m)	[tseh]
production site	производство (n)	[praiz'vɔtstvə]
industry	промышленность (f)	[pra'mɪʃlenastʲ]
industrial	промышленный	[pra'mɪʃlenij]
heavy industry	тяжелая промышленность (f)	[tʲaʒɜlaja pra'mɪʃlenastʲ]
light industry	лёгкая промышленность (f)	[lɜhkaja pra'mɪʃlenastʲ]
products	продукция (f)	[pra'dʊktsɪja]
to produce (vt)	производить	[praizva'dʲitʲ]
raw materials	сырьё (n)	[sɪ'rjo]
foreman	бригадир (m)	[briga'dʲir]

workers team	**бригада** (f)	[bri'gadə]
worker	**рабочий** (m)	[ra'botʃij]
workday	**рабочий день** (m)	[ra'botʃij deɲ]
pause	**остановка** (f)	[asta'nofkə]
meeting	**собрание** (n)	[sab'ranie]
to discuss (~ a problem)	**обсуждать**	[apsuʒ'datʲ]
plan	**план** (m)	[plan]
to fulfill the plan	**выполнять план**	[vɪpal'ɲatʲ plan]
rate (of output)	**норма** (f)	['nɔrmə]
quality	**качество** (n)	['katʃestvə]
checking (control)	**контроль** (m)	[kant'rɔʎ]
quality control	**контроль** (m) **качества**	[kant'rɔʎ 'katʃestvə]
safety of work	**безопасность** (f) **труда**	[biza'pasnastʲ tru'da]
discipline	**дисциплина** (f)	[distsip'linə]
violation (of rules)	**нарушение** (n)	[naru'ʃenie]
to violate (vt)	**нарушать**	[naru'ʃatʲ]
strike	**забастовка** (f)	[zabas'tofkə]
striker	**забастовщик** (m)	[zabas'tofɕik]
to be on strike	**бастовать**	[basta'vatʲ]
labor union	**профсоюз** (m)	[prafsa'jus]
to invent (machine etc.)	**изобретать**	[izabre'tatʲ]
invention	**изобретение** (n)	[izabre'tenie]
research	**исследование** (n)	[is'ledavanie]
to improve (make better)	**улучшать**	[ulutʃ'ʃatʲ]
technology	**технология** (f)	[tihna'logija]
technical drawing	**чертёж** (m)	[tʃir'tʒʃ]
load, cargo	**груз** (m)	[grus]
loader (person)	**грузчик** (m)	['gruɕik]
to load (vehicle etc.)	**грузить**	[gru'zitʲ]
loading (process)	**погрузка** (f)	[pag'ruskə]
to unload (vi, vt)	**разгружать**	[razgru'ʒatʲ]
unloading	**разгрузка** (f)	[razg'ruskə]
transportation	**транспорт** (m)	['transpart]
transportation company	**транспортная компания** (f)	['transpartnaja kampanija]
to transport (vt)	**транспортировать**	[transpar'tiravatʲ]
freight car	**вагон** (m)	[va'gɔn]
cistern	**цистерна** (f)	[tsɪs'ternə]
truck	**грузовик** (m)	[gruza'wik]
machine tool	**станок** (m)	[sta'nɔk]
mechanism	**механизм** (m)	[miha'nizm]
industrial waste	**отходы** (pl)	[at'hɔdɪ]
packing (process)	**упаковка** (f)	[upa'kofkə]
to pack (vt)	**упаковать**	[upaka'vatʲ]

107. Contract. Agreement

contract	контракт (m)	[kɑnt'rɑkt]
agreement	соглашение (n)	[sɑglɑ'ʃɛnie]
addendum	приложение (n)	[prilɑ'ʒɛnie]

to sign a contract	заключить контракт	[zɑkly'tʃitʲ kɑnt'rɑkt]
signature	подпись (f)	['pɔtpisʲ]
to sign (vt)	подписать	[pɑtpi'sɑtʲ]
stamp (on document)	печать (f)	[pi'tʃatʲ]

subject (of contract)	предмет (m) договора	[prid'met dɑgɑ'vɔrə]
clause	пункт (m)	[pʊnkt]
parties (in contract)	стороны (f pl)	['stɔrɑnı]
legal address	юридический адрес (m)	[juri'ditʃeskij 'ɑdres]

to break the contract	нарушить контракт	[nɑ'rʊʃitʲ kɑnt'rɑkt]
commitment	обязательство (n)	[ɑbi'zɑteʎstvə]
responsibility	ответственность (f)	[ɑt'wetstwenɑstʲ]
force majeure	форс-мажор (m)	[fɔrs mɑ'ʒɔr]
dispute	спор (m)	[spɔr]
penalties	штрафные санкции (f pl)	[ʃtrɑf'nıe 'sɑnktsıi]

108. Import & Export

import (activity)	импорт (m)	['impɑrt]
importer	импортёр (m)	[impɑr'tɜr]
to import (vt)	импортировать	[impɑr'tirɑvɑtʲ]
import (e.g., ~ goods)	импортный	['impɑrtnıj]

export (activity)	экспорт (m)	['ɛkspɑrt]
exporter	экспортёр (m)	[ɛkspɑr'tɜr]
to export (vi, vt)	экспортировать	[ɛkspɑr'tirɑvɑtʲ]
export (e.g., ~ goods)	экспортный	['ɛkspɑrtnıj]

| goods | товар (m) | [tɑ'vɑr] |
| load (e.g., carload) | партия (f) | ['pɑrtijɑ] |

weight	вес (m)	[wes]
volume	объём (m)	[ɑbʰɜm]
cubic meter	кубический метр (m)	[kʊ'bitʃiskij metr]

manufacturer	производитель (m)	[prɑizvɑ'diteʎ]
transportation company	транспортная компания (f)	['trɑnspɑrtnɑjɑ kɑmpɑnijɑ]
container (for cargo)	контейнер (m)	[kɑn'tɛjner]

| border (boundary) | граница (f) | [grɑ'nitsə] |
| customs | таможня (f) | [tɑ'mɔʒnɑ] |

customs duty	**таможенная пошлина** (f)	[ta'mɔʒɛnaja 'pɔʃlinə]
customs officer	**таможенник** (m)	[ta'mɔʒɛnik]
smuggling	**контрабанда** (f)	[kantra'bandə]
contraband (goods)	**контрабанда** (f)	[kantra'bandə]

109. Finances

share, stock	**акция** (f)	['aktsija]
bond (certificate)	**облигация** (f)	[abli'gatsija]
bill of exchange	**вексель** (m)	['wekseʎ]
stock exchange	**биржа** (f)	['birʒə]
stock price	**курс** (m) **акций**	[kurs 'aktsij]
to become cheaper	**подешеветь**	[padeʃe'wetʲ]
to rise in price	**подорожать**	[padara'ʒatʲ]
share	**доля** (f), **пай**	['dɔʎa], [paj]
controlling interest	**контрольный пакет** (m)	[kant'rɔʎnij pa'ket]
investment	**инвестиции** (f pl)	[inwes'titsii]
to invest (vi, vt)	**инвестировать**	[inwes'tiravatʲ]
percent	**процент** (m)	[pra'tsent]
interest (on investment)	**проценты** (m pl)	[pra'tsenti]
profit	**прибыль** (f)	['pribiʎ]
profitable	**прибыльный**	['pribiʎnij]
tax	**налог** (m)	[na'lɔk]
currency (foreign ~)	**валюта** (f)	[va'lytə]
national	**национальный**	[natsia'naʎnij]
exchange (of currency)	**обмен** (m)	[ab'men]
accountant	**бухгалтер** (m)	[bu'galter]
accounts department	**бухгалтерия** (f)	[bugal'terija]
bankruptcy	**банкротство** (n)	[bank'rɔtstvə]
collapse, crash	**крах** (m)	[krah]
ruin	**разорение** (n)	[raza'renie]
to be ruined	**разориться**	[raza'ritsə]
inflation	**инфляция** (f)	[inf'ʎatsija]
devaluation	**девальвация** (f)	[divaʎ'vatsija]
capital	**капитал** (m)	[kapi'tal]
income	**доход** (m)	[da'hɔt]
turnover	**оборот** (m)	[aba'rɔt]
resources	**ресурсы** (m pl)	[ri'sursi]
monetary resources	**денежные средства** (n pl)	['deneʒnie s'retstvə]
overhead	**накладные расходы** (pl)	[naklad'nie ras'hɔdi]
to reduce (expenses)	**сократить**	[sakra'titʲ]

110. Marketing

marketing	маркетинг (m)	[mar'ketink]
market	рынок (m)	['rınɑk]
market segment	сегмент (m) рынка	[seg'ment 'rınkə]
product	продукт (m)	[pra'dukt]
goods	товар (m)	[ta'var]
trademark	торговая марка (f)	[tar'gɔvaja 'markə]
logotype	фирменный знак (m)	['firmenıj znak]
logo	логотип (m)	[laga'tip]
demand	спрос (m)	[sprɔs]
offer	предложение (n)	[pridla'ʒenie]
need	потребность (f)	[pat'rebnastʲ]
consumer	потребитель (m)	[patre'biteʎ]
analysis	анализ (m)	[a'nalis]
to analyze (vt)	анализировать	[anali'ziravatʲ]
positioning	позиционирование (n)	[pazitsıa'niravanie]
to position (product)	позиционировать	[pazitsıa'niravatʲ]
price	цена (f)	[tsı'na]
pricing policy	ценовая политика (f)	[tsəna'vaja pa'litikə]
pricing	ценообразование (n)	[tsenaabraza'vanie]

111. Advertising

advertising	реклама (f)	[rik'lamə]
to advertise (vt)	рекламировать	[rikla'miravatʲ]
budget	бюджет (m)	[by'dʒet]
ad, advertisement	реклама (f)	[rik'lamə]
TV advertising	телереклама (f)	[telerek'lamə]
radio advertising	реклама (f) на радио	[rek'lama na 'radiə]
outdoor advertising	наружная реклама (f)	[na'ruʒnaja rek'lamə]
mass media	средства (n pl) массовой информации	['sretstva massavaj infar'matsıi]
periodical (noun)	периодическое издание (n)	[piria'ditʃeskae iz'danie]
image (public appearance)	имидж (m)	['imitʃ]
slogan	лозунг (m)	['lɔzunk]
motto (maxim)	девиз (m)	[di'wis]
campaign	кампания (f)	[kam'panija]
advertising campaign	рекламная кампания (f)	[rek'lamnaja kam'panija]
target group	целевая аудитория (f)	[tsele'vaja audi'torija]

business card	визитная карточка (f)	[wi'zitnaja 'kartatʃkə]
leaflet	листовка (f)	[lis'tɔfkə]
brochure	брошюра (f)	[bra'ʃyrə]
pamphlet	буклет (m)	[bʊk'let]
newsletter	бюллетень (m)	[byle'teɲ]
sign (on shop, bar etc.)	вывеска (f)	['vɪwiskə]
poster	плакат (m)	[pla'kat]
billboard	щит (m)	[ɕit]

112. Banking

bank	банк (m)	[bank]
branch (of bank etc.)	отделение (n)	[addi'lenie]
consultant	консультант (m)	[kansʊʎ'tant]
manager (boss)	управляющий (m)	[uprav'ʎajuɕij]
banking account	счёт (m)	['ɕɔt]
account number	номер (m) счёта	['nɔmer 'ɕɔtə]
checking account	текущий счёт (m)	[te'kuɕij 'ɕɔt]
savings account	накопительный счёт (m)	[naka'piteʎnɪj 'ɕɔt]
to open an account	открыть счёт	[atkrɪtʲ 'ɕɔt]
to close the account	закрыть счёт	[zak'rɪtʲ 'ɕɔt]
to deposit (vt)	положить на счёт	[pala'ʒitʲ na 'ɕɔt]
to withdraw (vt)	снять со счёта	['sɲatʲ sa 'ɕɔtə]
deposit	вклад (m)	[vklat]
to make a deposit	сделать вклад	['zdelatʲ fklat]
wire transfer	перевод (m)	[pere'vɔt]
to wire (money)	сделать перевод	['zdelatʲ pere'vɔt]
sum (amount of money)	сумма (f)	['sʊmmə]
How much?	Сколько?	['skɔʎka]
signature	подпись (f)	['pɔtpisʲ]
to sign (vt)	подписать	[patpi'satʲ]
credit card	кредитная карта (f)	[kri'ditnaja 'kartə]
code	код (m)	[kɔt]
credit card number	номер (m) кредитной карты	['nɔmer kre'ditnaj 'kartɪ]
ATM	банкомат (m)	[banka'mat]
check	чек (m)	[tʃek]
to write a check	выписать чек	['vɪpisatʲ tʃek]
checkbook	чековая книжка (f)	['tʃekavaja 'kniʃkə]
loan (bank ~)	кредит (m)	[kri'dit]
to ask for a loan	обращаться за кредитом	[abra'ɕatsa za kre'ditam]

to take a loan	брать кредит	[bratʲ kreˈdit]
to grant a credit	предоставлять кредит	[pridastavˈʎatʲ kriˈdit]
guarantee	гарантия (f)	[gaˈrantija]

113. Telephone. Phone conversation

telephone	телефон (m)	[tileˈfɔn]
mobile phone	мобильный телефон (m)	[maˈbiʎnɨj teleˈfɔn]
answering machine	автоответчик (m)	[aftaatˈwetʃik]

| to call (telephone) | звонить | [zvaˈnitʲ] |
| phone call | звонок (m) | [zvaˈnɔk] |

to dial a number	набрать номер	[nabˈratʲ ˈnɔmer]
Hello!	Алло!	[aˈlɔ]
to ask (vi, vt)	спросить	[spraˈsitʲ]
to answer (vi, vt)	ответить	[atˈwetitʲ]

to hear (vi, vt)	слышать	[ˈslɨʃʌtʲ]
well	хорошо	[haraˈʃɔ]
not good, bad (adv)	плохо	[ˈplɔhə]
noises	помехи (f pl)	[paˈmehi]

receiver	трубка (f)	[ˈtrupkə]
to pick up (~ the phone)	снять трубку	[sɲatʲ ˈtrupkʊ]
to hang up (~ the phone)	положить трубку	[palaˈʒitʲ ˈtrupkʊ]

busy	занятый	[ˈzanitɨj]
to ring (about phone)	звонить	[zvaˈnitʲ]
telephone book	телефонная книга (f)	[teleˈfɔnnaja ˈknigə]

local	местный	[ˈmesnɨj]
local call	местный звонок (m)	[ˈmesnɨj zvaˈnɔk]
international call	междугородний звонок (m)	[miʒdʊgaˈrɔdnij zvaˈnɔk]

| long distance (e.g., ~ call) | междугородний | [miʒdʊgaˈrɔdnij] |
| international | международный | [miʒdʊnaˈrɔdnɨj] |

114. Mobile telephone

mobile phone	мобильный телефон (m)	[maˈbiʎnɨj teleˈfɔn]
display	дисплей (m)	[dispˈlej]
button	кнопка (f)	[ˈknɔpkə]
SIM card	SIM-карта (f)	[sim ˈkartə]

battery	батарея (f)	[bataˈreja]
to be dead (battery)	разрядиться	[razriˈditsə]
charger	зарядное устройство (n)	[zaˈrʲadnae ustˈrɔjstvə]

menu	**меню** (n)	[mi'ny]
settings	**настройки** (f pl)	[nɑst'rɔjki]
tune (melody)	**мелодия** (f)	[mi'lɔdijə]
to choose (select)	**выбрать**	['vɪbratʲ]
calculator	**калькулятор** (m)	[kaʌkʊ'ʌatər]
answering machine	**автоответчик** (m)	[aftɑat'wetʃik]
alarm clock	**будильник** (m)	[bʊ'diʌnik]
contacts	**телефонная книга** (f)	[tele'fɔnnaja 'knigə]
SMS (text message)	**SMS-сообщение** (n)	[ɛsɛ'mɛs saap'ɕenie]
subscriber	**абонент** (m)	[aba'nent]

115. Stationery

fountain pen	**ручка** (f) **перьевая**	['rʊtʃka perje'vaja]
pencil	**карандаш** (m)	[karan'daʃ]
highlighter	**маркер** (m)	['marker]
felt-tip pen	**фломастер** (m)	[fla'master]
notepad	**блокнот** (m)	[blak'nɔt]
datebook	**ежедневник** (m)	[eʒɪd'nevnik]
ruler	**линейка** (f)	[li'nejkə]
calculator	**калькулятор** (m)	[kaʌkʊ'ʌatər]
eraser	**ластик** (m)	['lastik]
thumbtack	**кнопка** (f)	['knɔpkə]
paper clip	**скрепка** (f)	['skrepkə]
glue	**клей** (m)	[klej]
stapler	**степлер** (m)	['stepler]
hole punch	**дырокол** (m)	[dɪra'kɔl]
pencil sharpener	**точилка** (f)	[ta'tʃilkə]
pointer	**указка** (f)	[u'kaskə]
card index	**картотека** (f)	[karta'tekə]
label	**этикетка** (f)	[ɛti'ketkə]

116. Various kinds of documents

account (report)	**отчёт** (m)	[a'tʃɔt]
agreement	**соглашение** (n)	[sagla'ʃenie]
application form	**заявка** (f)	[za'jafkə]
authentic	**подлинный**	['pɔdlinɪj]
badge (identity tag)	**бэдж** (m)	[bɛdʃ]
business card	**визитная карточка** (f)	[wi'zitnaja 'kartatʃkə]
certificate (~ of quality)	**сертификат** (m)	[sirtifi'kat]
check (e.g., draw a ~)	**чек** (m)	[tʃek]

check (in restaurant)	счёт (m)	[ˈɕɜt]
constitution	конституция (f)	[kɐnstiˈtutsɪja]
contract	договор (m)	[dɐgɐˈvɔr]
copy	копия (f)	[ˈkɔpija]
copy (of contract etc.)	экземпляр (m)	[ɛkzempˈʎar]

declaration	декларация (f)	[diklɐˈratsija]
document	документ (m)	[dɐkʊˈment]
driver's license	водительские права (pl)	[vɐˈditeʎskie prɐˈva]
attachment (to the contract)	приложение (n)	[prilɐˈʒenie]
form	анкета (f)	[ɐˈŋketə]
identity card, ID	удостоверение (n)	[udɐstɐweˈrenie]
inquiry (request)	запрос (m)	[zɐpˈrɔs]
invitation	приглашение (n)	[priglɐˈʃɛnie]
invoice	счёт (m)	[ˈɕɜt]

law	закон (m)	[zɐˈkɔn]
letter (mail)	письмо (n)	[pisʲˈmɔ]
letterhead	бланк (m)	[blɑnk]
list (of names etc.)	список (m)	[ˈspisɑk]
manuscript	рукопись (f)	[ˈrʊkɑpisʲ]
newsletter	бюллетень (m)	[byleˈteɲ]
note (short letter)	записка (f)	[zɐˈpiskə]

pass (for worker, visitor)	пропуск (m)	[ˈprɔpʊsk]
passport	паспорт (m)	[ˈpɑspart]
permit	разрешение (n)	[rɐzreˈʃɛnie]
résumé	резюме (n)	[rizyˈme]
debt note, iou	расписка (f)	[rɐsˈpiskə]
receipt (for purchase etc.)	квитанция (f)	[kwiˈtɑntsija]
sales slip (receipt)	чек (m)	[ʧek]
report	рапорт (m)	[ˈrɑpart]

to show (ID etc.)	предъявлять	[pridʰevˈʎatʲ]
to sign (vt)	подписать	[pɐtpiˈsatʲ]
signature	подпись (f)	[ˈpɔtpisʲ]
stamp (on document)	печать (f)	[piˈʧatʲ]
text	текст (m)	[tekst]
ticket (for entry)	билет (m)	[biˈlet]

| to cross out | зачеркнуть | [zɐʧerkˈnʊtʲ] |
| to fill out (~ a form etc.) | заполнить | [zɐˈpɔlnitʲ] |

| waybill | накладная (f) | [nɐklɐdˈnaja] |
| will | завещание (n) | [zɐweˈɕanie] |

117. Kinds of business

| accounting services | бухгалтерские услуги (f pl) | [bʊˈgalterskie usˈlugi] |

advertising	**реклама** (f)	[rik'lamə]
advertising agency	**рекламное агентство** (n)	[rek'lamnae a'gentstvə]
air-conditioners	**кондиционеры** (m pl)	[kanditsɪa'nerɪ]
airline	**авиакомпания** (f)	[awiakam'panija]
alcoholic drinks	**спиртные напитки** (m pl)	[spirt'nɪe na'pitki]
antiques	**антиквариат** (m)	[antikvari'at]
art gallery	**галерея** (f)	[gale'reja]
audit services	**аудиторские услуги** (f pl)	[au'ditarskie us'lugi]
banks	**банковский бизнес** (m)	['bankafskij 'biznɛs]
bar	**бар** (m)	[bar]
beauty parlor	**салон** (m) **красоты**	[sa'lon krasa'tɪ]
bookstore	**книжный магазин** (m)	['knɪʒnɪj maga'zin]
brewery	**пивоварня** (f)	[piva'varɲa]
business center	**бизнес-центр** (m)	['biznɛs 'tsentr]
business school	**бизнес-школа** (f)	['biznɛs 'ʃkolə]
casino	**казино** (n)	[kazi'nɔ]
construction	**строительство** (n)	[stra'iteʎstvə]
consulting	**консалтинг** (m)	[kan'saltink]
dentistry	**стоматология** (f)	[stamata'lɔgija]
design	**дизайн** (m)	[di'zajn]
drugstore, pharmacy	**аптека** (f)	[ap'tekə]
dry cleaners	**химчистка** (f)	[him'tʃistkə]
employment agency	**кадровое агентство** (n)	['kadravae a'genstvə]
financial services	**финансовые услуги** (f pl)	[fi'nansavɪe us'lugi]
food (industry)	**продукты** (m pl) **питания**	[pra'duktɪ pi'tanija]
funeral home	**похоронное бюро** (n)	[paha'rɔnnae by'rɔ]
furniture (for house)	**мебель** (f)	['mebeʎ]
garment	**одежда** (f)	[a'deʒdə]
hotel	**гостиница** (f)	[gas'tinitsə]
ice-cream	**мороженое** (n)	[ma'rɔʒnae]
industry	**промышленность** (f)	[pra'mɪʃlenastʲ]
insurance	**страхование** (n)	[straha'vanie]
Internet	**интернет** (m)	[inter'net]
investment	**инвестиции** (f pl)	[inwes'titsɪi]
jeweler	**ювелир** (m)	[juwi'lir]
jewelry	**ювелирные изделия** (n pl)	[juwi'lirnɪe iz'delija]
laundry (room, shop)	**прачечная** (f)	['pratʃetʃnaja]
legal advisor	**юридические услуги** (f pl)	[juri'ditʃeskie us'lugi]
light industry	**лёгкая промышленность** (f)	[lɜhkaja pra'mɪʃlenastʲ]
magazine	**журнал** (m)	[ʒur'nal]
mail-order selling	**торговля** (f) **по каталогу**	[tar'gɔvʎa pa kata'lɔgu]

medicine	**медицина** (f)	[midi'tsınə]
movie theater	**кинотеатр** (m)	[kinati'atr]
museum	**музей** (m)	[mʊ'zej]
news agency	**информационное агентство** (n)	[infarmatsı'ɔnae a'genstvə]
newspaper	**газета** (f)	[ga'zetə]
nightclub	**ночной клуб** (m)	[natʃ'nɔj klup]
oil (petroleum)	**нефть** (f)	[neftʲ]
parcels service	**курьерская служба** (f)	[kʊ'rjerskaja 'sluʒbə]
pharmaceuticals	**фармацевтика** (f)	[farma'tsəftikə]
printing (industry)	**полиграфия** (f)	[paligra'fija]
publishing house	**издательство** (n)	[iz'dateʎstvə]
radio	**радио** (n)	['radiɔ]
real estate	**недвижимость** (f)	[nid'wiʒımastʲ]
restaurant	**ресторан** (m)	[rista'ran]
security agency	**охранное агентство** (n)	[ah'ranae a'genstvə]
sports	**спорт** (m)	[spɔrt]
stock exchange	**биржа** (f)	['birʒə]
store	**магазин** (m)	[maga'zin]
supermarket	**супермаркет** (m)	[sʊper'market]
swimming pool	**бассейн** (m)	[ba'sɛjn]
tailors	**ателье** (n)	[atɛ'ʎje]
television	**телевидение** (n)	[tile'widenie]
theater	**театр** (m)	[ti'atr]
trade	**торговля** (f)	[tar'gɔvʎa]
transportation	**перевозки** (f pl)	[pire'vɔski]
travel	**туризм** (m)	[tʊ'rizm]
veterinarian	**ветеринар** (m)	[witeri'nar]
warehouse	**склад** (m)	[sklat]
waste management	**вывоз** (m) **мусора**	['vıvaz 'mʊsarə]

Job. Business. Part 2

118. Show. Exhibition

exhibition, show	**выставка** (f)	['vɪstafkə]
trade show	**торговая выставка** (f)	[tar'gɔvaja 'vɪstafkə]
participation	**участие** (n)	[u'ʧastie]
to participate (vi)	**участвовать**	[u'ʧastvavatʲ]
participant	**участник** (m)	[u'ʧasnik]
director	**директор** (m)	[di'rektar]
organizer's office	**дирекция** (f)	[di'rektsija]
organizer	**организатор** (m)	[argani'zatar]
to organize (vt)	**организовывать**	[argani'zɔvɪvatʲ]
participation form	**заявка** (f) **на участие**	[za'jafka na u'ʧastie]
to fill out (vt)	**заполнить**	[za'pɔlnitʲ]
details	**детали** (f pl)	[di'tali]
information	**информация** (f)	[infar'matsija]
price	**цена** (f)	[tsɪ'na]
including	**включая**	[fkly'ʧaja]
to include (vt)	**включать**	[fkly'ʧatʲ]
to pay (vi, vt)	**платить**	[pla'titʲ]
registration fee	**регистрационный взнос** (m)	[registratsɪ'ɔnɪj vznɔs]
entrance	**вход** (m)	[vhɔt]
pavilion, hall	**павильон** (m)	[pawi'ʎɔn]
to register (vt)	**регистрировать**	[rigist'riravatʲ]
badge (identity tag)	**бэдж** (m)	[bɛdʃ]
booth, stand	**выставочный стенд** (m)	['vɪstavaʧnɪj stɛnt]
to reserve, to book	**резервировать**	[rezir'wiravatʲ]
display case	**витрина** (f)	[wit'rinə]
spotlight	**светильник** (m)	[swi'tiʎnik]
design	**дизайн** (m)	[di'zajn]
to place (put, set)	**располагать**	[raspala'gatʲ]
to be placed	**располагаться**	[raspala'gatsə]
distributor	**дистрибьютор** (m)	[distri'bjytar]
supplier	**поставщик** (m)	[pastaf'ɕik]
to supply (vt)	**поставлять**	[pastav'ʎatʲ]
country	**страна** (f)	[stra'na]

| foreign | иностранный | [inast'rannɪj] |
| product | продукт (m) | [pra'dukt] |

association (grouping)	ассоциация (f)	[asatsɪ'atsɪja]
conference hall	конференц-зал (m)	[kanfe'rents 'zal]
congress	конгресс (m)	[kahg'res]
contest (competition)	конкурс (m)	['konkurs]

visitor	посетитель (m)	[pase'titeʎ]
to visit (vi, vt)	посещать	[pase'ɕatʲ]
customer	заказчик (m)	[za'kaɕik]

119. Mass Media

newspaper	газета (f)	[ga'zetə]
magazine	журнал (m)	[ʒur'nal]
press (printed media)	пресса (f)	['pressə]
radio	радио (n)	['radiɔ]
radio station	радиостанция (f)	[radias'tantsɪja]
television	телевидение (n)	[tile'widenie]

anchorman	ведущий (m)	[wi'duɕij]
newscaster	диктор (m)	['diktar]
commentator	комментатор (m)	[kamen'tatar]

journalist	журналист (m)	[ʒurna'list]
correspondent (reporter)	корреспондент (m)	[karespan'dent]
press photographer	фотокорреспондент (m)	[fotakarespan'dent]
reporter	репортёр (m)	[ripar'tɜr]

| editor | редактор (m) | [ri'daktar] |
| editor-in-chief | главный редактор (m) | ['glavnɪj ri'daktar] |

to subscribe to …	подписаться	[patpi'satsə]
subscription	подписка (f)	[pat'piskə]
subscriber	подписчик (m)	[pat'piɕik]
to read (vi, vt)	читать	[ʧi'tatʲ]
reader	читатель (m)	[ʧi'tateʎ]

circulation (of newspaper)	тираж (m)	[ti'raʃ]
monthly	ежемесячный	[eʒɪ'mesitʃnɪj]
weekly (adj)	еженедельный	[eʒɪni'deʎnɪj]
issue (edition)	номер (m)	['nɔmer]
recent (new)	свежий	['sweʒɪj]

headline	заголовок (m)	[zaga'lovak]
short article	заметка (f)	[za'metkə]
column (regular article)	рубрика (f)	['rubrikə]
article	статья (f)	[sta'tja]
page	страница (f)	[stra'nitsə]

reportage, report	репортаж (m)	[ripar'taʃ]
event	событие (n)	[sa'bɪtie]
sensation (news)	сенсация (f)	[sin'satsɪja]
scandal	скандал (m)	[skan'dal]
scandalous	скандальный	[skan'daʎnɪj]
great (e.g., ~ scandal)	громкий	['grɔmkij]

program	передача (f)	[piri'datʃe]
interview	интервью (n)	[inter'vjy]
live broadcast	прямая трансляция (f)	[prʲa'maja transˈʎatsɪja]
channel	канал (m)	[ka'nal]

120. Agriculture

agriculture	сельское хозяйство (n)	['seʎskae ha'zʲajstve]
peasant (man)	крестьянин (m)	[kris'tjanin]
peasant (woman)	крестьянка (f)	[kris'tjanke]
farmer	фермер (m)	['fermer]

| tractor | трактор (m) | ['traktar] |
| combine, harvester | комбайн (m) | [kam'bajn] |

plow	плуг (m)	[pluk]
to plow (vi, vt)	пахать	[pa'hatʲ]
plowland	пашня (f)	['paʃna]
furrow (in field)	борозда (f)	[baraz'da]

to sow (vi, vt)	сеять	['seitʲ]
seeder	сеялка (f)	['seilke]
sowing (process)	посев (m)	[pa'sef]

| scythe | коса (f) | [ka'sa] |
| to mow, to scythe | косить | [ka'sitʲ] |

| shovel (tool) | лопата (f) | [la'pate] |
| to dig (vi, vt) | копать | [ka'patʲ] |

hoe	тяпка (f)	['tʲapke]
to hoe, to weed	полоть	[pa'lotʲ]
weed (plant)	сорняк (m)	[sar'ɲak]

watering can	лейка (f)	['lejke]
to water (plants)	поливать	[pali'vatʲ]
watering (act)	полив (m)	[pa'lif]

| pitchfork | вилы (pl) | ['wilɪ] |
| rake | грабли (pl) | ['grabli] |

| fertilizer | удобрение (n) | [udab'renie] |
| to fertilize (vt) | удобрять | [udab'rʲatʲ] |

manure (fertilizer)	навоз (m)	[na'vɔs]
field	поле (n)	['pɔle]
meadow	луг (m)	[luk]
vegetable garden	огород (m)	[aga'rɔt]
orchard (e.g., apple ~)	сад (m)	[sat]

to herd (livestock)	пасти	[pas'ti]
herdsman	пастух (m)	[pas'tuh]
pastureland	пастбище (n)	['pasbiɕe]

| cattle breeding | животноводство (n) | [ʒɪvatna'vɔtstve] |
| sheep farming | овцеводство (n) | [avtsɪ'vɔtstve] |

plantation	плантация (f)	[plan'tatsɪja]
row (garden bed ~s)	грядка (f)	['grʲatke]
greenhouse	парник (m)	[par'nik]
hothouse	теплица (f)	[tip'litse]

| drought (lack of rain) | засуха (f) | ['zasʊhe] |
| dry (~ summer) | засушливый | [za'sʊʃlivɪj] |

grain	зерно (n)	[zer'nɔ]
cereal plants	зерновые (pl)	[zerna'vɪe]
to harvest, to gather	убирать	[ubi'ratʲ]

miller (person)	мельник (m)	['melʲnik]
mill (e.g., gristmill)	мельница (f)	['melʲnitse]
to grind (grain)	молоть	[ma'lotʲ]
flour	мука (f)	[mʊ'ka]
straw	солома (f)	[sa'lɔme]

121. Building. Building process

construction site	стройка (f)	['strɔjke]
to build (vt)	строить	['strɔitʲ]
construction worker	строитель (m)	[stra'iteʎ]

project	проект (m)	[pra'ɛkt]
architect	архитектор (m)	[arhi'tektar]
worker	рабочий (m)	[ra'bɔtʃij]

foundation (of building)	фундамент (m)	[fʊn'dament]
roof	крыша (f)	['krɪʃe]
pile (foundation ~)	свая (f)	['svaja]
wall	стена (f)	[sti'na]

reinforcing bars	арматура (f)	[arma'tʊre]
scaffolding	строительные леса (pl)	[stra'iteʎnɪe le'sa]
concrete	бетон (m)	[bi'tɔn]
granite	гранит (m)	[gra'nit]

| stone | камень (m) | ['kameɲ] |
| brick | кирпич (m) | [kir'pitʃ] |

sand	песок (m)	[pi'sɔk]
cement	цемент (m)	[tsɪ'ment]
plaster (for walls)	штукатурка (f)	[ʃtʊka'tʊrkə]
to plaster (vt)	штукатурить	[ʃtʊka'tʊritʲ]
paint	краска (f)	['krɑskə]
to paint (e.g., ~ a wall)	красить	['krɑsitʲ]
barrel	бочка (f)	['bɔtʃkə]

crane	кран (m)	[krɑn]
to lift (vt)	поднимать	[padni'matʲ]
to lower (vt)	опускать	[apʊs'katʲ]

bulldozer	бульдозер (m)	[bʊʎ'dozer]
excavator	экскаватор (m)	[ɛska'vatar]
scoop, bucket	ковш (m)	[kɔvʃ]
to dig (excavate)	копать	[ka'patʲ]
hard hat	каска (f)	['kɑskə]

122. Science. Research. Scientists

science	наука (f)	[na'ukə]
scientific	научный	[na'utʃnɪj]
scientist	учёный (m)	[u'tʃɔnɪj]
theory	теория (f)	[ti'ɔrija]

axiom	аксиома (f)	[aksi'ɔmə]
analysis	анализ (m)	[a'nalis]
to analyze (vt)	анализировать	[anali'ziravatʲ]
argument (reasoning)	аргумент (m)	[argʊ'ment]
substance (matter)	вещество (n)	[wiçest'vɔ]

hypothesis	гипотеза (f)	[gi'potezə]
dilemma	дилемма (f)	[di'lemə]
dissertation	диссертация (f)	[diser'tatsɪja]
dogma	догма (f)	['dɔgmə]

doctrine	доктрина (f)	[dakt'rinə]
research	исследование (n)	[is'ledavanie]
to do research	исследовать	[is'ledavatʲ]
testing	контроль (m)	[kant'rɔʎ]
laboratory	лаборатория (f)	[labara'tɔrija]

method	метод (m)	['metat]
molecule	молекула (f)	[ma'lekʊlə]
monitoring	мониторинг (m)	[mani'tɔrink]
discovery (act, event)	открытие (n)	[atk'rɪtie]
postulate	постулат (m)	[pastʊ'lat]

principle	**принцип** (m)	['printsɪp]
forecast	**прогноз** (m)	[prag'nɔs]
to forecast (vt)	**прогнозировать**	[pragna'ziravatʲ]
synthesis	**синтез** (m)	['sintes]
trend (tendency)	**тенденция** (f)	[tɛn'dɛntsɪja]
theorem	**теорема** (f)	[tia'remə]
teachings	**учение** (n)	[u'tʃenie]
fact	**факт** (m)	[fakt]
expedition (to go on an ~)	**экспедиция** (f)	[ɛkspe'ditsɪja]
experiment	**эксперимент** (m)	[ɛksperi'ment]
academician	**академик** (m)	[aka'demik]
bachelor (e.g., ~ of Arts)	**бакалавр** (m)	[baka'lavr]
doctor (PhD)	**доктор** (m)	['dɔktar]
Associate Professor	**доцент** (m)	[da'tsənt]
Master (e.g., ~ of Arts)	**магистр** (m)	[ma'gistr]
professor	**профессор** (m)	[pra'fesar]

Professions and occupations

123. Job search. Dismissal

job	работа (f)	[ra'botə]
personnel, staff	персонал (m)	[pirsa'nal]
career	карьера (f)	[ka'rjerə]
prospect	перспектива (f)	[pirspek'tivə]
skills (expertise)	мастерство (n)	[masterst'vo]
selection (for job)	подбор (m)	[pad'bor]
employment agency	кадровое агентство (n)	['kadravae a'genstvə]
résumé	резюме (n)	[rizy'me]
interview (for job)	собеседование (n)	[sabe'sedavanie]
vacancy, opening	вакансия (f)	[va'kansija]
salary, pay	зарплата (f)	[zarp'latə]
fixed pay	оклад (m)	[ak'lat]
pay, compensation	оплата (f)	[ap'latə]
position (job)	должность (f)	['doʒnastʲ]
duty (of employee)	обязанность (f)	[a'bʲazanastʲ]
range of duties	круг (m)	[krʊk]
busy	занятой	[zani'toj]
to fire (dismiss)	уволить	[u'volitʲ]
dismissal	увольнение (n)	[uvaʎ'nenie]
unemployment	безработица (f)	[bizra'botitsə]
unemployed (noun)	безработный (m)	[bizra'botnıj]
retirement	пенсия (f)	['peɲsija]
to retire (from job)	уйти на пенсию	[uj'ti na 'peɲsiju]

124. Business people

director	директор (m)	[di'rektar]
manager (director)	управляющий (m)	[uprav'ʎajuɕij]
boss	руководитель, шеф (m)	[rʊkava'diteʎ], [ʃɛf]
superior	начальник (m)	[na'ʧaʎnik]
management	начальство (n)	[na'ʧaʎstvə]
president	президент (m)	[prizi'dent]
chairman	председатель (m)	[pritse'dateʎ]
deputy (substitute)	заместитель (m)	[zamis'titeʎ]

assistant	помощник (m)	[pɑ'mɔʃnik]
secretary	секретарь (m)	[sikre'tarʲ]
personal assistant	личный секретарь (m)	['litʃnɪj sikri'tarʲ]

businessman	бизнесмен (m)	[biznes'men]
entrepreneur	предприниматель (m)	[pritprini'mateʎ]
founder	основатель (m)	[asnɑ'vateʎ]
to found (vt)	основать (m)	[asnɑ'vatʲ]

associate	учредитель (m)	[utʃre'diteʎ]
partner	партнёр (m)	[part'nɜr]
shareholder	акционер (m)	[aktsɪɑ'ner]

millionaire	миллионер (m)	[milia'ner]
billionaire	миллиардер (m)	[miliar'der]
owner	владелец (m)	[vla'delets]
landowner	землевладелец (m)	[zemlevla'delets]

customer	заказчик (m)	[za'kaɕik]
client	клиент (m)	[kli'ent]
regular client	постоянный клиент (m)	[pasta'janɪj kli'ent]
buyer (customer)	покупатель (m)	[paku'pateʎ]
visitor	посетитель (m)	[pase'titeʎ]

professional (noun)	профессионал (m)	[prafesia'nal]
expert	эксперт (m)	[ɛks'pert]
specialist	специалист (m)	[spitsɪɑ'list]

| banker | банкир (m) | [ba'ŋkir] |
| broker | брокер (m) | ['brɔker] |

cashier, teller	кассир (m)	[kas'sir]
accountant	бухгалтер (m)	[bu'galter]
security guard	охранник (m)	[ah'rannik]

| investor | инвестор (m) | [in'westar] |
| debtor | должник (m) | [daʒ'nik] |

| creditor | кредитор (m) | [kridi'tor] |
| borrower | заёмщик (m) | [zaзmɕik] |

| importer | импортёр (m) | [impar'tзr] |
| exporter | экспортёр (m) | [ɛkspar'tзr] |

manufacturer	производитель (m)	[praizva'diteʎ]
distributor	дистрибьютор (m)	[distri'bjytar]
middleman	посредник (m)	[pas'rednik]

consultant	консультант (m)	[kansuʎ'tant]
representative	представитель (m)	[pritsta'witeʎ]
agent	агент (m)	[a'gent]
insurance agent	страховой агент (m)	[straha'vɔj a'gent]

125. Service professions

cook	повар (m)	['povar]
chef	шеф-повар (m)	[ʃɛf'povar]
baker	пекарь (m)	['pekarʲ]
bartender	бармен (m)	[bar'men]
waiter	официант (m)	[afitsɪ'ant]
waitress	официантка (f)	[afitsɪ'antkə]
lawyer, attorney	адвокат (m)	[adva'kat]
lawyer (legal expert)	юрист (m)	[ju'rist]
notary	нотариус (m)	[na'tarius]
electrician	электрик (m)	[ɛ'lektrik]
plumber	сантехник (m)	[san'tehnik]
carpenter	плотник (m)	['plotnik]
masseur	массажист (m)	[masa'ʒist]
masseuse	массажистка (f)	[masa'ʒistkə]
doctor	врач (m)	[vratʃ]
taxi driver	таксист (m)	[tak'sist]
driver	шофёр (m)	[ʃʌ'fɜr]
courier	курьер (m)	[kʊ'rjer]
chambermaid	горничная (f)	['gorniʧnaja]
security guard	охранник (m)	[ah'rannik]
flight attendant	стюардесса (f)	[styar'desə]
teacher (in primary school)	учитель (m)	[u'ʧiteʎ]
librarian	библиотекарь (m)	[biblia'tekarʲ]
translator	переводчик (m)	[pire'votʃik]
interpreter	переводчик (m)	[pire'votʃik]
guide (person)	гид (m)	[git]
hairdresser	парикмахер (m)	[parih'maher]
mailman	почтальон (m)	[patʃta'ʎjon]
salesman	продавец (m)	[prada'wets]
gardener	садовник (m)	[sa'dovnik]
servant (in household)	слуга (f)	[slu'ga]
maid	служанка (f)	[slu'ʒankə]
cleaner (cleaning lady)	уборщица (f)	[u'borçitsə]

126. Military professions and ranks

private	рядовой (m)	[rida'voj]
sergeant	сержант (m)	[sir'ʒant]

lieutenant	**лейтенант** (m)	[lijte'nant]
captain	**капитан** (m)	[kapi'tan]
major	**майор** (m)	[maɜr]
colonel	**полковник** (m)	[pal'kɔvnik]
general	**генерал** (m)	[gine'ral]
marshal	**маршал** (m)	['marʃʌl]
admiral	**адмирал** (m)	[admi'ral]
military man	**военный** (m)	[va'ennɪj]
soldier	**солдат** (m)	[sal'dat]
officer	**офицер** (m)	[afi'ʦer]
commander	**командир** (m)	[kaman'dir]
border guard	**пограничник** (m)	[pagra'nitʃnik]
radio operator	**радист** (m)	[ra'dist]
scout (searcher)	**разведчик** (m)	[raz'wetʃik]
pioneer (sapper)	**сапёр** (m)	[sa'pɜr]
marksman	**стрелок** (m)	[stre'lɔk]
navigator	**штурман** (m)	['ʃturman]

127. Officials. Priests

king	**король** (m)	[ka'rɔʎ]
queen	**королева** (f)	[kara'levə]
prince	**принц** (m)	[prinʦ]
princess	**принцесса** (f)	[prin'ʦəsə]
tsar, czar	**царь** (m)	[ʦarʲ]
czarina	**царица** (f)	[ʦa'riʦə]
president	**президент** (m)	[prizi'dent]
Secretary (~ of State)	**министр** (m)	[mi'nistr]
prime minister	**премьер-министр** (m)	[pri'mjer mi'nistr]
senator	**сенатор** (m)	[si'natər]
diplomat	**дипломат** (m)	[dipla'mat]
consul	**консул** (m)	['kɔnsul]
ambassador	**посол** (m)	[pa'sɔl]
councelor, advisor	**советник** (m)	[sa'wetnik]
official (civil servant)	**чиновник** (m)	[tʃi'nɔvnik]
prefect	**префект** (m)	[pri'fekt]
mayor	**мэр** (m)	[mɛr]
judge	**судья** (f)	[su'dja]
district attorney	**прокурор** (m)	[praku'rɔr]
missionary	**миссионер** (m)	[misia'ner]
monk	**монах** (m)	[ma'nah]

abbot	аббат (m)	[a'bat]
rabbi	раввин (m)	[ra'win]
vizier	визирь (m)	[wi'zir']
shah	шах (m)	[ʃʌh]
sheikh	шейх (m)	[ʃɛjh]

128. Agricultural professions

beekeeper	пчеловод (m)	[ptʃila'vot]
herdsman	пастух (m)	[pas'tʊh]
agronomist	агроном (m)	[agra'nɔm]
cattle breeder	животновод (m)	[ʒıvatna'vot]
veterinarian	ветеринар (m)	[witeri'nar]
farmer	фермер (m)	['fermer]
winemaker	винодел (m)	[wina'del]
potter	гончар (m)	[gaɲ'tʃar]
zoologist	зоолог (m)	[za'ɔlak]
cowboy	ковбой (m)	[kav'bɔj]

129. Art professions

actor	актёр (m)	[ak'tɜr]
actress	актриса (f)	[akt'risə]
singer (man)	певец (m)	[pi'wets]
singer (woman)	певица (f)	[pi'witsə]
dancer (man)	танцор (m)	[tan'tsɔr]
dancer (woman)	танцовщица (f)	[tan'tsɔfɕitsə]
performing artist (masc.)	артист (m)	[ar'tist]
performing artist (fem.)	артистка (f)	[ar'tistkə]
musician	музыкант (m)	[mʊzı'kant]
pianist	пианист (m)	[pia'nist]
guitar player	гитарист (m)	[gita'rist]
conductor (of musicians)	дирижёр (m)	[diri'ʒɜr]
composer	композитор (m)	[kampa'zitar]
impresario	импресарио (m)	[impre'sariə]
movie director	режиссёр (m)	[riʒı'sɜr]
producer	продюсер (m)	[pra'dyser]
scriptwriter	сценарист (m)	[stsına'rist]
critic	критик (m)	['kritik]
writer	писатель (m)	[pi'sateʎ]

poet	поэт (m)	[pɑˈɛt]
sculptor	скульптор (m)	[ˈskʊˈʎptɑr]
artist (painter)	художник (m)	[hʊˈdɔʒnik]

juggler	жонглёр (m)	[ʒɑhgˈlɜr]
clown	клоун (m)	[ˈklɔun]
acrobat	акробат (m)	[ɑkrɑˈbɑt]
magician	фокусник (m)	[ˈfɔkʊsnik]

130. Various professions

doctor	врач (m)	[vrɑtʃ]
nurse (in hospital)	медсестра (f)	[mitsestˈrɑ]
psychiatrist	психиатр (m)	[psihiˈɑtr]
dentist	стоматолог (m)	[stɑmɑˈtɔlɑk]
surgeon	хирург (m)	[hiˈrʊrk]

| astronaut | астронавт (m) | [ɑstrɑˈnɑft] |
| astronomer | астроном (m) | [ɑstrɑˈnɔm] |

driver (of car, taxi etc.)	водитель (m)	[vɑˈditeʎ]
engineer (train driver)	машинист (m)	[mɑʃiˈnist]
mechanic	механик (m)	[miˈhɑnik]

miner	шахтёр (m)	[ʃʌhˈtɜr]
worker	рабочий (m)	[rɑˈbɔtʃij]
metalworker	слесарь (m)	[ˈslesɑrʲ]
joiner, carpenter	столяр (m)	[stɑˈʎɑr]
turner	токарь (m)	[ˈtɔkɑrʲ]
construction worker	строитель (m)	[strɑˈiteʎ]
welder	сварщик (m)	[ˈsvɑrɕik]

professor	профессор (m)	[prɑˈfesɑr]
architect	архитектор (m)	[ɑrhiˈtektɑr]
historian	историк (m)	[isˈtɔrik]
scientist	учёный (m)	[uˈtʃɔnıj]
physicist	физик (m)	[ˈfizik]
chemist (scientist)	химик (m)	[ˈhimik]

archeologist	археолог (m)	[ɑrheˈɔlɑk]
geologist	геолог (m)	[giˈɔlɑk]
researcher	исследователь (m)	[isˈledavɑteʎ]

| babysitter | няня (f) | [ˈɲɑɲɑ] |
| teacher | учитель (m) | [uˈtʃiteʎ] |

editor	редактор (m)	[riˈdɑktɑr]
editor-in-chief	главный редактор (m)	[ˈglɑvnıj riˈdɑktɑr]
correspondent	корреспондент (m)	[kɑrespɑnˈdent]
typist (woman)	машинистка (f)	[mɑʃiˈnistkə]

designer	дизайнер (m)	[di'zajner]
computer expert	компьютерщик (m)	[kam'pjuterçik]
programmer	программист (m)	[pragra'mist]
engineer (designer)	инженер (m)	[inʒɪ'ner]

seaman	моряк (m)	[ma'rʲak]
sailor	матрос (m)	[mat'rɔs]
rescuer	спасатель (m)	[spa'sateʎ]

fireman	пожарный (m)	[pa'ʒarnɪj]
policeman	полицейский (m)	[pali'tsejskij]
watchman	сторож (m)	['stɔraʃ]
detective	сыщик (m)	['sɪçik]

customs officer	таможенник (m)	[ta'mɔʒɛnik]
bodyguard	телохранитель (m)	[tilahra'niteʎ]
prison guard	охранник (m)	[ah'rannik]
inspector	инспектор (m)	[ins'pektar]

sportsman	спортсмен (m)	[sparts'men]
trainer, coach	тренер (m)	['trener]
butcher	мясник (m)	[mis'nik]
cobbler	сапожник (m)	[sa'pɔʒnik]
businessman	коммерсант (m)	[kamer'sant]
loader (person)	грузчик (m)	['gruçik]

| fashion designer | модельер (m) | [madɛ'ʎjer] |
| model (woman) | модель (f) | [ma'dɛʎ] |

131. Occupations. Social status

| schoolboy | школьник (m) | ['ʃkɔʎnik] |
| student (college ~) | студент (m) | [stʊ'dent] |

philosopher	философ (m)	[fi'lɔsaf]
economist	экономист (m)	[ɛkana'mist]
inventor	изобретатель (m)	[izabre'tateʎ]

unemployed (noun)	безработный (m)	[bizra'botnɪj]
retiree	пенсионер (m)	[pinsia'ner]
spy, secret agent	шпион (m)	[ʃpi'ɔn]

prisoner	заключённый (m)	[zakly'tʃɔnnɪj]
striker	забастовщик (m)	[zabas'tɔfçik]
bureaucrat	бюрократ (m)	[byrak'rat]
traveler	путешественник (m)	[pʊte'ʃɛstwenik]

homosexual	гомосексуалист (m)	[gomɔsɛksʊa'list]
hacker	хакер (m)	['haker]
hippie	хиппи (m)	['hippi]

bandit	бандит (m)	[bɑn'dit]
hit man, killer	наёмный убийца (m)	[nɑзmnɪj u'bijtsə]
drug addict	наркоман (m)	[nɑrkɑ'mɑn]
drug dealer	торговец (m) наркотиками	[tɑr'gɔwets nɑr'kɔtikɑmi]
prostitute (woman)	проститутка (f)	[prɑsti'tʊtkə]
pimp	сутенёр (m)	[sʊte'nзr]

sorcerer	колдун (m)	[kɑl'dʊn]
sorceress	колдунья (f)	[kɑl'dʊɲjɑ]
pirate	пират (m)	[pi'rɑt]
slave	раб (m)	[rɑp]
samurai	самурай (m)	[sɑmʊ'rɑj]
savage (primitive)	дикарь (m)	[di'kɑrʲ]

Sports

132. Kinds of sports. Sportspersons

sportsman	спортсмен (m)	[sparʦ'men]
kind of sports	вид (m) спорта	[wit 'sportə]
basketball	баскетбол (m)	[basked'bɔl]
basketball player	баскетболист (m)	[baskedba'list]
baseball	бейсбол (m)	[bejz'bɔl]
baseball player	бейсболист (m)	[bejzba'list]
soccer	футбол (m)	[fʊd'bɔl]
soccer player	футболист (m)	[fʊdba'list]
goalkeeper	вратарь (m)	[vra'tarʲ]
hockey	хоккей (m)	[ha'kej]
hockey player	хоккеист (m)	[hake'ist]
volleyball	волейбол (m)	[valej'bɔl]
volleyball player	волейболист (m)	[valejba'list]
boxing	бокс (m)	[bɔks]
boxer	боксёр (m)	[bak'sзr]
wrestling	борьба (f)	[barʲ'ba]
wrestler	борец (m)	[ba'reʦ]
karate	карате (n)	[kara'tɛ]
karate fighter	каратист (m)	[kara'tist]
judo	дзюдо (n)	[ʣy'dɔ]
judo athlete	дзюдоист (m)	[ʣyda'ist]
tennis	теннис (m)	['tɛnis]
tennis player	теннисист (m)	[tɛni'sist]
swimming	плавание (n)	['plavanie]
swimmer	пловец (m)	[pla'weʦ]
fencing	фехтование (n)	[fihta'vanie]
fencer	фехтовальщик (m)	[fihta'vaʎɕik]
chess	шахматы (pl)	['ʃʌhmatɪ]
chess player	шахматист (m)	[ʃʌhma'tist]

| alpinism | **альпинизм** (m) | [aʎpiˈnizm] |
| alpinist | **альпинист** (m) | [aʎpiˈnist] |

| running | **бег** (m) | [bek] |
| runner | **бегун** (m) | [biˈgʊn] |

| athletics | **лёгкая атлетика** (f) | [ˈlɜhkaja atˈletikə] |
| athlete | **атлет** (m) | [atˈlet] |

| horseback riding | **конный спорт** (m) | [ˈkɔnnɪj ˈspɔrt] |
| rider | **наездник** (m) | [naˈeznik] |

figure skating	**фигурное катание** (n)	[fiˈgʊrnae kaˈtanie]
figure skater (man)	**фигурист** (m)	[figʊˈrist]
figure skater (woman)	**фигуристка** (f)	[figʊˈristkə]

| weightlifting | **тяжёлая атлетика** (f) | [tʲaˈʒзlaja atˈletikə] |
| weightlifter | **штангист** (m) | [ʃtaˈŋist] |

| car racing | **автогонки** (f pl) | [aftaˈgɔnki] |
| racing driver | **гонщик** (m) | [ˈgɔɲɕik] |

| cycling | **велоспорт** (m) | [wilasˈpɔrt] |
| cyclist | **велосипедист** (m) | [wilasipeˈdist] |

broad jump	**прыжки** (m pl) **в длину**	[prɪʃˈki v ˈdlinʊ]
pole vault	**прыжки** (m pl) **с шестом**	[prɪʃˈki s ʃəsˈtɔm]
jumper	**прыгун** (m)	[prɪˈgʊn]

133. Kinds of sports. Miscellaneous

football	**американский футбол** (m)	[amiriˈkanskij fʊdˈbɔl]
badminton	**бадминтон** (m)	[badminˈtɔn]
biathlon	**биатлон** (m)	[biatˈlɔn]
billiards	**бильярд** (m)	[biˈʎjart]

bobsled	**бобслей** (m)	[bapsˈlej]
bodybuilding	**бодибилдинг** (m)	[badiˈbildink]
water polo	**водное поло** (n)	[ˈvɔdnae ˈpɔlə]
handball	**гандбол** (m)	[gandˈbɔl]
golf	**гольф** (m)	[gɔʎf]

rowing	**гребля** (f)	[ˈgrebʎa]
diving	**дайвинг** (m)	[ˈdajwink]
cross-country skiing	**лыжные гонки** (f pl)	[ˈlɪʒnɪe ˈgɔnki]
ping-pong	**настольный теннис** (m)	[nasˈtɔʎnɪj ˈtɛnis]

| sailing | **парусный спорт** (m) | [ˈparʊsnɪj spɔrt] |
| rally | **ралли** (n) | [ˈralli] |

rugby	регби (n)	['rɛgbi]
snowboarding	сноуборд (m)	[snɔu'bɔrt]
archery	стрельба (f) из лука	[strɛʎ'ba iz 'lukə]

134. Gym

| barbell | штанга (f) | ['ʃtahgə] |
| dumbbells | гантели (f pl) | [gan'tɛli] |

training machine	тренажёр (m)	[trena'ʒɜr]
bicycle trainer	велотренажёр (m)	[wilatrena'ʒɜr]
treadmill	беговая дорожка (f)	[biga'vaja da'rɔʃkə]

horizontal bar	перекладина (f)	[perek'ladinə]
parallel bars	брусья (pl)	['brusja]
vaulting horse	конь (m)	[kɔɲ]
mat (in gym)	мат (m)	[mat]

jump rope	скакалка (f)	[ska'kalkə]
aerobics	аэробика (f)	[aə'rɔbikə]
yoga	йога (f)	['jogə]

135. Hockey

hockey	хоккей (m)	[ha'kej]
hockey player	хоккеист (m)	[hake'ist]
to play hockey	играть в хоккей	[ig'ratʲ f ha'kej]
ice	лёд (m)	['lɜt]

puck	шайба (f)	['ʃʌjbə]
hockey stick	клюшка (f)	['klyʃkə]
ice skates	коньки (m pl)	[kaɲ'ki]
board	борт (m)	[bɔrt]
shot	бросок (m)	[bra'sɔk]
goaltender	вратарь (m)	[vra'tarʲ]
goal (score)	гол (m)	[gɔl]
to score a goal	забить гол	[za'bitʲ gɔl]

period	период (m)	[pi'riat]
second period	2-й период	[fta'rɔj pi'riat]
substitutes bench	скамейка (f) запасных	[ska'mejka zapas'nɪh]

136. Football

| soccer | футбол (m) | [fʊd'bɔl] |
| soccer player | футболист (m) | [fʊdba'list] |

to play soccer	**играть в футбол**	[ig'ratʲ f fud'bɔl]
major league	**высшая лига** (f)	['vɪʃʌja 'ligə]
soccer club	**футбольный клуб** (m)	[fud'bɔlnɪj 'klup]
coach	**тренер** (m)	['trener]
owner	**владелец** (m)	[vla'delets]
team	**команда** (f)	[ka'mandə]
team captain	**капитан** (m) **команды**	[kapi'tan ka'mandɪ]
player	**игрок** (m)	[ig'rɔk]
substitute	**запасной игрок** (m)	[zapas'nɔj ig'rɔk]
forward	**нападающий** (m)	[napa'dajuɕij]
center forward	**центральный нападающий** (m)	[tsent'ralnɪj napa'dajuɕij]
striker, scorer	**бомбардир** (m)	[bambar'dir]
defender, back	**защитник** (m)	[za'ɕitnik]
halfback	**полузащитник** (m)	[poluza'ɕitnik]
match	**матч** (m)	[matʃ]
to meet (vi, vt)	**встречаться**	[fstre'tʃatsə]
final	**финал** (m)	[fi'nal]
semi-final	**полуфинал** (m)	[polufi'nal]
championship	**чемпионат** (m)	[tʃimpiɔ'nat]
period, half	**тайм** (m)	[tajm]
first period	**1-й тайм** (m)	['pervɪj tajm]
half-time	**перерыв** (m)	[pere'rɪf]
goal	**ворота** (pl)	[va'rɔtə]
goalkeeper	**вратарь** (m)	[vra'tarʲ]
goalpost	**штанга** (f)	['ʃtahgə]
crossbar	**перекладина** (f)	[perek'ladinə]
net	**сетка** (f)	['setkə]
to miss (fail to catch)	**пропустить**	[prapus'titʲ]
to miss the ball	**пропустить гол**	[prapus'titʲ gɔl]
ball	**мяч** (m)	[mʲatʃ]
pass	**пас, передача** (f)	[pas], [piri'datʃə]
kick	**удар** (m)	[u'dar]
to kick (~ the ball)	**нанести удар**	[nanes'ti u'dar]
free kick	**штрафной удар** (m)	[ʃtraf'nɔj u'dar]
corner kick	**угловой удар** (m)	[ugla'vɔj u'dar]
attack	**атака** (f)	[a'takə]
counterattack	**контратака** (f)	[kontra'takə]
combination	**комбинация** (f)	[kambi'natsɪja]
referee	**арбитр** (m)	[ar'bitr]
to whistle (vi)	**свистеть**	[swis'tetʲ]
whistle (sound)	**свисток** (m)	[swis'tɔk]
foul, misconduct	**нарушение** (n)	[naru'ʃɛnie]
to commit a foul	**нарушить**	[na'ruʃitʲ]

to send off	удалить с поля	[uda'litʲ s 'poʎa]
yellow card	жёлтая карточка (f)	['ʒɜltaja 'kartatʃkə]
red card	красная карточка (f)	['krasnaja 'kartatʃkə]
disqualification	дисквалификация (f)	[diskvalifi'katsija]
to disqualify (vt)	дисквалифицировать	[diskvalifi'tsɪravatʲ]

penalty kick	пенальти (m)	[pi'naʎti]
wall	стенка (f)	['stenkə]
to score (vi, vt)	забить	[za'bitʲ]
goal (score)	гол (m)	[gɔl]
to score a goal	забить гол	[za'bitʲ gɔl]

replacement	замена (f)	[za'menə]
to replace (vt)	заменить	[zame'nitʲ]
rules	правила (n pl)	['prawilə]
tactics	тактика (f)	['taktikə]

stadium	стадион (m)	[stadi'ɔn]
stand (at stadium)	трибуна (f)	[tri'bʊnə]
fan, supporter	болельщик (m)	[ba'leʎɕik]
to shout (vi, vt)	кричать	[kri'tʃatʲ]

| scoreboard | табло (n) | [tab'lo] |
| score | счёт (m) | ['ɕɜt] |

defeat	поражение (n)	[para'ʒɛnie]
to lose (not win)	проиграть	[praig'ratʲ]
draw	ничья (f)	[ni'tʃja]
to draw (vi)	сыграть вничью	[sɪg'ratʲ vni'tʃjy]

victory	победа (f)	[pa'bedə]
to win (vi, vt)	победить	[pabe'ditʲ]
champion	чемпион (m)	[tʃimpi'ɔn]
the best	лучший	['lutʃʃij]
to congratulate (vt)	поздравлять	[pazdrav'ʎatʲ]

commentator	комментатор (m)	[kamen'tatar]
to commentate (vi, vt)	комментировать	[kamen'tiravatʲ]
broadcast	трансляция (f)	[trans'ʎatsija]

137. Alpine skiing

skis	лыжи (f pl)	['lɪʒɪ]
to ski (vi)	кататься на лыжах	[ka'tatsa na 'lɪʒah]
mountain-ski resort	горнолыжный курорт (m)	[garna'lɪʒnɪj kʊ'rɔrt]
ski lift	подъёмник (m)	[padʰɜmnik]

ski poles	палки (f pl)	['palki]
slope	склон (m)	[sklɔn]
slalom	слалом (m)	['slalam]

138. Tennis. Golf

golf	гольф (m)	[gɔʎf]
golf club	гольф-клуб (m)	[gɔʎf 'klup]
golfer	игрок в гольф (m)	[ig'rɔk v 'gɔʎf]

hole	лунка (f)	['lunkə]
club	клюшка (f)	['klyʃkə]
golf trolley	тележка (f) для клюшек	[te'leʃka dʎa 'klyʃək]

tennis	теннис (m)	['tɛnis]
court (for tennis)	корт (m)	[kɔrt]
serve	подача (f)	[pa'datʃə]
to serve (vt)	подавать	[pada'vatʲ]
racket	ракетка (f)	[ra'ketkə]
net	сетка (f)	['setkə]
ball	мяч (m)	[mʲatʃ]

139. Chess

chess	шахматы (pl)	['ʃʌhmatɪ]
chessmen	шахматы (pl)	['ʃʌhmatɪ]
chess player	шахматист (m)	[ʃʌhma'tist]
chessboard	шахматная доска (f)	['ʃʌhmatnaja das'ka]
chessman	фигура (f)	[fi'gʊrə]

| White (white pieces) | белые (pl) | ['belɪe] |
| Black (black pieces) | чёрные (pl) | ['tʃɔrnɪe] |

pawn	пешка (f)	['peʃkə]
bishop	слон (m)	[slɔn]
knight	конь (m)	[kɔnʲ]
castle	ладья (f)	[la'dja]
queen	ферзь (m)	[fersʲ]
king	король (m)	[ka'rɔʎ]

move	ход (m)	[hɔt]
to move (vi, vt)	ходить	[ha'ditʲ]
to sacrifice	пожертвовать	[pa'ʒertvavatʲ]
castling	рокировка (f)	[raki'rɔfkə]

| check | шах (m) | [ʃʌh] |
| checkmate | мат (m) | [mat] |

chess tournament	шахматный турнир (m)	['ʃʌhmatnɪj tʊr'nir]
Grand Master	гроссмейстер (m)	[gras'mejster]
combination	комбинация (f)	[kambi'natsija]
game (in chess)	партия (f)	['partija]
checkers	шашки (f pl)	['ʃʌʃki]

140. Boxing

boxing	**бокс** (m)	[bɔks]
fight	**бой** (m)	[bɔj]
boxing match	**поединок** (m)	[pai'dinak]
round (in boxing)	**раунд** (m)	['raunt]
ring	**ринг** (m)	[rink]
gong	**гонг** (m)	[gɔnk]
punch	**удар** (m)	[u'dar]
knock-down	**нокдаун** (m)	[nak'daun]
knockout	**нокаут** (m)	[na'kaut]
to knock out	**нокаутировать**	[nakau'tiravatʲ]
boxing glove	**боксёрская перчатка** (f)	[bak'sзrskaja per'tʃatkə]
referee	**рефери** (m)	['referi]
lightweight	**легкий вес** (m)	['lзhkij wes]
middleweight	**средний вес** (m)	['srednij wes]
heavyweight	**тяжелый вес** (m)	[ti'ʒзlɪj wes]

141. Sports. Miscellaneous

Olympic Games	**Олимпийские игры** (f pl)	[alim'pijskie 'igrɪ]
winner	**победитель** (m)	[pabe'diteʌ]
to be winning	**побеждать**	[pabeʒ'datʲ]
to win (vi)	**выиграть**	['vɪigratʲ]
leader	**лидер** (m)	['lider]
to lead (vi)	**лидировать**	[li'diravatʲ]
first place	**первое место** (n)	['pervae 'mestə]
second place	**второе место** (n)	[fta'rɔe 'mestə]
third place	**третье место** (n)	['tretje 'mestə]
medal	**медаль** (f)	[mi'daʌ]
trophy	**трофей** (m)	[tra'fej]
cup (trophy)	**кубок** (m)	['kubak]
prize (in game)	**приз** (m)	[pris]
main prize	**главный приз** (m)	['glavnɪj pris]
record	**рекорд** (m)	[ri'kɔrt]
to set a record	**ставить рекорд**	['stawitʲ re'kɔrt]
final	**финал** (m)	[fi'nal]
final (adj)	**финальный**	[fi'naʌnɪj]
champion	**чемпион** (m)	[tʃimpi'ɔn]
championship	**чемпионат** (m)	[tʃimpia'nat]

stadium	стадион (m)	[stadi'ɔn]
stand (at stadium)	трибуна (f)	[tri'bʊnə]
fan, supporter	болельщик (m)	[ba'leʌɕik]
opponent, rival	противник (m)	[pra'tivnik]

| start | старт (m) | [start] |
| finish | финиш (m) | ['finiʃ] |

| defeat | поражение (n) | [para'ʒɛnie] |
| to lose (not win) | проиграть | [praig'ratʲ] |

referee	судья (f)	[sʊ'dja]
judges	жюри (n)	['ʒyri]
score	счёт (m)	['ɕɔt]
draw	ничья (f)	[ni'tʃja]
to draw (vi)	сыграть вничью	[sɪg'ratʲ vni'tʃjy]
point	очко (n)	[atʃ'kɔ]
result (of match)	результат (m)	[rizuʌ'tat]

half-time	перерыв (m)	[pere'rɪf]
dope (for athlete, horse)	допинг (m)	['dɔpink]
to penalize (vt)	штрафовать	[ʃtrafa'vatʲ]
to disqualify (vt)	дисквалифицировать	[diskvalifi'tsɪravatʲ]

apparatus	снаряд (m)	[sna'rʲat]
javelin	копьё (n)	[ka'pjo]
shot (metal ball)	ядро (n)	[jad'rɔ]
ball (in snooker, croquet)	шар (m)	[ʃʌr]

target (objective)	цель (f)	[tseʌ]
target (e.g., for archery)	мишень (f)	[mi'ʃəŋ]
to shoot (vi)	стрелять	[stri'ʌatʲ]
precise (shot)	точный	['tɔtʃnɪj]

trainer, coach	тренер (m)	['trener]
to train sb	тренировать	[trinira'vatʲ]
to train (vi)	тренироваться	[trinira'vatsə]
training	тренировка (f)	[trini'rɔfkə]

gym	спортзал (m)	[sport'zal]
exercise (physical)	упражнение (n)	[upraʒ'nenie]
warm-up (of athlete)	разминка (f)	[raz'minkə]

Education

142. School

school	**школа** (f)	[ˈʃkolə]
headmaster	**директор** (m) **школы**	[diˈrektar ˈʃkolɪ]
pupil (boy)	**ученик** (m)	[utʃiˈnik]
pupil (girl)	**ученица** (f)	[utʃiˈnitsə]
schoolboy	**школьник** (m)	[ˈʃkoʎnik]
schoolgirl	**школьница** (f)	[ˈʃkoʎnitsə]
to teach (sb)	**учить**	[uˈtʃitʲ]
to learn (language etc.)	**учить**	[uˈtʃitʲ]
to learn by heart	**учить наизусть**	[uˈtʃitʲ naiˈzustʲ]
to study (vi)	**учиться**	[uˈtʃitsə]
to be in school	**учиться**	[uˈtʃitsə]
to go to school	**идти в школу**	[itʲˈti f ˈʃkolu]
alphabet	**алфавит** (m)	[alfaˈwit]
subject (at school)	**предмет** (m)	[pridˈmet]
classroom	**класс** (m)	[klas]
classes	**занятие** (n)	[zaˈɲatie]
lesson	**урок** (m)	[uˈrok]
recess	**перемена** (f)	[pireˈmenə]
school bell	**звонок** (m)	[zvaˈnok]
desk (for pupil)	**парта** (f)	[ˈpartə]
chalkboard	**доска** (f)	[dasˈka]
grade	**отметка** (f)	[atˈmetkə]
good grade	**хорошая отметка** (f)	[haˈroʃʎja atˈmetkə]
bad grade	**плохая отметка** (f)	[plaˈhaja atˈmetkə]
to give a grade	**ставить отметку**	[ˈstawitʲ atˈmetku]
mistake	**ошибка** (f)	[aˈʃipkə]
to make mistakes	**делать ошибки**	[ˈdelatʲ aˈʃipki]
to correct (vt)	**исправлять**	[ispravˈʎatʲ]
cheat sheet	**шпаргалка** (f)	[ʃparˈgalkə]
homework	**домашнее задание** (n)	[daˈmaʃnee zaˈdanie]
exercise (in education)	**упражнение** (n)	[upraʒˈnenie]
to be present	**присутствовать**	[priˈsutstvavatʲ]
to be absent	**отсутствовать**	[aˈtsutstvavatʲ]

to miss classes	пропускать уроки	[prapus'katʲ u'rɔki]
to punish (vt)	наказывать	[na'kazıvatʲ]
punishment	наказание (n)	[naka'zanie]
conduct (behavior)	поведение (n)	[pawi'denie]

report card	дневник (m)	[dniv'nik]
pencil	карандаш (m)	[karan'daʃ]
eraser	ластик (m)	['lastik]
chalk	мел (m)	[mel]
pencil case	пенал (m)	[pi'nal]

schoolbag	портфель (m)	[part'feʎ]
pen	ручка (f)	['rʊtʃkə]
school notebook	тетрадь (f)	[tit'ratʲ]
textbook	учебник (m)	[u'tʃebnik]
compasses	циркуль (m)	['tsırkʊʎ]

| to draw (a blueprint etc.) | чертить | [tʃir'titʲ] |
| technical drawing | чертёж (m) | [tʃir'tɜʃ] |

poem	стихотворение (n)	[stihatva'renie]
by heart	наизусть	[nai'zustʲ]
to learn by heart	учить наизусть	[u'tʃitʲ nai'zustʲ]

school vacation	каникулы (pl)	[ka'nikʊlı]
to be on vacation	быть на каникулах	[bıtʲ na ka'nikʊlah]
to spend one's vacation	провести каникулы	[prawes'ti ka'nikʊlı]

quiz (at school)	контрольная работа (f)	[kant'rɔʎnaja ra'bɔtə]
essay (composition)	сочинение (n)	[satʃi'nenie]
dictation	диктант (m)	[dik'tant]
exam	экзамен (m)	[ɛk'zamen]
to take an exam	сдавать экзамены	[sda'vatʲ ɛk'zamenı]
experiment (chemical ~)	опыт (m)	['ɔpıt]

143. College. University

academy	академия (f)	[aka'demija]
university	университет (m)	[uniwersi'tet]
faculty (section)	факультет (m)	[fakʊʎ'tet]

student (man)	студент (m)	[stu'dent]
student (woman)	студентка (f)	[stu'dentkə]
lecturer (teacher)	преподаватель (m)	[pripada'vateʎ]
professor	профессор (m)	[pra'fesar]

lecture hall, room	аудитория (f)	[aʊdi'tɔrija]
graduate (of high school)	выпускник (m)	[vıpusk'nik]
diploma	диплом (m)	[dip'lɔm]
dissertation	диссертация (f)	[diser'tatsıja]

| study (report) | исследование (n) | [isˈledavanie] |
| laboratory | лаборатория (f) | [labaraˈtɔrija] |

lecture	лекция (f)	[ˈlektsɪja]
schoolmate	однокурсник (m)	[adnaˈkʊrsnik]
stipend	стипендия (f)	[stiˈpendija]
academic degree	учёная степень (f)	[uˈtɕɔnaja ˈstepeɲ]

144. Sciences. Disciplines

mathematics	математика (f)	[mateˈmatikə]
algebra	алгебра (f)	[ˈalgebrə]
geometry	геометрия (f)	[giaˈmetrija]

astronomy	астрономия (f)	[astraˈnɔmija]
biology	биология (f)	[biaˈlɔgija]
geography	география (f)	[giagˈrafija]
geology	геология (f)	[giaˈlɔgija]
history	история (f)	[isˈtɔrija]

medicine	медицина (f)	[midiˈtsɪnə]
pedagogy	педагогика (f)	[pidaˈgɔgikə]
law (e.g., student of ~)	право (n)	[ˈpravə]

physics	физика (f)	[ˈfizikə]
chemistry	химия (f)	[ˈhimija]
philosophy	философия (f)	[filaˈsɔfija]
psychology	психология (f)	[psihaˈlɔgija]

145. Writing system. Orthography

grammar	грамматика (f)	[graˈmatikə]
vocabulary	лексика (f)	[ˈleksikə]
phonetics	фонетика (f)	[faˈnɛtikə]

noun	существительное (n)	[sʊɕestˈwiteʎnae]
adjective	прилагательное (n)	[prilaˈgateʎnae]
verb	глагол (m)	[glaˈgɔl]
adverb	наречие (n)	[naˈretɕie]

pronoun	местоимение (n)	[mistaiˈmenie]
interjection	междометие (n)	[meʒdaˈmetie]
preposition	предлог (m)	[pridˈlɔk]

root (base form)	корень (m) слова	[ˈkɔreɲ ˈslɔvə]
ending	окончание (n)	[akaɲˈtɕanie]
prefix	приставка (f)	[prisˈtafkə]
syllable	слог (m)	[slɔk]

suffix	**суффикс** (m)	['sufiks]
stress mark	**ударение** (n)	[uda'renie]
apostrophe	**апостроф** (m)	[a'postraf]

period, dot	**точка** (f)	['tɔtʃkə]
comma	**запятая** (f)	[zapi'taja]
semicolon	**точка** (f) **с запятой**	['tɔtʃka s zapi'tɔj]
colon	**двоеточие** (n)	[dvae'tɔtʃie]
ellipsis	**многоточие** (n)	[mnaga'tɔtʃie]

| question mark | **вопросительный знак** (m) | [vapra'siteʌnıj znak] |
| exclamation point | **восклицательный знак** (m) | [vaskli'tsateʌnıj z'nak] |

quotation marks	**кавычки** (f pl)	[ka'vıtʃki]
in quotation marks	**в кавычках**	[f ka'vıtʃkah]
parenthesis	**скобки** (f pl)	['skɔpki]
in parenthesis	**в скобках**	[f 'skɔpkah]

hyphen	**дефис** (m)	[di'fis]
dash	**тире** (n)	[ti'rɛ]
space (between words)	**пробел** (m)	[pra'bel]
hyphen (end of a line)	**перенос** (m)	[pire'nɔs]

| letter | **буква** (f) | ['bukvə] |
| capital letter | **большая буква** (f) | [baʌ'ʃʌja 'bukvə] |

| vowel (noun) | **гласный звук** (m) | ['glasnıj zvuk] |
| consonant (noun) | **согласный звук** (m) | [sag'lasnıj zvuk] |

sentence	**предложение** (n)	[pridla'ʒenie]
subject	**подлежащее** (n)	[padle'ʒaɕee]
predicate	**сказуемое** (n)	[ska'zuemae]

line (in writing)	**строка** (f)	[stra'ka]
on a new line	**с новой строки**	[s 'nɔvaj stra'ki]
paragraph	**абзац** (m)	[ab'zats]

word	**слово** (n)	['slɔvə]
word group	**словосочетание** (n)	[slovasatʃi'tanie]
expression	**выражение** (n)	[vıra'ʒɛnie]
synonym	**синоним** (m)	[si'nɔnim]
antonym	**антоним** (m)	[an'tɔnim]

rule	**правило** (n)	['prawilə]
exception	**исключение** (n)	[iskly'tʃenie]
right (correct)	**верный**	['wernıj]

conjugation	**спряжение** (n)	[spri'ʒɛnie]
declension	**склонение** (n)	[skla'nenie]
nominal case	**падеж** (m)	[pa'deʃ]

question	вопрос (m)	[vap'rɔs]
to underline (vt)	подчеркнуть	[patʃerk'nutʲ]
dotted line	пунктир (m)	[punk'tir]

146. Foreign languages

language	язык (m)	[ja'zık]
foreign	иностранный	[inast'rannıj]
foreign language	иностранный язык (m)	[inast'rannıj ja'zık]
to study (vt)	изучать	[izu'tʃatʲ]
to learn (language etc.)	учить	[u'tʃitʲ]

to read (vi, vt)	читать	[tʃi'tatʲ]
to speak (vi, vt)	говорить	[gava'ritʲ]
to understand (vt)	понимать	[pani'matʲ]
to write (vi, vt)	писать	[pi'satʲ]

fast	быстро	['bıstrə]
slowly	медленно	['medlenə]
fluently	свободно	[sva'bɔdnə]

rules	правила (n pl)	['prawilə]
grammar	грамматика (f)	[gra'matikə]
vocabulary	лексика (f)	['leksikə]
phonetics	фонетика (f)	[fa'nɛtikə]

textbook	учебник (m)	[u'tʃebnik]
dictionary	словарь (m)	[sla'varʲ]
teach-yourself book	самоучитель (m)	[samau'tʃiteʎ]
phrasebook	разговорник (m)	[razga'vɔrnik]

cassette	кассета (f)	[ka'setə]
videotape	видеокассета (f)	[wideaka'setə]
CD (compact disc)	CD-диск (m)	[si'di disk]
DVD	DVD-диск (m)	[diwi'di 'disk]

alphabet	алфавит (m)	[alfa'wit]
to spell (vt)	говорить по буквам	[gava'ritʲ pa 'bukvam]
pronunciation	произношение (n)	[praizna'ʃɛnie]

accent	акцент (m)	[ak'ʦənt]
with an accent	с акцентом	[s ak'ʦəntam]
without an accent	без акцента	[bez ak'ʦəntə]

| word | слово (n) | ['slɔvə] |
| meaning | смысл (m) | [smısl] |

course (e.g., a French ~)	курсы (pl)	['kursı]
to sign up	записаться	[zapi'saʦə]
teacher	преподаватель (m)	[pripada'vateʎ]

translation (process)	перевод (m)	[pere'vɔt]
translation (text etc.)	перевод (m)	[pere'vɔt]
translator	переводчик (m)	[pire'vɔtʃik]
interpreter	переводчик (m)	[pire'vɔtʃik]
polyglot	полиглот (m)	[palig'lɔt]
memory	память (f)	['pamitʲ]

147. Fairy tale characters

Santa Claus	Санта Клаус (m)	['santa 'klaus]
Cinderella	Золушка (f)	['zɔluʃkə]
mermaid	русалка (f)	[rʊ'salkə]
Neptune	Нептун (m)	[nip'tʊn]
magician, wizard	волшебник (m)	[val'ʃɛbnik]
good witch	волшебница (f)	[val'ʃɛbnitsə]
magic	волшебный	[val'ʃɛbnɪj]
magic wand	волшебная палочка (f)	[val'ʃɛbnaja 'palatʃkə]
fairy tale	сказка (f)	['skaskə]
miracle	чудо (n)	['tʃudə]
dwarf	гном (m)	[gnɔm]
to turn into …	превратиться в …	[privra'titsa f]
ghost	привидение (n)	[priwi'denie]
phantom	призрак (m)	['prizrak]
monster	чудовище (n)	[tʃu'dɔwiɕe]
dragon	дракон (m)	[dra'kɔn]
giant	великан (m)	[wili'kan]

148. Zodiac Signs

Aries	Овен (m)	['ɔwen]
Taurus	Телец (m)	[ti'lets]
Gemini	Близнецы (pl)	[blizne'tsɪ]
Cancer	Рак (m)	[rak]
Leo	Лев (m)	[lef]
Virgo	Дева (f)	['devə]
Libra	Весы (pl)	[wi'sɪ]
Scorpio	Скорпион (m)	[skarpi'ɔn]
Sagittarius	Стрелец (m)	[stre'lets]
Capricorn	Козерог (m)	[kaze'rɔk]
Aquarius	Водолей (m)	[vada'lej]
Pisces	Рыбы (pl)	['rɪbɪ]

character	**характер** (m)	[hɑ'rakter]
features of character	**черты** (f pl) **характера**	[ʧer'tɪ hɑ'rakterə]
behavior	**поведение** (n)	[pɑwi'denie]
to tell fortunes	**гадать**	[gɑ'datʲ]
fortune-teller	**гадалка** (f)	[gɑ'dalkə]
horoscope	**гороскоп** (m)	[gɑras'kɔp]

Arts

149. Theater

theater	театр (m)	[ti'atr]
opera	опера (f)	['ɔperə]
operetta	оперетта (f)	[api'retə]
ballet	балет (m)	[ba'let]

playbill	афиша (f)	[a'fiʃə]
company	труппа (f)	['truppə]
tour	гастроли (pl)	[gast'roli]
to be on tour	гастролировать	[gastra'liravatʲ]
to rehearse (vi, vt)	репетировать	[ripe'tiravatʲ]
rehearsal	репетиция (f)	[ripe'titsija]
repertoire	репертуар (m)	[riper'tʋar]

performance	представление (n)	[pritstav'lenie]
show, play	спектакль (m)	[spik'takʌ]
play	пьеса (f)	['pjesə]

ticket	билет (m)	[bi'let]
ticket office	билетная касса (f)	[bi'letnaja 'kassə]
lobby, foyer	холл (m)	[hɔl]
coat check	гардероб (m)	[garde'rɔp]
coat check tag	номерок (m)	[name'rɔk]
binoculars	бинокль (m)	[bi'nɔkʌ]
usher	контролёр (m)	[kantra'lɜr]

orchestra seats	партер (m)	[par'tɛr]
balcony	балкон (m)	[bal'kɔn]
dress circle	бельэтаж (m)	[biʌje'taʃ]
box	ложа (f)	['lɔʒə]
row	ряд (m)	[rʲat]
seat	место (n)	['mestə]

audience	публика (f)	['publikə]
spectator	зритель (m)	['zriteʌ]
to clap (vi, vt)	хлопать	['hlɔpatʲ]
applause	аплодисменты (pl)	[apladis'mentɪ]
ovation	овации (f pl)	[a'vatsɪi]

stage	сцена (f)	['stsɜnə]
curtain	занавес (m)	['zanawes]
scenery	декорация (f)	[dika'ratsɪja]
backstage	кулисы (pl)	[kʋ'lisɪ]

scene (e.g., the last ~)	сцена (f)	['stsɛnə]
act	акт (m)	[akt]
intermission	антракт (m)	[ant'rakt]

150. Cinema

actor	актёр (m)	[ak'tɜr]
actress	актриса (f)	[akt'risə]
movies (industry)	кино (n)	[ki'nɔ]
movie	кино, фильм (m)	[ki'nɔ], [fiʌm]
episode	серия (f)	['serija]
detective	детектив (m)	[dɛtɛk'tif]
action movie	боевик (m)	[bae'wik]
adventure movie	приключенческий фильм (m)	[prikly'tʃɛɲtʃeskij fiʌm]
science fiction movie	фантастический фильм (m)	[fantas'titʃeskij fiʌm]
horror movie	фильм (m) ужасов	[fiʌm 'uʒasaf]
comedy movie	кинокомедия (f)	[kinaka'medija]
melodrama	мелодрама (f)	[milad'ramə]
drama	драма (f)	['dramə]
fictional movie	художественный фильм (m)	[hʊ'dɔʒɛstwennɪj 'fiʌm]
documentary	документальный фильм (m)	[dakʊmen'taʌnɪj fiʌm]
cartoon	мультфильм (m)	[mʊʌt'fiʌm]
silent movies	немое кино (n)	[ne'mɔe ki'nɔ]
role	роль (f)	[rɔʌ]
leading role	главная роль (f)	['glavnaja rɔʌ]
to play (vi, vt)	играть	[ig'ratʲ]
movie star	кинозвезда (f)	[kinazwez'da]
well-known	известный	[iz'wesnɪj]
famous	знаменитый	[zname'nitɪj]
popular	популярный	[papʊ'ʌarnɪj]
script (screenplay)	сценарий (m)	[stsɪ'narij]
scriptwriter	сценарист (m)	[stsɪna'rist]
movie director	режиссёр (m)	[riʒɪ'sɜr]
producer	продюсер (m)	[pra'dyser]
assistant	ассистент (m)	[asis'tent]
cameraman	оператор (m)	[api'ratar]
stuntman	каскадёр (m)	[kaska'dɜr]
double	дублёр (m)	[dʊb'lɜrʲ]
to shoot a movie	снимать фильм	[sni'matʲ fiʌm]

audition, screen test	пробы (pl)	['prɔbɪ]
shooting	съёмки (pl)	[sʰɜmkɪ]
movie crew	съёмочная группа (f)	[sʰɜmatʃnaja 'grupə]
movie set	съёмочная площадка (f)	[sʰɜmatʃnaja plɑ'ɕatkə]
camera	кинокамера (f)	[kina'kamerə]
movie theater	кинотеатр (m)	[kinatɪ'atr]
screen (e.g., big ~)	экран (m)	[ɛk'ran]
to show a movie	показывать фильм	[pa'kazıvatʲ fiʌm]
soundtrack	звуковая дорожка (f)	[zvʊka'vaja da'rɔʃkə]
special effects	специальные эффекты (m pl)	[spetsɪ'aʌnɪe ɛ'fektɪ]
subtitles	субтитры (pl)	[sʊp'titrɪ]
credits	титры (pl)	['titrɪ]
translation	перевод (m)	[pere'vɔt]

151. Painting

art	искусство (n)	[is'kʊstvə]
fine arts	изящные искусства (n pl)	[i'zʲaɕnɪe is'kʊstvə]
art gallery	галерея (f)	[gale'reja]
art exhibition	выставка (f) картин	['vɪstafka kar'tin]
painting	живопись (f)	['ʒɪvapisʲ]
graphic art	графика (f)	['grafikə]
abstract art	абстракционизм (m)	[apstraktsɪa'nizm]
impressionism	импрессионизм (m)	[impresɪa'nizm]
picture (painting)	картина (f)	[kar'tinə]
drawing	рисунок (m)	[ri'sʊnak]
poster	плакат (m)	[pla'kat]
illustration (picture)	иллюстрация (f)	[ilyst'ratsɪja]
miniature	миниатюра (f)	[minia'tʲurə]
copy (of painting etc.)	копия (f)	['kɔpija]
reproduction	репродукция (f)	[ripra'dʊktsɪja]
mosaic	мозаика (f)	[ma'zaikə]
stained glass	витраж (m)	[wit'raʃ]
fresco	фреска (f)	['freskə]
engraving	гравюра (f)	[gra'wyrə]
bust (sculpture)	бюст (m)	[byst]
sculpture	скульптура (f)	[skuʌp'tʊrə]
statue	статуя (f)	['statʊja]
plaster of Paris	гипс (m)	[gips]
plaster (e.g., ~ statue)	из гипса	[iz 'gipsə]
portrait	портрет (m)	[part'ret]

self-portrait	**автопортрет** (m)	[aftapart'ret]
landscape	**пейзаж** (m)	[pij'zaʃ]
still life	**натюрморт** (m)	[natyr'mɔrt]
caricature	**карикатура** (f)	[karika'turə]
sketch	**набросок** (m)	[nab'rɔsak]
paint	**краска** (f)	['kraskə]
watercolor	**акварель** (f)	[akva'reʎ]
oil (paint)	**масло** (n)	['maslə]
pencil	**карандаш** (m)	[karan'daʃ]
Indian ink	**тушь** (f)	[tuʃ]
charcoal	**уголь** (m)	['ugaʎ]
to draw (vi, vt)	**рисовать**	[risa'vatʲ]
to pose (vi)	**позировать**	[pa'ziravatʲ]
artist's model (man)	**натурщик** (m)	[na'turɕik]
artist's model (woman)	**натурщица** (f)	[na'turɕitsə]
artist (painter)	**художник** (m)	[hu'dɔʒnik]
work of art	**произведение** (n)	[praizwe'denie]
masterpiece	**шедевр** (m)	[ʃi'devr]
workshop (of artist)	**мастерская** (f)	[masters'kaja]
canvas (cloth)	**холст** (m)	[hɔlst]
easel	**мольберт** (m)	[maʎ'bert]
palette	**палитра** (f)	[pa'litrə]
frame (of picture etc.)	**рама** (f)	['ramə]
restoration	**реставрация** (f)	[ristav'ratsija]
to restore (vt)	**реставрировать**	[ristav'riravatʲ]

152. Literature & Poetry

literature	**литература** (f)	[litera'turə]
author (writer)	**автор** (m)	['aftar]
pseudonym	**псевдоним** (m)	[psivda'nim]
book	**книга** (f)	['knigə]
volume	**том** (m)	[tɔm]
contents list	**оглавление** (n)	[aglav'lenie]
page	**страница** (f)	[stra'nitsə]
main character	**главный герой** (m)	['glavnɨj ge'rɔj]
autograph	**автограф** (m)	[af'tɔgraf]
short story	**рассказ** (m)	[ras'kas]
story (novella)	**повесть** (f)	['pɔwestʲ]
novel	**роман** (m)	[ra'man]
work (writing)	**сочинение** (n)	[satɕi'nenie]
fable	**басня** (f)	['basɲa]
detective novel	**детектив** (m)	[dɛtɛk'tif]

poem (verse)	стихотворение (n)	[stihatva'renie]
poetry	поэзия (f)	[pa'ɛzija]
poem (epic, ballad)	поэма (f)	[pa'ɛmə]
poet	поэт (m)	[pa'ɛt]

fiction	беллетристика (f)	[bilet'ristikə]
science fiction	научная фантастика (f)	[na'utʃnaja fan'tastikə]
adventures	приключения (f)	[prikly'tʃenija]
educational literature	учебная литература (f)	[u'tʃebnaja litera'turə]
children's literature	детская литература (f)	['detskaja litera'turə]

153. Circus

circus	цирк (m)	[tsɪrk]
big top (circus)	цирк-шапито (m)	[tsɪrk ʃʌpi'tɔ]
program	программа (f)	[prag'rammə]
performance	представление (n)	[pritstav'lenie]

| act (circus ~) | номер (m) | ['nɔmer] |
| circus ring | арена (f) | [a'renə] |

| pantomime (act) | пантомима (f) | [panta'mimə] |
| clown | клоун (m) | ['kloun] |

acrobat	акробат (m)	[akra'bat]
acrobatics	акробатика (f)	[akra'batikə]
gymnast	гимнаст (m)	[gim'nast]
gymnastics	гимнастика (f)	[gim'nastikə]
somersault	сальто (n)	['saʎtə]
athlete	атлет (m)	[at'let]
animal-tamer	укротитель (m)	[ukra'titeʎ]
rider	наездник (m)	[na'eznik]
assistant	ассистент (m)	[asis'tent]

stunt	трюк (m)	[tryk]
conjuring trick	фокус (m)	['fɔkʊs]
conjurer, magician	фокусник (m)	['fɔkʊsnik]

juggler	жонглёр (m)	[ʒɑhg'lɜr]
to juggle (vi, vt)	жонглировать	[ʒɑhg'liravatʲ]
animal trainer	дрессировщик (m)	[drisi'rɔfɕik]
animal training	дрессировка (f)	[drisi'rɔfkə]
to train (animals)	дрессировать	[drisira'vatʲ]

154. Music. Pop music

| music | музыка (f) | ['mʊzɪkə] |
| musician | музыкант (m) | [mʊzɪ'kant] |

musical instrument	**музыкальный инструмент** (m)	[muzɪˈkaʎnɪj instruˈment]
to play ...	**играть на ...**	[igˈratʲ na]
guitar	**гитара** (f)	[giˈtarə]
violin	**скрипка** (f)	[ˈskrɪpkə]
cello	**виолончель** (f)	[wialanˈtʃeʎ]
double bass	**контрабас** (m)	[kantraˈbas]
harp	**арфа** (f)	[ˈarfə]
piano	**пианино** (n)	[piaˈninə]
grand piano	**рояль** (m)	[raˈjaʎ]
organ	**орган** (m)	[arˈgan]
wind instruments	**духовые инструменты** (m pl)	[duhaˈvɪe instruˈmentɪ]
oboe	**гобой** (m)	[gaˈbɔj]
saxophone	**саксофон** (m)	[saksaˈfon]
clarinet	**кларнет** (m)	[klarˈnet]
flute	**флейта** (f)	[ˈflejtə]
trumpet	**труба** (f)	[truˈba]
accordion	**аккордеон** (m)	[akardeˈɔn]
drum	**барабан** (m)	[baraˈban]
duo	**дуэт** (m)	[duˈɛt]
trio	**трио** (n)	[ˈtriə]
quartet	**квартет** (m)	[kvarˈtet]
choir	**хор** (m)	[hɔr]
orchestra	**оркестр** (m)	[arˈkestr]
pop music	**поп-музыка** (f)	[pɔp ˈmuzɪkə]
rock music	**рок-музыка** (f)	[rɔk ˈmuzɪkə]
rock group	**рок-группа** (f)	[rɔk ˈgrupə]
jazz	**джаз** (m)	[dʒas]
idol	**кумир** (m)	[kuˈmir]
admirer, fan	**поклонник** (m)	[pakˈlɔnnik]
concert	**концерт** (m)	[kanˈtsert]
symphony	**симфония** (f)	[simˈfɔnija]
composition	**сочинение** (n)	[satʃiˈnenie]
to compose (write)	**сочинить**	[satʃiˈnitʲ]
singing	**пение** (n)	[ˈpenie]
song	**песня** (f)	[ˈpesʲɲa]
tune (melody)	**мелодия** (f)	[miˈlodija]
rhythm	**ритм** (m)	[ritm]
blues	**блюз** (m)	[blys]
sheet music	**ноты** (f pl)	[ˈnotɪ]
baton	**палочка** (f)	[ˈpalatʃkə]

bow	**смычок** (m)	[smɪˈʧɔk]
string	**струна** (f)	[struˈnɑ]
case (e.g., for guitar)	**футляр** (m)	[futˈʎar]

Rest. Entertainment. Travel

155. Trip. Travel

tourism	**туризм** (m)	[tʊˈrizm]
tourist	**турист** (m)	[tʊˈrist]
trip, voyage	**путешествие** (n)	[pʊtɛˈʃɛstwiɛ]
adventure	**приключение** (n)	[priklʲuˈʧɛniɛ]
trip, journey	**поездка** (f)	[paˈeztkə]
vacation	**отпуск** (m)	[ˈɔtpʊsk]
to be on vacation	**быть в отпуске**	[bɪtʲ v ˈɔtpʊskɛ]
rest	**отдых** (m)	[ˈɔddɪh]
train	**поезд** (m)	[ˈpɔɛzt]
by train	**поездом**	[ˈpɔizdam]
airplane	**самолёт** (m)	[samaˈlʲɜt]
by airplane	**самолётом**	[samaˈlʲɜtam]
by car	**на автомобиле**	[na aftamaˈbilɛ]
by ship	**на корабле**	[na karabˈlʲe]
luggage	**багаж** (m)	[baˈgaʃ]
suitcase, luggage	**чемодан** (m)	[ʧimaˈdan]
luggage cart	**тележка** (f) **для багажа**	[tiˈlʲeʃka dʲʎa bagaˈʒa]
passport	**паспорт** (m)	[ˈpaspart]
visa	**виза** (f)	[ˈwizə]
ticket	**билет** (m)	[biˈlʲet]
air ticket	**авиабилет** (m)	[awiabiˈlʲet]
guidebook	**путеводитель** (m)	[pʊtevaˈditɛʎ]
map	**карта** (f)	[ˈkartə]
area (place)	**местность** (f)	[ˈmɛsnastʲ]
place, site	**место** (n)	[ˈmɛstə]
exotica	**экзотика** (f)	[ɛkˈzɔtikə]
exotic	**экзотический**	[ɛkzaˈtiʧeskij]
amazing	**удивительный**	[udiˈwitɛʎnɪj]
group	**группа** (f)	[ˈgrʊpə]
excursion	**экскурсия** (f)	[ɛksˈkʊrsija]
guide (person)	**экскурсовод** (m)	[ɛkskʊrsaˈvot]

156. Hotel

hotel	**гостиница** (f)	[gɑs'tinitsə]
motel	**мотель** (m)	[mɑ'teʎ]
three-star	**3 звезды**	[tri zwez'dɪ]
five-star	**5 звёзд**	[pʲatʲ 'zwɜst]
to stay (in hotel etc.)	**остановиться**	[əstɑnɑ'witsə]
room	**номер** (m)	['nɔmer]
single room	**одноместный номер** (m)	[ɑdnɑ'mesnɪj 'nɔmer]
double room	**двухместный номер** (m)	[dvʊh'mesnɪj 'nɔmer]
to book a room	**бронировать номер**	[brɑ'nirɑvɑtʲ 'nɔmer]
half board	**полупансион** (m)	[pɑlupɑnsi'ɔn]
full board	**полный пансион** (m)	['pɔlnɪj pɑnsi'ɔn]
with bath	**с ванной**	[s 'vɑnnɑj]
with shower	**с душем**	[s 'dʊʃəm]
satellite television	**спутниковое телевидение** (n)	['spʊtnikɑvɑe telewidenie]
air-conditioner	**кондиционер** (m)	[kɑnditsɪɑ'ner]
towel	**полотенце** (n)	[pɑlɑ'tentsə]
key	**ключ** (m)	[klytʃ]
administrator	**администратор** (m)	[ɑdminist'rɑtɑr]
chambermaid	**горничная** (f)	['gɔrnitʃnɑjɑ]
porter, bellboy	**носильщик** (m)	[nɑ'siʎɕik]
doorman	**портье** (n)	[pɑr'tʲe]
restaurant	**ресторан** (m)	[ristɑ'rɑn]
pub, bar	**бар** (m)	[bɑr]
café	**кафе** (n)	[kɑ'fɛ]
breakfast	**завтрак** (m)	['zɑftrɑk]
dinner	**ужин** (m)	['ʊʒɪn]
buffet	**шведский стол** (m)	['ʃwetskij 'stɔl]
lobby	**вестибюль** (m)	[wisti'byʎ]
elevator	**лифт** (m)	[lift]
DO NOT DISTURB	**НЕ БЕСПОКОИТЬ**	[ne bespɑ'kɔitʲ]
NO SMOKING	**НЕ КУРИТЬ!**	[ne kʊ'ritʲ]

157. Books. Reading

book	**книга** (f)	['knigə]
author	**автор** (m)	['ɑftɑr]
writer	**писатель** (m)	[pi'sɑteʎ]
to write (e.g., ~ a book)	**написать**	[nɑpi'sɑtʲ]

reader	**читатель** (m)	[tʃiˈtatɛʎ]
to read (vi, vt)	**читать**	[tʃiˈtatʲ]
reading (activity)	**чтение** (n)	[ˈtʃtenie]

| silently | **про себя** | [pra seˈbʲa] |
| aloud | **вслух** | [vsluh] |

to publish (vt)	**издавать**	[izdaˈvatʲ]
publication	**издание** (n)	[izˈdanie]
publisher	**издатель** (m)	[izˈdatɛʎ]
publishing house	**издательство** (n)	[izˈdatɛʎstvə]

to come out	**выйти**	[ˈvɪjti]
publication	**выход** (m)	[ˈvɪhat]
print run	**тираж** (m)	[tiˈraʃ]

| bookstore | **книжный магазин** (m) | [ˈkniʒnɪj magaˈzin] |
| library | **библиотека** (f) | [bibliaˈtekə] |

story (novella)	**повесть** (f)	[ˈpowestʲ]
short story	**рассказ** (m)	[rasˈkas]
novel	**роман** (m)	[raˈman]
detective novel	**детектив** (m)	[dɛtɛkˈtif]

memoirs	**мемуары** (pl)	[mimʊˈarɪ]
legend	**легенда** (f)	[liˈgendə]
myth	**миф** (m)	[mif]

poetry, poems	**стихи** (m pl)	[stiˈhi]
autobiography	**автобиография** (f)	[aftabiagˈrafija]
collected works	**избранное** (n)	[ˈizbrannae]
science fiction	**фантастика** (f)	[fanˈtastikə]

title	**название** (n)	[nazˈvanie]
introduction	**введение** (n)	[vwiˈdenie]
title page	**титульный лист** (m)	[ˈtitʊʎnɪj list]

chapter	**глава** (f)	[glaˈva]
extract	**отрывок** (m)	[atˈrɪvak]
episode	**эпизод** (m)	[ɛpiˈzot]

thread (of story)	**сюжет** (m)	[syˈʒet]
contents	**содержание** (n)	[sadɛrˈʒanie]
table of contents	**оглавление** (n)	[aglavˈlenie]
main character	**главный герой** (m)	[ˈglavnɪj geˈrɔj]

volume	**том** (m)	[tom]
cover	**обложка** (f)	[abˈlɔʃkə]
binding	**переплёт** (m)	[pirepˈlɜt]
bookmark	**закладка** (f)	[zakˈlatkə]
page	**страница** (f)	[straˈnitsə]
to flick through	**листать**	[lisˈtatʲ]

margins	поля (f)	[pɑ'ʎa]
note (in margins)	пометка (f)	[pɑ'metkə]
annotation	примечание (n)	[primi'ʧanie]

text	текст (m)	[tekst]
type, font	шрифт (m)	[ʃrift]
misprint, typo	опечатка (f)	[ɑpi'ʧatkə]

translation	перевод (m)	[pere'vɔt]
to translate (vi, vt)	переводить	[pireva'ditʲ]
original (read in the ~)	подлинник (m)	['pɔdlinnik]

famous	знаменитый	[znɑme'nitɪj]
unknown	неизвестный	[niiz'wesnɪj]
interesting	интересный	[inti'resnɪj]
bestseller	бестселлер (m)	[bes'tsɛler]

dictionary	словарь (m)	[slɑ'varʲ]
textbook	учебник (m)	[u'ʧebnik]
encyclopedia	энциклопедия (f)	[intsɪklɑ'pedija]

158. Hunting. Fishing

hunt (of animal)	охота (f)	[ɑ'hɔtə]
to hunt (vi, vt)	охотиться	[ɑ'hɔtitsə]
hunter	охотник (m)	[ɑ'hɔtnik]

to shoot (vi)	стрелять	[stri'ʎatʲ]
rifle	ружьё (n)	[ru'ʒjo]
bullet (cartridge)	патрон (m)	[pat'rɔn]
shotgun pellets	дробь (f)	[drɔpʲ]

trap (e.g., bear ~)	капкан (m)	[kap'kɑn]
snare (for birds etc.)	ловушка (f)	[lɑ'vuʃkə]
to fall into the trap	попасться в капкан	[pɑ'pastsa f kap'kɑn]
to lay a trap	ставить капкан	['stɑwitʲ kap'kɑn]

poacher	браконьер (m)	[brɑkɑ'ɲjer]
game (in hunting)	дичь (f)	[diʧ]
hound	охотничья собака (f)	[ɑ'hɔtniʧja sɑ'bɑkə]
safari	сафари (n)	[sɑ'fɑri]
mounted animal	чучело (n)	['ʧuʧelə]

fisherman	рыбак (m)	[rɪ'bɑk]
fishing	рыбалка (f)	[rɪ'bɑlkə]
to fish (vi)	ловить рыбу	[lɑ'witʲ 'rɪbʊ]

fishing rod	удочка (f)	['udɑʧkə]
fishing line	леска (f)	['leskə]
hook	крючок (m)	[kry'ʧɔk]

| float | поплавок (m) | [papla'vɔk] |
| bait | наживка (f) | [na'ʒifkə] |

to cast a line	забросить удочку	[zab'rositʲ 'udatʃkʊ]
to bite (about fish)	клевать	[kli'vatʲ]
catch (of fish)	улов (m)	[u'lɔf]
ice-hole	прорубь (f)	['prorʊpʲ]

net	сеть (f)	[setʲ]
boat	лодка (f)	['lɔtkə]
to net (catch with net)	ловить сетью	[la'witʲ 'setʲy]
to cast the net	забрасывать сеть	[zab'rasıvatʲ setʲ]
to haul in the net	вытаскивать сеть	[vı'taskivatʲ setʲ]

whaler (person)	китобой (m)	[kita'bɔj]
whaleboat	китобойное судно (n)	[kita'bɔjnae 'sʊdnə]
harpoon	гарпун (m)	[gar'pʊn]

159. Games. Billiards

billiards	бильярд (m)	[bi'ʎjart]
billiard room, hall	бильярдная (f)	[bi'ʎjardnaja]
ball	бильярдный шар (m)	[bi'ʎjardnıj 'ʃʌr]

to pocket a ball	загнать шар	[zag'natʲ ʃʌr]
cue	кий (m)	[kij]
pocket	луза (f)	['luzə]

160. Games. Playing cards

diamonds	бубны (pl)	['bʊbnı]
spades	пики (pl)	['piki]
hearts	черви (pl)	['tʃerwi]
clubs	трефы (pl)	['trefı]

ace	туз (m)	[tʊs]
king	король (m)	[ka'rɔʎ]
queen	дама (f)	['damə]
jack, knave	валет (m)	[va'let]

playing card	игральная карта (f)	[ig'raʎnaja 'kartə]
cards	карты (f pl)	['kartı]
trump	козырь (m)	['kɔzırʲ]
deck of cards	колода (f)	[ka'lodə]

point	очко (n)	[atʃ'kɔ]
to deal (vi, vt)	сдавать	[sda'vatʲ]
to shuffle (in card games)	тасовать	[tasa'vatʲ]

| lead, turn (noun) | ход (m) | [hɔt] |
| card sharp | шулер (m) | [ˈʃuler] |

161. Casino. Roulette

casino	казино (n)	[kaziˈnɔ]
roulette (game)	рулетка (f)	[rʊˈletkə]
bet, stake	ставка (f)	[ˈstafkə]
to place bets	делать ставки	[ˈdelatʲ ˈstafki]

red (in roulette)	красное (n)	[ˈkrasnəe]
black	чёрное (n)	[ˈtʃɔrnəe]
to bet on red	ставить на красное	[ˈstawitʲ na ˈkrasnəe]
to bet on black	ставить на чёрное	[ˈstawitʲ na ˈtʃɔrnəe]

croupier	крупье (m, f)	[krʊˈpje]
to turn the wheel	вращать барабан	[vraˈɕatʲ baraˈban]
rules (of game)	правила (n pl) игры	[ˈprawila igˈrɪ]
chip	фишка (f)	[ˈfiʃkə]

| to win (vi, vt) | выиграть | [ˈvɪigratʲ] |
| winnings | выигрыш (m) | [ˈvɪigrɪʃ] |

| to lose (not win) | проиграть | [praigˈratʲ] |
| loss | проигрыш (m) | [ˈprɔigrɪʃ] |

player	игрок (m)	[igˈrɔk]
blackjack (card game)	блэк джек (m)	[blɛk ˈdʒɛk]
game of dice	игра в кости	[igˈra f ˈkɔsti]
dice	кости (pl)	[ˈkɔsti]
slot machine	игральный автомат (m)	[igˈraʎnɪj aftaˈmat]

162. Rest. Games. Miscellaneous

to walk, to stroll (vi)	гулять	[gʊˈʎatʲ]
walk, stroll	прогулка (f)	[praˈgʊlkə]
pleasure-ride, trip	поездка	[paˈestka]
adventure	приключение (n)	[priklyˈtʃenie]
picnic	пикник (m)	[pikˈnik]

game (chess etc.)	игра (f)	[igˈra]
player	игрок (m)	[igˈrɔk]
game (one ~ of chess)	партия (f)	[ˈpartija]

collector (e.g., philatelist)	коллекционер (m)	[kalektsaˈner]
to collect (vt)	коллекционировать	[kalektsaˈniravatʲ]
collection	коллекция (f)	[kaˈlektsɪja]
crossword	кроссворд (m)	[krasˈvɔrt]

dominoes	**домино**	[dɑmi'nɔ]
racecourse (for horses)	**ипподром** (m)	[ipɑd'rɔm]
disco (place)	**дискотека** (f)	[diskɑ'tekə]
sauna	**сауна** (f)	['saunə]
lottery	**лотерея** (f)	[latɛ'reja]
camping trip	**похо́д** (m)	[pa'hɔt]
camp	**лагерь** (m)	['lagerʲ]
tent (for camping)	**палатка** (f)	[pa'latkə]
compass	**компас** (m)	['kɔmpɑs]
camper	**турист** (m)	[tʊ'rist]
to watch (movie etc.)	**смотреть**	[smat'retʲ]
viewer	**телезритель** (m)	[tilez'riteʎ]
TV show	**телепередача** (f)	[tilepere'datʃə]

163. Photography

camera (photo)	**фотоаппарат** (m)	[fɔtɑpɑ'rat]
photo, picture	**фото, фотография** (f)	['fɔta], [fatag'rafija]
photographer	**фотограф** (m)	[fa'tɔgraf]
photo studio	**фотостудия** (f)	[fatɑs'tʊdija]
photo album	**фотоальбом** (m)	[fɔtaaʎ'bɔm]
camera lens	**объектив** (m)	[abʰek'tif]
telephoto lens	**телеобъектив** (m)	[teleabʰek'tif]
filter	**фильтр** (m)	[fiʎtr]
lens	**линза** (f)	['linzə]
set of lenses	**оптика** (f)	['ɔptikə]
diaphragm (aperture)	**диафрагма** (f)	[diaf'ragmə]
exposure time	**выдержка** (f)	['vɪderʃkə]
viewfinder	**видоискатель** (m)	[widais'kateʎ]
digital camera	**цифровая камера** (f)	[tsɪfra'vaja 'kamerə]
tripod	**штатив** (m)	[ʃta'tif]
flash	**вспышка** (f)	['fspɪʃkə]
to photograph (vt)	**фотографировать**	[fatagra'firavatʲ]
to take pictures	**снимать**	[sni'matʲ]
to be photographed	**фотографироваться**	[fatagra'firavatsə]
focus	**резкость** (f)	['reskastʲ]
to adjust the focus	**наводить на резкость**	[nava'ditʲ na 'reskastʲ]
sharp, in focus	**резкий**	['reskij]
sharpness	**резкость** (f)	['reskastʲ]
contrast	**контраст** (m)	[kant'rast]
contrasty	**контрастный**	[kant'rasnɪj]

picture (photo)	снимок (m)	['snimak]
negative (noun)	негатив (m)	[niga'tif]
film (e.g., a roll of ~)	фотоплёнка (f)	['fɔtaplɜnkə]
shot, frame	кадр (m)	[kadr]
to print (photos)	печатать	[pi'ʧatatʲ]

164. Beach. Swimming

beach	пляж (m)	[pʌaʃ]
sand	песок (m)	[pi'sɔk]
deserted (beach)	пустынный	[pʊs'tɪnnɪj]

suntan	загар (m)	[za'gar]
to get a tan	загорать	[zaga'ratʲ]
tan (adj)	загорелый	[zaga'relɪj]
sunscreen	крем для загара (f)	[krem dʌa za'garə]

bikini	бикини (n)	[bi'kini]
bathing suit	купальник (m)	[kʊ'paʌnik]
swim briefs	плавки (pl)	['plafki]

swimming pool	бассейн (m)	[ba'sɛjn]
to swim (vi)	плавать	['plavatʲ]
shower	душ (m)	[dʊʃ]
to change (one's clothes)	переодеваться	[pireade'vatsə]
towel	полотенце (n)	[pala'tentse]

| boat | лодка (f) | ['lɔtkə] |
| motorboat | катер (m) | ['kater] |

water ski	водные лыжи (pl)	['vɔdnɪe 'lɪʒɪ]
pedal boat	водный велосипед (m)	['vɔdnɪj welasi'pet]
surfing	серфинг (m)	['serfink]
surfer	серфингист (m)	[sirfi'ɲist]

scuba set	акваланг (m)	[akva'lank]
flippers	ласты (f pl)	['lastɪ]
mask	маска (f)	['maskə]
diver, snorkeler	ныряльщик (m)	[nɪ'rʲaʌɕik]
to dive (vi)	нырять	[nɪ'rʲatʲ]
underwater (adv)	под водой	[pad va'dɔj]

beach umbrella	зонт (m)	[zɔnt]
beach chair	шезлонг (m)	[ʃɛz'lɔnk]
sunglasses	очки (pl)	[aʧ'ki]
air mattress	плавательный матрац (m)	['plavatiʌnɪj matrats]

| to play (amuse oneself) | играть | [ig'ratʲ] |
| to go for a swim | купаться | [kʊ'patsə] |

beach ball	мяч (m)	[mʲatʃ]
to inflate (vt)	**надувать**	[nadu'vatʲ]
inflatable, air	**надувной**	[naduv'nɔj]
wave	**волна** (f)	[val'na]
buoy	**буй** (m)	[buj]
to drown (ab. person)	**тонуть**	[ta'nutʲ]
to save, to rescue	**спасать**	[spa'satʲ]
life vest	**спасательный жилет** (m)	[spa'sateʎnɪj ʒɪ'let]
to observe, to watch	**наблюдать**	[nably'datʲ]
lifeguard	**спасатель** (m)	[spa'sateʎ]

TECHNICAL EQUIPMENT. TRANSPORT

Technical equipment

165. Computer

computer	компьютер (m)	[kam'pjyter]
notebook, laptop	ноутбук (m)	[naud'buk]
to switch on (vt)	включить	[fkly'tʃitʲ]
to turn off	выключить	['vɪklytʃitʲ]
keyboard	клавиатура (f)	[klawia'turə]
key	клавиша (f)	['klawiʃə]
mouse	мышь (f)	[mɪʃ]
mouse pad	коврик (m)	['kovrik]
button	кнопка (f)	['knɔpkə]
cursor	курсор (m)	[kur'sɔr]
monitor	монитор (m)	[mani'tɔr]
screen	экран (m)	[ɛk'ran]
hard disk	жёсткий диск (m)	['ʒɜskij disk]
hard disk volume	объём (m)	[abjɔm
	жесткого диска	'ʒeskava 'diskə]
memory	память (f)	['pamitʲ]
random access memory	оперативная память (f)	[apera'tivnaja 'pamitʲ]
file	файл (m)	[fajl]
folder	папка (f)	['papkə]
to open (a file)	открыть	[atk'rɪtʲ]
to close (vt)	закрыть	[zak'rɪtʲ]
to save (vt)	сохранить	[sahra'nitʲ]
to delete (vt)	удалить	[uda'litʲ]
to copy (vt)	скопировать	[ska'piravatʲ]
to sort (vt)	сортировать	[sartira'vatʲ]
to copy (vt)	переписать	[perepi'satʲ]
program	программа (f)	[prag'rammə]
software	программное	[prag'ramnae
	обеспечение (n)	abes'petʃenie]
programmer	программист (m)	[pragra'mist]
to program (vi)	программировать	[pragra'miravatʲ]

hacker	хакер (m)	['haker]
password	пароль (m)	[pɑ'rɔʎ]
virus	вирус (m)	['wirʊs]
to find, to detect	обнаружить	[abnɑ'rʊʒɪtʲ]

| byte | байт (m) | [bajt] |
| megabyte | мегабайт (m) | [migɑ'bajt] |

| data | данные (pl) | ['dɑnnɪe] |
| database | база (f) данных | ['bɑzɑ 'dɑnnɪh] |

cable (wire)	кабель (m)	['kɑbeʎ]
to disconnect (vt)	отсоединить	[atsɑedi'nitʲ]
to connect (sth to sth)	подсоединить	[patsɑedi'nitʲ]

166. Internet. E-mail

Internet	интернет (m)	[inter'net]
browser	браузер (m)	['brɑuzɛr]
search engine	поисковый ресурс (m)	[pɑis'kɔvij re'sʊrs]
provider	провайдер (m)	[prɑ'vɑjder]

web master	веб-мастер (m)	[vɛb 'mɑster]
website	веб-сайт (m)	[vɛb 'sɑjt]
web page	веб-страница (f)	[web strɑ'nitsə]

| address | адрес (m) | ['ɑdres] |
| address book | адресная книга (f) | ['ɑdresnɑjɑ 'knigə] |

mailbox	почтовый ящик (m)	[patʃ'tɔvɪj 'jɑɕik]
mail	почта (f)	['pɔtʃtə]
overfull	переполненный	[pire'pɔlnennɪj]

message	сообщение (n)	[sɑɑp'ɕenie]
incoming messages	входящие сообщения (n pl)	[fhɑ'dʲaɕie sɑɑp'ɕenija]
outgoing messages	исходящие сообщения (n pl)	[ishɑ'dʲaɕie sɑɑp'ɕenija]

sender	отправитель (m)	[atprɑ'witeʎ]
to send (vt)	отправить	[atp'rawitʲ]
sending (of mail)	отправка (f)	[atp'rafkə]

| receiver | получатель (m) | [palu'tʃateʎ] |
| to receive (vt) | получить | [palu'tʃitʲ] |

correspondence	переписка (f)	[pire'piskə]
to correspond (vi)	переписываться	[pire'pisɪvatsə]
file	файл (m)	[fajl]
to download (vt)	скачать	[skɑ'tʃatʲ]

to create (vt)	создать	[saz'datʲ]
to delete (vt)	удалить	[uda'litʲ]
deleted	удалённый	[uda'lɜnnɪj]

connection (good, bad ~)	связь (f)	[svʲasʲ]
speed	скорость (f)	['skɔrastʲ]
modem	модем (m)	[ma'dem]
access	доступ (m)	['dɔstʊp]
port (e.g., input ~)	порт (m)	[pɔrt]

| connection | подключение (n) | [patkly'tʃenie] |
| to connect to … (vi) | подключиться | [patkly'tʃitsə] |

| to choose (vt) | выбрать | ['vɪbratʲ] |
| to search for … | искать … | [is'katʲ] |

167. Electricity

electricity	электричество (n)	[ɛlikt'ritʃestvə]
electrical	электрический	[ɛlikt'ritʃeskij]
electric power station	электростанция (f)	[ɛlektras'tantsɪja]
energy	энергия (f)	[ɛ'nergija]
electric power	электроэнергия (f)	[ɛlektraɛ'nergija]

light bulb	лампочка (f)	['lampatʃkə]
flashlight	фонарь (m)	[fa'narʲ]
street light	фонарь (m)	[fa'narʲ]

light	свет (m)	[swet]
to turn on	включать	[fkly'tʃatʲ]
to turn off	выключать	[vɪkly'tʃatʲ]
to turn off the light	погасить свет	[paga'sitʲ swet]

to burn out (vi)	перегореть	[pirega'retʲ]
short circuit	короткое замыкание (n)	[ka'rɔtkae zamɪ'kanie]
broken wire	обрыв (m)	[ab'rɪf]
contact	контакт (m)	[kan'takt]

switch (for light)	выключатель (m)	[vɪkly'tʃateʎ]
wall socket	розетка (f)	[ra'zetkə]
plug	вилка (f)	['wilkə]
extension cord	удлинитель (m)	[udli'niteʎ]

fuse	предохранитель (m)	[pridahra'niteʎ]
cable, wire	провод (m)	['prɔvat]
wiring	проводка (f)	[pra'vɔtkə]

ampere	ампер (m)	[am'per]
amperage	сила (f) тока	['sila 'tɔkə]
volt	вольт (m)	[vɔʎt]

voltage	напряжение (n)	[napriˈʒenie]
electrical device	электроприбор (m)	[ɛlektrapriˈbɔr]
indicator	индикатор (m)	[indiˈkatar]
electrician	электрик (m)	[ɛˈlektrik]
to solder (vt)	паять	[paˈjatʲ]
soldering iron	паяльник (m)	[paˈjaʎnik]
current	ток (m)	[tɔk]

168. Tools

tool, instrument	инструмент (m)	[instrʊˈment]
tools	инструменты (m pl)	[instrʊˈmentɪ]
equipment (factory ~)	оборудование (n)	[abaˈrʊdavanie]
hammer	молоток (m)	[malaˈtɔk]
screwdriver	отвёртка (f)	[atˈwɜrtkə]
ax	топор (m)	[taˈpɔr]
saw	пила (f)	[piˈla]
to saw (vt)	пилить	[piˈlitʲ]
plane (tool)	рубанок (m)	[rʊˈbanak]
to plane (vt)	строгать	[straˈgatʲ]
soldering iron	паяльник (m)	[paˈjaʎnik]
to solder (vt)	паять	[paˈjatʲ]
file (for metal)	напильник (m)	[naˈpiʎnik]
carpenter pincers	клещи (pl)	[ˈkleɕi]
lineman's pliers	плоскогубцы (pl)	[plaskaˈgʊbtsɪ]
chisel	стамеска (f)	[staˈmeskə]
drill bit	сверло (n)	[swirˈlɔ]
electric drill	дрель (f)	[dreʎ]
to drill (vi, vt)	сверлить	[swirˈlitʲ]
knife	нож (m)	[nɔʃ]
pocket knife	карманный нож (m)	[karˈmanɪj nɔʃ]
folding (knife etc.)	складной	[skladˈnɔj]
blade	лезвие (n)	[ˈlezwie]
sharp (knife)	острый	[ˈɔstrɪj]
blunt	тупой	[tʊˈpɔj]
to become blunt	затупиться	[zatʊˈpitsə]
to sharpen (vt)	точить	[taˈtʃitʲ]
bolt	болт (m)	[bɔlt]
nut	гайка (f)	[ˈgajkə]
thread (of a screw)	резьба (f)	[rizʲˈba]
screw (for wood)	шуруп (m)	[ʃʊˈrʊp]
nail	гвоздь (m)	[gvɔsʲtʲ]

nailhead	**шляпка** (f)	[ˈʃʎapkə]
ruler (for measuring)	**линейка** (f)	[liˈnejkə]
tape measure	**рулетка** (f)	[rʊˈletkə]
level (tool)	**уровень** (m)	[ˈurəweɲ]
magnifying glass	**лупа** (f)	[ˈlupə]
measuring instrument	**измерительный прибор** (m)	[izmeˈriteʎnɪj priˈbɔr]
to measure (vt)	**измерять**	[izmeˈrʲatʲ]
scale (of thermometer etc.)	**шкала** (f)	[ʃkaˈla]
readings	**показание** (n)	[pakaˈzanie]
compressor	**компрессор** (m)	[kampˈresar]
microscope	**микроскоп** (m)	[mikrasˈkɔp]
pump (e.g., water ~)	**насос** (m)	[naˈsɔs]
robot	**робот** (m)	[ˈrobat]
laser	**лазер** (m)	[ˈlazɛr]
wrench	**гаечный ключ** (m)	[ˈgaitʃnɪj klytʃ]
adhesive tape	**лента-скотч** (m)	[ˈlenta skɔtʃ]
glue	**клей** (m)	[klej]
emery paper	**наждачная бумага** (f)	[naʒˈdatʃnaja bʊˈmagə]
spring	**пружина** (f)	[prʊˈʒinə]
magnet	**магнит** (m)	[magˈnit]
gloves	**перчатки** (f pl)	[pirˈtʃatki]
rope	**верёвка** (f)	[wiˈrɜfkə]
cord	**шнур** (m)	[ʃnʊr]
wire (e.g., telephone ~)	**провод** (m)	[ˈprɔvat]
cable	**кабель** (m)	[ˈkabeʎ]
sledgehammer	**кувалда** (f)	[kʊˈvaldə]
crowbar	**лом** (m)	[lɔm]
ladder	**лестница** (f)	[ˈlesnitsə]
stepladder	**стремянка** (f)	[striˈmʲankə]
to screw (tighten)	**закручивать**	[zakˈrʊtʃivatʲ]
to unscrew (vt)	**откручивать**	[atkˈrʊtʃivatʲ]
to tighten (vt)	**зажимать**	[zaʒɪˈmatʲ]
to glue, to stick	**приклеивать**	[prikˈleivatʲ]
to cut (vt)	**резать**	[ˈrezatʲ]
malfunction (fault)	**неисправность** (f)	[niispˈravnastʲ]
fault, problems	**неполадки** (f pl)	[nipaˈlatki]
repair (mending)	**починка** (f)	[paˈtʃinkə]
to repair, to mend (vt)	**ремонтировать**	[rimanˈtiravatʲ]
to adjust (machine etc.)	**регулировать**	[rigʊˈliravatʲ]
to check (to examine)	**проверять**	[praweˈrʲatʲ]
checking	**проверка** (f)	[praˈwerkə]

readings	**показание** (n)	[paka′zanie]
to reduce (vt)	**понижать**	[pani′ʒatʲ]
reduction	**понижение** (n)	[pani′ʒenie]
reliable (machine)	**надёжный**	[na′dʒʒnɪj]
complicated	**сложный**	[′slɔʒnɪj]
to rust (vi)	**ржаветь**	[rʒa′wetʲ]
rusty, rusted	**ржавый**	[′rʒavɪj]
rust	**ржавчина** (f)	[′rʒaftʃɪnə]

Transport

169. Airplane

airplane	самолёт (m)	[sama'lɜt]
air ticket	авиабилет (m)	[awiabi'let]
airline	авиакомпания (f)	[awiakam'panija]
airport	аэропорт (m)	[aəra'port]
supersonic	сверхзвуковой	[swerhzvʊka'vɔj]

captain	командир (m) корабля	[kaman'dir karab'ʎa]
crew	экипаж (m)	[ɛki'paʃ]
pilot	пилот (m)	[pi'lɔt]
flight attendant	стюардесса (f)	[styar'desə]
navigator	штурман (m)	['ʃturman]

wings	крылья (n pl)	['krɪʎja]
tail	хвост (m)	[hvɔst]
cockpit	кабина (f)	[ka'binə]
engine	двигатель (m)	['dwigateʎ]
undercarriage	шасси (n)	[ʃʌ'si]
turbine	турбина (f)	[tʊr'binə]

propeller	пропеллер (m)	[prɑ'peler]
black box	чёрный ящик (m)	['tʃɔrnɪj 'jaɕik]
control column	штурвал (m)	[ʃtʊr'val]
fuel	горючее (n)	[ga'rytʃee]

instructions	инструкция (f)	[inst'rʊktsɪja]
oxygen mask	кислородная маска (f)	[kisla'rɔdnaja 'maskə]
uniform	униформа (f)	[uni'formə]
life vest	спасательный жилет (m)	[spa'sateʎnɪj ʒɪ'let]
parachute	парашют (m)	[para'ʃyt]

takeoff	взлёт (m)	['vzlɜt]
to take off (vi)	взлетать	[vzle'tatʲ]
runway	взлётная полоса (f)	['vzlɜtnaja pala'sa]

visibility	видимость (f)	['widiməstʲ]
flight (act of flying)	полёт (m)	[pa'lɜt]
altitude	высота (f)	[vɪsa'ta]
air pocket	воздушная яма (f)	[vaz'dʊʃnaja 'jamə]

seat	место (n)	['mestə]
headphones	наушники (m pl)	[na'uʃniki]
folding tray	откидной столик (m)	[atkid'nɔj 'stɔlik]

window (in plane)	иллюминатор (m)	[ilymi'natər]
No smoking!	Курить запрещено!	[ku'ritɪ zapreɕe'nɔ]
aisle	проход (m)	[pra'hɔt]

170. Train

train	поезд (m)	['pɔezt]
suburban train	электричка (f)	[ɛlikt'ritʃkə]
fast train	скорый поезд (m)	['skɔrɪj 'pɔezt]
diesel locomotive	тепловоз (m)	[tepla'vɔs]
steam engine	паровоз (m)	[para'vɔs]

| passenger car | вагон (m) | [va'gɔn] |
| dining car | вагон-ресторан (m) | [va'gɔn resta'ran] |

rails	рельсы (pl)	['reʌsɪ]
railroad	железная дорога (f)	[ʒɛ'lʲeznaja da'rɔgə]
railway tie	шпала (f)	['ʃpalə]

platform (railway ~)	платформа (f)	[plat'fɔrmə]
track (e.g., ~ 1, 2 etc.)	путь (m)	[putʲ]
semaphore	семафор (m)	[sima'fɔr]
station	станция (f)	['stantsija]

engineer	машинист (m)	[maʃi'nist]
porter (of luggage)	носильщик (m)	[na'siʌɕik]
train steward	проводник (m)	[pravad'nik]
passenger	пассажир (m)	[pasa'ʒir]
conductor	контролёр (m)	[kantra'lɜr]

| corridor (in train) | коридор (m) | [kari'dɔr] |
| emergency break | стоп-кран (m) | [stɔp 'kran] |

compartment	купе (n)	[ku'pɛ]
berth	полка (f)	['pɔlkə]
upper berth	верхняя полка (f)	['werhnija 'pɔlkə]
lower berth	нижняя полка (f)	['niʒnija 'pɔlkə]
linen	постельное бельё (n)	[pas'teʌnae be'ʌjo]

ticket	билет (m)	[bi'let]
schedule	расписание (n)	[raspi'sanie]
timetable	табло (n)	[tab'lɔ]

to leave, to depart	отходить	[atha'ditʲ]
departure	отправление (n)	[atprav'lenie]
to arrive (about train)	прибывать	[pribɪ'vatʲ]
arrival	прибытие (n)	[pri'bɪtie]

| to be late (about train) | опаздывать | [a'pazdɪvatʲ] |
| to arrive by train | приехать поездом | [pri'ehatɪ 'pɔizdam] |

| to get on the train | сесть на поезд | [sestʲ na ˈpɔezt] |
| to get off the train | сойти с поезда | [sajˈti s ˈpɔezdə] |

| train wreck | крушение (n) | [kruˈʃɛnie] |
| to be derailed | сойти с рельс | [sajˈti s reʌs] |

steam engine	паровоз (m)	[paraˈvɔs]
stoker, fireman	кочегар (m)	[katʃeˈgar]
firebox	топка (f)	[ˈtɔpkə]
coal	уголь (m)	[ˈugaʌ]

171. Ship

| ship | корабль (m) | [kaˈrabʌ] |
| vessel | судно (n) | [ˈsudnə] |

steamship	пароход (m)	[paraˈhɔt]
riverboat	теплоход (m)	[tiplaˈhɔt]
ocean liner	лайнер (m)	[ˈlajner]
cruiser	крейсер (m)	[ˈkrejser]

yacht	яхта (f)	[ˈjahtə]
tug	буксир (m)	[bukˈsir]
barge	баржа (f)	[ˈbarʒə]
ferry	паром (m)	[paˈrɔm]

| sailing ship | парусник (m) | [ˈparusnik] |
| brigantine | бригантина (f) | [briganˈtinə] |

| ice breaker | ледокол (m) | [lidaˈkɔl] |
| submarine | подводная лодка (f) | [padˈvɔdnaja ˈlɔtkə] |

boat	лодка (f)	[ˈlɔtkə]
dinghy	шлюпка (f)	[ˈʃlypkə]
lifeboat	спасательная	[spaˈsateʌnaja
	шлюпка (f)	ʃlypkə]
motorboat	катер (m)	[ˈkater]

captain	капитан (m)	[kapiˈtan]
seaman	матрос (m)	[matˈrɔs]
sailor	моряк (m)	[maˈrʲak]
crew	экипаж (m)	[ɛkiˈpaʃ]

boatswain	боцман (m)	[ˈbɔtsman]
ship's boy	юнга (m)	[ˈjuhgə]
cook	кок (m)	[kɔk]
ship's doctor	судовой врач (m)	[sudaˈvɔj vratʃ]

| deck | палуба (f) | [ˈpalubə] |
| mast | мачта (f) | [ˈmatʃtə] |

sail	**парус** (m)	['parʊs]
hold	**трюм** (m)	[trym]
bow	**нос** (m)	[nɔs]
stern	**корма** (f)	[kar'ma]
oar	**весло** (n)	[wis'lɔ]
propeller	**винт** (m)	[wint]
cabin	**каюта** (f)	[ka'jutə]
wardroom	**кают-компания** (f)	[ka'jut kam'panija]
engine room	**машинное отделение** (n)	[ma'ʃinnae atde'lenie]
the bridge	**капитанский мостик** (m)	[kapi'tanskij 'mɔstik]
radio room	**радиорубка** (f)	[radia'rʊpkə]
wave (radio)	**волна** (f)	[val'na]
logbook	**судовой журнал** (m)	[sʊda'vɔj ʒur'nal]
spyglass	**подзорная труба** (f)	[pa'dzɔrnaja trʊ'ba]
bell	**колокол** (m)	['kɔlakal]
flag	**флаг** (m)	[flak]
rope (mooring ~)	**канат** (m)	[ka'nat]
knot (bowline etc.)	**узел** (m)	['uzel]
handrail	**поручень** (m)	['pɔrʊtʃeɲ]
gangway	**трап** (m)	[trap]
anchor	**якорь** (m)	['jakarʲ]
to weigh anchor	**поднять якорь**	[pad'natʲ 'jakarʲ]
to drop anchor	**бросить якорь**	['brɔsitʲ 'jakarʲ]
anchor chain	**якорная цепь** (f)	['jakarnaja 'tsepʲ]
port (harbor)	**порт** (m)	[pɔrt]
wharf, quay	**причал** (m)	[pri'tʃal]
to berth (moor)	**причаливать**	[pri'tʃalivatʲ]
to cast off	**отчаливать**	[a'tʃalivatʲ]
trip (voyage)	**путешествие** (n)	[pʊte'ʃɛstwie]
cruise (sea trip)	**круиз** (m)	[krʊ'is]
course (route)	**курс** (m)	[kʊrs]
route (itinerary)	**маршрут** (m)	[marʃ'rʊt]
fairway	**фарватер** (m)	[far'vater]
shallows (shoal)	**мель** (f)	[meʎ]
to run aground	**сесть на мель**	[sestʲ na 'meʎ]
storm	**буря** (f)	['bʊrʲa]
signal	**сигнал** (m)	[sig'nal]
to sink (about boat)	**тонуть**	[ta'nʊtʲ]
Man overboard!	**Человек за бортом!**	[tʃela'wek za 'bortam]
SOS	**SOS** (m)	[sɔs]
life buoy	**спасательный круг** (m)	[spa'sateʎnɪj krʊk]

172. Airport

airport	аэропорт (m)	[aera'pɔrt]
airplane	самолёт (m)	[sama'lɔt]
airline	авиакомпания (f)	[awiakam'panija]
air-traffic controller	диспетчер (m)	[dis'petʃer]

departure	вылет (m)	['vɪlet]
arrival	прилёт (m)	[pri'lɔt]
to arrive (vi)	прилететь	[prile'tetʲ]

| departure time | время (n) вылета | ['vremʲa 'vɪletə] |
| arrival time | время (n) прилёта | ['vremʲa pri'lɔtə] |

| to be delayed | задерживаться | [za'derʒɪvatsə] |
| flight delay | задержка (f) вылета | [za'derʃka 'vɪletə] |

information board	информационное табло (n)	[infarmatsɪ'ɔnae tab'lɔ]
information	информация (f)	[infar'matsɪja]
to announce (vt)	объявлять	[abʰiv'ʎatʲ]
flight (e.g., next ~)	рейс (m)	[rejs]

| customs | таможня (f) | [ta'mɔʒna] |
| customs officer | таможенник (m) | [ta'mɔʒɛnik] |

declaration	декларация (f)	[dikla'ratsɪja]
to fill out (~ a declaration)	заполнить	[za'pɔlnitʲ]
to fill out a declaration	заполнить декларацию	[za'pɔlnitʲ dekla'ratsɪju]
passport control	паспортный контроль (m)	['paspartnɪj kant'rɔʎ]

luggage	багаж (m)	[ba'gaʃ]
hand luggage	ручная кладь (f)	[rʊtʃ'naja klatʲ]
LOST-AND-FOUND	розыск (m) багажа	['rɔzɪsk baga'ʒa]
luggage cart	тележка (f) для багажа	[ti'leʃka dʎa baga'ʒa]

landing	посадка (f)	[pa'satkə]
runway	посадочная полоса (f)	[pa'sadatʃnaja pala'sa]
to land (vi)	садиться	[sa'ditsə]
airstairs	трап (m)	[trap]

check-in	регистрация (f)	[regist'ratsɪja]
check-in desk	стойка (f) регистрации	['stɔjka regist'ratsii]
to check-in (vi)	зарегистрироваться	[zaregist'riravatsə]
boarding pass	посадочный талон (m)	[pa'sadatʃnɪj ta'lɔn]
departure gate	выход (m)	['vɪhat]

transit	транзит (m)	[tran'zit]
to wait (vi, vt)	ждать	[ʒdatʲ]
departure lounge	зал (m) ожидания	[zal aʒɪ'danija]

| to see off | провожать | [prava'ʒatʲ] |
| to say goodbye | прощаться | [pra'ɕatsə] |

173. Bicycle. Motorcycle

bicycle	велосипед (m)	[wilasi'pet]
scooter	мотороллер (m)	[mata'roler]
motorcycle, bike	мотоцикл (m)	[mata'tsɪkl]

to go by bicycle	ехать на велосипеде	['ehatʲ na wilasi'pede]
handlebars	руль (m)	[ruʎ]
pedal	педаль (f)	[pi'daʎ]
brake	тормоза (m pl)	[tarma'za]
bicycle seat	седло (n)	[sid'lɔ]

pump	насос (m)	[na'sɔs]
rack	багажник (m)	[ba'gaʒnik]
front lamp	фонарь (m)	[fa'narʲ]
helmet	шлем (m)	[ʃlem]

wheel	колесо (n)	[kale'sɔ]
mudguard	крыло (n)	[krɪ'lɔ]
rim	обод (m)	['ɔbat]
spoke	спица (f)	['spitsə]

Cars

174. Types of cars

| automobile, car | автомобиль (m) | [aftama'biʎ] |
| sports car | спортивный автомобиль (m) | [spar'tivnɨj aftama'biʎ] |

limousine	лимузин (m)	[limu'zin]
off-road vehicle	внедорожник (m)	[vneda'roʒnik]
convertible	кабриолет (m)	[kabria'let]
minibus	микроавтобус (m)	[mikraaf'tobus]

| ambulance | скорая помощь (f) | ['skoraja 'pomac] |
| snowplow | снегоуборочная машина (f) | [snegau'boraʧnaja ma'ʃinə] |

truck	грузовик (m)	[gruza'wik]
tank truck	бензовоз (m)	[binza'vos]
van	фургон (m)	[fur'gon]
road tractor	тягач (m)	[ti'gaʧ]
trailer	прицеп (m)	[pri'tsep]

| comfortable | комфортабельный | [kamfar'tabeʎnɨj] |
| second hand | подержанный | [pa'derʒenɨj] |

175. Cars. Bodywork

hood	капот (m)	[ka'pot]
fender	крыло (n)	[krɨ'lo]
roof	крыша (f)	['krɨʃə]

| windshield | ветровое стекло (n) | [wetra'voe stek'lo] |
| rear-view mirror | зеркало (n) заднего вида | ['zerkalo 'zadneva 'widə] |

| windshield washer | омыватель (m) | [amɨ'vateʎ] |
| windshield wipers | дворники (pl) | ['dvorniki] |

side window	боковое стекло (n)	[baka'voe stek'lo]
window crank	стеклоподъёмник (m)	[stiklapadʰ'ɜmnik]
antenna	антенна (f)	[an'tɛnə]
sun roof	люк (m)	[lyk]
bumper	бампер (m)	['bamper]
trunk	багажник (m)	[ba'gaʒnik]

luggage rack, roof rack	багажник (m)	[ba'gaʒnik]
door	дверца (f)	['dwertsə]
door handle	ручка (f)	['rʊtʃkə]
door lock	замок (m)	[za'mɔk]

license plate	номер (m)	['nɔmer]
muffler	глушитель (m)	[glu'ʃiteʎ]
gas tank	бензобак (m)	[binza'bak]
tail pipe	выхлопная труба (f)	[vɪhlap'naja trʊ'ba]

gas, accelerator	газ (m)	[gas]
pedal	педаль (f)	[pi'daʎ]
gas pedal	педаль (f) газа	[pi'daʎ 'gazə]

brake	тормоз (m)	['tɔrmas]
brake pedal	педаль (f) тормоза	[pi'daʎ 'tɔrmazə]
to slow down (to brake)	тормозить	[tarma'zitʲ]
parking brake	стояночный тормоз (m)	[sta'janatʃnɪj 'tɔrmas]

clutch	сцепление (n)	[stsɪp'lenie]
clutch pedal	педаль (f) сцепления	[pi'daʎ stsɪp'lenija]
clutch plate	диск (m) сцепления	[disk stsɪp'lenija]
shock absorber	амортизатор (m)	[amarti'zatar]

wheel	колесо (n)	[kale'sɔ]
spare tire	запасное колесо (n)	[zapas'nɔe kale'sɔ]
wheel cover (hubcap)	колпак (m)	[kal'pak]

driving wheels	ведущие колёса (n pl)	[wi'duɕie ka'lɜsə]
front-wheel drive	переднеприводный	[pirednep'rivadnɪj]
rear-wheel drive	заднеприводный	[zadnep'rivadnɪj]
all-wheel drive	полноприводный	[polnap'rivadnɪj]

gearbox	коробка (f) передач	[ka'rɔpka pere'datʃ]
automatic	автоматический	[aftama'titʃeskij]
mechanical	механический	[miha'nitʃeskij]
gear shift	рычаг (m) коробки передач	[rɪ'tʃak ka'rɔpki pere'datʃ]

| headlight | фара (f) | ['farə] |
| headlights | фары (f pl) | ['farɪ] |

low beam	ближний свет (m)	['bliʒnij swet]
high beam	дальний свет (m)	['daʎnij swet]
brake light	стоп-сигнал (m)	[stɔp sig'nal]

parking lights	габаритные огни (pl)	[gaba'ritnɪe ag'ni]
hazard lights	аварийные огни (pl)	[ava'rijnɪe ag'ni]
fog lights	противотуманные фары (f pl)	[prativatu'mannɪe 'farɪ]

| turn signal | поворотник (m) | [pava'rɔtnik] |
| back-up light | задний ход (m) | ['zadnij hɔt] |

176. Cars. Passenger compartment

car inside	салон (m)	[sa'lɔn]
leather (attr)	кожаный	['kɔʒɛnɪj]
velour (attr)	велюровый	[wi'lyravɪj]
upholstery	обивка (f)	[a'bifkə]
instrument (gage)	прибор (m)	[pri'bɔr]
dashboard	приборный щиток (m)	[pri'bɔrnɪj ɕi'tɔk]
speedometer	спидометр (m)	[spi'dɔmetr]
needle (pointer)	стрелка (f)	['strelkə]
odometer	счётчик (m)	['ɕɜtʃik]
indicator	датчик (m)	['datʃik]
level	уровень (m)	['urawɛɲ]
indicator light	лампочка (f)	['lampatʃkə]
steering wheel	руль (m)	[ruʎ]
horn	сигнал (m)	[sig'nal]
button	кнопка (f)	['knɔpkə]
switch	переключатель (m)	[pirekly'tʃateʎ]
seat	сиденье (n)	[si'deɲje]
seat back	спинка (f)	['spinkə]
headrest	подголовник (m)	[padga'lɔvnik]
seat belt	ремень (m) безопасности	[ri'meɲ beza'pasnasti]
to fasten the belt	пристегнуть ремень	[pristeg'nutʲ ri'meɲ]
adjustment (of seats)	регулировка (f)	[riguli'rɔfkə]
airbag	воздушная подушка (f)	[vaz'duʃnaja pa'duʃkə]
air-conditioner	кондиционер (m)	[kanditsia'ner]
radio	радио (n)	['radiɔ]
CD player	CD-проигрыватель (m)	[si'di pra'igrɪvateʎ]
to turn on	включить	[fkly'tʃitʲ]
antenna	антенна (f)	[an'tɛnə]
glove box	бардачок (m)	[barda'tʃɔk]
ashtray	пепельница (f)	['pepeʎnitsə]

177. Cars. Engine

engine	двигатель (m)	['dwigateʎ]
motor	мотор (m)	[ma'tɔr]
diesel (e.g., ~ engine)	дизельный	['dizeʎnɪj]
gasoline (e.g., ~ engine)	бензиновый	[bin'zinavɪj]
engine volume	объём (m) двигателя	[a'bjom 'dwigateʎa]
power	мощность (f)	['mɔɕnastʲ]

horsepower	лошадиная сила (f)	[laʃʌ'dinaja 'silə]
piston	поршень (m)	['porʃɛɲ]
cylinder	цилиндр (m)	[tsɪ'lindr]
valve	клапан (m)	['klapan]

injector	инжектор (m)	[in'ʒɛktar]
generator	генератор (m)	[gine'ratar]
carburetor	карбюратор (m)	[karby'ratar]
engine oil	моторное масло (n)	[ma'tornae 'maslə]

radiator	радиатор (m)	[radi'atar]
cooling liquid	охлаждающая жидкость (f)	[ahlaʒ'dajuɕeja 'ʒitkastʲ]
cooling fan	вентилятор (m)	[winti'ʎatar]

battery (accumulator)	аккумулятор (m)	[akumu'ʎatar]
starter	стартер (m)	['starter]
ignition	зажигание (n)	[zaʒɪ'ganie]
spark plug	свеча (f) зажигания	[swe'tʃa zaʒɪ'ganija]

terminal (of battery)	клемма (f)	['klemmə]
plus (positive terminal)	плюс (m)	[plys]
minus (negative terminal)	минус (m)	['minʊs]
fuse	предохранитель (m)	[pridahra'niteʎ]

air filter	воздушный фильтр (m)	[vaz'duʃnɪj fiʎtr]
oil filter	масляный фильтр (m)	['maslinɪj fiʎtr]
fuel filter	топливный фильтр (m)	['toplivnɪj fiʎtr]

178. Cars. Crash. Repair

car accident	авария (f)	[a'varija]
road accident	дорожное происшествие (n)	[da'roʒnae prai'ʃestwie]
to run into ...	врезаться	['vrezatsə]
to have an accident	разбиться	[raz'bitsə]
damage	повреждение (n)	[pavreʒ'denie]
intact	целый	['tselɪj]

breakdown	авария (f), поломка (f)	[a'varija], [pa'lomkə]
to break down (vi)	сломаться	[sla'matsə]
towrope	буксировочный трос (m)	[buksi'rovatʃnɪj tros]

puncture	прокол (m)	[pra'kol]
to be flat	спустить	[spʊs'titʲ]
to pump up	накачивать	[na'katʃivatʲ]
pressure	давление (n)	[dav'lenie]
to check (to examine)	проверить	[pra'weritʲ]
repair	ремонт (m)	[ri'mont]
auto repair shop	автосервис (m)	[avto'sɛrwis]

spare part	запчасть (f)	[zɑpˈtʃastʲ]
part	деталь (f)	[diˈtaʎ]
bolt	болт (m)	[bɔlt]
screw bolt	винт (m)	[wint]
nut	гайка (f)	[ˈgajkə]
washer	шайба (f)	[ˈʃʌjbə]
bearing	подшипник (m)	[patˈʃipnik]
tube	трубка (f)	[ˈtrʊpkə]
gasket, washer	прокладка (f)	[prakˈlatkə]
cable, wire	провод (m)	[ˈprɔvat]
jack	домкрат (m)	[damkˈrat]
wrench	гаечный ключ (m)	[ˈgaitʃnij klytʃ]
hammer	молоток (m)	[malaˈtɔk]
pump	насос (m)	[naˈsɔs]
screwdriver	отвёртка (f)	[atˈwɜrtkə]
fire extinguisher	огнетушитель (m)	[agnetuˈʃiteʎ]
warning triangle	аварийный	[avaˈrijnij
	треугольник (m)	triuˈgoʎnik]
to stall (vi)	глохнуть	[ˈglohnʊtʲ]
stall	остановка (f)	[astaˈnɔfkə]
to be broken	быть сломанным	[bɪtʲ ˈslɔmanɪm]
to overheat (vi)	перегреться	[piregˈretsə]
to be clogged up	засориться	[zasaˈritsə]
to freeze (about pipe etc.)	замёрзнуть	[zaˈmɜrznʊtʲ]
to burst (vi)	лопнуть	[ˈlɔpnʊtʲ]
pressure	давление (n)	[davˈlenie]
level	уровень (m)	[ˈuraweɲ]
slack (e.g., ~ belt)	слабый	[ˈslabɪj]
dent	вмятина (f)	[ˈvmʲatinə]
knock (in motor)	стук (m)	[stʊk]
crack	трещина (f)	[ˈtreçinə]
scratch	царапина (f)	[tsaˈrapinə]

179. Cars. Road

road	дорога (f)	[daˈrɔgə]
highway, freeway	автомагистраль (f)	[aftamagistˈraʎ]
freeway	шоссе (n)	[ʃʌsˈsɛ]
direction (way)	направление (n)	[napravˈlenie]
distance	расстояние (n)	[rastaˈjanie]
bridge	мост (m)	[mɔst]
parking lot	паркинг (m)	[ˈparkink]

square	площадь (f)	['ploɕatʲ]
interchange	развязка (f)	[raz'vʲaskə]
tunnel	тоннель (m)	[ta'neʎ]

gas station	автозаправка (f)	[aftazap'rafkə]
parking lot	автостоянка (f)	[aftasta'jankə]
gas pump	бензоколонка (f)	[binzaka'lonkə]
auto repair shop	гараж (m)	[ga'raʃ]
to get gas	заправить	[zap'rawitʲ]
fuel	топливо (n)	['toplivə]
jerrycan	канистра (f)	[ka'nistrə]

asphalt	асфальт (m)	[as'faʎt]
road markings	разметка (f)	[raz'metkə]
curb	бордюр (m)	[bar'dyr]
guardrail	ограждение (n)	[agraʒ'denie]
ditch	кювет (m)	[ky'wet]
roadside	обочина (f)	[a'botʃinə]
street light	столб (m)	[stolp]

to drive (a car)	вести	[wis'ti]
to turn (steering wheel)	крутить	[kru'titʲ]
to turn (left, right etc.)	поворачивать	[pava'ratʃivatʲ]
to make a U-turn	разворачиваться	[razva'ratʃivatsə]
reverse	задний ход (m)	['zadnij hot]

to honk (about car)	сигналить	[sig'nalitʲ]
honk (sound)	звуковой сигнал (m)	[zvuka'voj sig'nal]
to get stuck	застрять	[zast'rʲatʲ]
to spin (in the mud)	буксовать	[buksa'vatʲ]
to cut, to turn off	глушить	[glu'ʃitʲ]

speed	скорость (f)	['skorostʲ]
to exceed the speed limit	превысить скорость	[pri'visitʲ 'skorostʲ]
to give sb a ticket	штрафовать	[ʃtrafa'vatʲ]
traffic lights	светофор (m)	[swita'for]
driver's license	водительские права (pl)	[va'diteʎskie pra'va]

grade crossing	переезд (m)	[pire'ezt]
intersection	перекрёсток (m)	[pirek'rɜstak]
crosswalk	пешеходный переход (m)	[peʃi'hodnɪj pere'hot]
turn (curve in road)	поворот (m)	[pava'rot]
pedestrian zone	пешеходная зона (f)	[peʃi'hodnaja 'zonə]

180. Traffic signs

| rules of the road | правила дорожного движения (f) | ['prawila da'roʒnava dwi'ʒenija] |
| traffic sign | знак (m) | [znak] |

passing (overtaking)	обгон (m)	[ab'gɔn]
curve	поворот (m)	[pava'rɔt]
U-turn	разворот (m)	[razva'rɔt]
traffic circle	круговое движение (n)	[kruga'vɔe dwi'ʒenie]
No entry	въезд запрещён	[vʰezt zapre'ɕɜn]
No vehicles allowed	движение запрещено	[dwi'ʒenie zapreɕe'nɔ]
No passing	обгон (m) запрещён	[ab'gɔn zapre'ɕɜn]
No parking	стоянка (f) запрещена	[sta'janka zapreɕe'na]
No stopping	остановка (f) запрещена	[asta'nɔfka zapreɕe'na]
dangerous turn	крутой поворот (m)	[kru'tɔj pava'rɔt]
steep descent	крутой спуск (m)	[kru'tɔj spusk]
one-way traffic	одностороннее движение (n)	[adnasta'rɔnee dwi'ʒenie]
pedestrian crossing	пешеходный переход (m)	[peʃi'hɔdnɪj pere'hɔt]
slippery road	скользкая дорога (f)	['skɔʌskaja da'rɔgə]
YIELD	уступи дорогу	[ustu'pi da'rɔgu]

PEOPLE. LIFE EVENTS

Life events

181. Holidays. Event

celebration, holiday	праздник (m)	['praznik]
national day	национальный праздник (m)	[natsɪa'naʌnɪj p'raznik]
public holiday	праздничный день (m)	['praznitʃnɪj deɲ]
to celebrate (vi, vt)	праздновать	['praznavatʲ]
event (happening)	событие (n)	[sa'bɪtie]
event (organized activity)	мероприятие (n)	[mɪrapri'jatie]
banquet (party)	банкет (m)	[ba'ɳket]
reception (formal party)	приём (m)	[priзm]
feast	пир (m)	[pir]
anniversary	годовщина (f)	[gadaf'ɕinə]
jubilee	юбилей (m)	[jubi'lej]
to celebrate (jubilee etc.)	отметить	[at'metitʲ]
New Year	Новый год (m)	['novɪj got]
Happy New Year!	С Новым Годом!	[s 'novɪm 'godam]
Christmas tree	Новогодняя ёлка (f)	[nava'godɲaja зlkə]
Christmas	Рождество (n)	[raʒdest'vo]
Merry Christmas!	Весёлого Рождества!	[wi'sзlava raʒdest'va]
Christmas tree	Рождественская ёлка (f)	[raʒ'destwenskaja зlkə]
fireworks	салют (m)	[sa'lyt]
wedding	свадьба (f)	['svadʲbə]
groom	жених (m)	[ʒɛ'nih]
bride	невеста (f)	[ni'westə]
to invite (vt)	приглашать	[prigla'ʃʌtʲ]
invitation	приглашение (n)	[prigla'ʃɛnie]
guest	гость (m)	[gɔstʲ]
to visit with sb	идти в гости	[itʲ'ti v 'gɔsti]
to greet the guests	встречать гостей	[fstre'tʃatʲ gas'tej]
gift, present	подарок (m)	[pa'darak]
to give (sth as present)	дарить	[da'ritʲ]
to receive gifts	получать подарки	[palu'tʃatʲ pa'darki]

bouquet (of flowers)	**букет** (m)	[bʊˈket]
congratulations	**поздравление** (n)	[pazdrɑvˈlenie]
to congratulate (vt)	**поздравлять**	[pazdrɑvˈʎatʲ]
greeting card	**поздравительная открытка** (f)	[pazdrɑˈwiteʎnɑja atkˈrɪtkə]
to send a postcard	**отправить открытку**	[atpˈrawitʲ atkˈrɪtkʊ]
to get a postcard	**получить открытку**	[palʊˈtʃitʲ atkˈrɪtkʊ]
toast	**тост** (m)	[tɔst]
to offer (a drink etc.)	**угощать**	[ugaˈɕatʲ]
champagne	**шампанское** (n)	[ʃʌmˈpanskae]
to have fun	**веселиться**	[wiseˈlitsə]
fun, merriment	**веселье** (n)	[wiˈseʎje]
joy	**радость** (f)	[ˈradastʲ]
dance	**танец** (m)	[ˈtanets]
to dance (vi, vt)	**танцевать**	[tantsɪˈvatʲ]
waltz	**вальс** (m)	[vaʎs]
tango	**танго** (n)	[ˈtahgə]

182. Funerals. Burial

cemetery	**кладбище** (n)	[ˈkladbiɕe]
grave, tomb	**могила** (f)	[maˈgilə]
cross	**крест** (m)	[krest]
gravestone	**надгробие** (n)	[nadgˈrɔbie]
fence	**ограда** (f)	[agˈradə]
chapel	**часовня** (f)	[tʃiˈsɔvɲa]
death	**смерть** (f)	[smertʲ]
to die (vi, vt)	**умереть**	[umiˈretʲ]
the deceased	**покойник** (m)	[paˈkɔjnik]
mourning	**траур** (m)	[ˈtraur]
to bury (vt)	**хоронить**	[haraˈnitʲ]
funeral home	**похоронное бюро** (n)	[pahaˈrɔnnae byˈrɔ]
funeral	**похороны** (pl)	[ˈpɔharanɪ]
wreath	**венок** (m)	[wiˈnɔk]
casket	**гроб** (m)	[grɔp]
hearse	**катафалк** (m)	[kataˈfalk]
shroud	**саван** (m)	[ˈsavan]
procession	**процессия** (f)	[praˈtsessija]
funeral procession	**траурная процессия** (f)	[ˈtraurnaja praˈtsesija]
cremation urn	**урна** (f)	[ˈurnə]
crematory	**крематорий** (m)	[krimaˈtorij]

obituary	некролог (m)	[nikra'lɔk]
to cry (weep)	плакать	['plakat^j]
to sob (vi)	рыдать	[rɪ'dat^j]

183. War. Soldiers

platoon	взвод (m)	[vzvɔt]
company	рота (f)	['rɔtə]
regiment	полк (m)	[pɔlk]
army	армия (f)	['armijə]
division	дивизия (f)	[di'wizijə]

| detachment | отряд (m) | [at'r^jat] |
| host (army) | войско (n) | ['vɔjskə] |

| soldier | солдат (m) | [sal'dɑt] |
| officer | офицер (m) | [afi'tser] |

private	рядовой (m)	[rida'vɔj]
sergeant	сержант (m)	[sir'ʒant]
lieutenant	лейтенант (m)	[lijte'nant]
captain	капитан (m)	[kapi'tan]
major	майор (m)	[maзr]
colonel	полковник (m)	[pal'kɔvnik]
general	генерал (m)	[gine'ral]

sailor	моряк (m)	[ma'r^jak]
captain	капитан (m)	[kapi'tan]
boatswain	боцман (m)	['bɔtsman]

artilleryman	артиллерист (m)	[artile'rist]
paratrooper	десантник (m)	[di'santnik]
pilot	лётчик (m)	['lɔtʃik]
navigator	штурман (m)	['ʃturman]
mechanic	механик (m)	[mi'hanik]

pioneer (sapper)	сапёр (m)	[sa'pзr]
parachutist	парашютист (m)	[paraʃy'tist]
scout	разведчик (m)	[raz'wetʃik]
sniper	снайпер (m)	['snajper]

patrol (group)	патруль (m)	[pat'rʊʎ]
to patrol (vi, vt)	патрулировать	[patrʊ'liravat^j]
sentry, guard	часовой (m)	[tʃisa'vɔj]

warrior	воин (m)	['vɔin]
hero	герой (m)	[gi'rɔj]
heroine	героиня (f)	[gira'iɲa]
patriot	патриот (m)	[patri'ɔt]
traitor	предатель (m)	[pri'dateʎ]

betrayer	изменник (m)	[iz'mennik]
deserter	дезертир (m)	[dizer'tir]
to desert (vi)	дезертировать	[dizer'tiravatʲ]

mercenary	наёмник (m)	[naᴣmnik]
recruit	новобранец (m)	[navab'ranets]
volunteer	доброволец (m)	[dabra'volets]

dead	убитый (m)	[u'bitɪj]
wounded	раненый (m)	['ranenɪj]
prisoner of war	пленный (m)	['plennɪj]

184. War. Military actions. Part 1

war	война (f)	[vaj'na]
to be at war	воевать	[vai'vatʲ]
civil war	гражданская война (f)	[graʒ'danskaja vaj'na]

treacherously	вероломно	[wira'lomnə]
declaration (~ of war)	объявление (n)	[abʰiv'lenie]
to declare (~ war)	объявить	[abʰi'witʲ]
aggression	агрессия (f)	[ag'resija]
to attack (invade)	нападать	[napa'datʲ]

to invade (vt)	захватывать	[zah'vatɪvatʲ]
invader	захватчик (m)	[zah'vatʃik]
conqueror	завоеватель (m)	[zavae'vateʌ]

defense	оборона (f)	[aba'rɔnə]
to defend (a country etc.)	оборонять	[abara'ɲatʲ]
to defend oneself	обороняться	[abara'ɲatsə]
enemy	враг (m)	[vrak]
hostile (noun)	противник (m)	[pra'tivnik]
hostile (attr)	вражеский	['vraʒɪskij]

| strategy | стратегия (f) | [stra'tegija] |
| tactics | тактика (f) | ['taktikə] |

order	приказ (m)	[pri'kas]
command (order)	команда (f)	[ka'mandə]
to order (vi, vt)	приказывать	[pri'kazɪvatʲ]
mission	задание (n)	[za'danie]
secret (adj)	секретный	[sik'retnɪj]

| battle | сражение (n) | [sra'ʒenie] |
| combat | бой (m) | [bɔj] |

attack	атака (f)	[a'takə]
storming (assault)	штурм (m)	[ʃturm]
to storm (vt)	штурмовать	[ʃturma'vatʲ]

siege (to be under ~)	осада (f)	[ɑ'sɑdə]
offensive (noun)	наступление (n)	[nɑstup'lenie]
to go on the offensive	наступать	[nɑstu'patʲ]

| retreat | отступление (n) | [ɑtstup'lenie] |
| to retreat (vi) | отступать | [ɑtstu'patʲ] |

| encirclement | окружение (n) | [ɑkru'ʒenie] |
| to encircle (vt) | окружать | [ɑkru'ʒatʲ] |

bombing (by aircraft)	бомбёжка (f)	[bam'bʒʃkə]
to drop a bomb	сбросить бомбу	['zbrɔsitʲ 'bɔmbu]
to bomb (vt)	бомбить	[bam'bitʲ]
explosion	взрыв (m)	[fzrɪf]

shot	выстрел (m)	['vɪstrel]
to fire a shot	выстрелить	['vɪstrelitʲ]
shooting	стрельба (f)	[streʎ'ba]

to take aim (at …)	целиться	['tselitsə]
to point (a gun)	навести	[nɑwes'ti]
to hit (the target)	попасть	[pɑ'pastʲ]

to sink (e.g., ~ a ship)	потопить	[pɑtɑ'pitʲ]
hole (in a ship)	пробоина (f)	[prɑ'bɔinə]
to founder, to sink	идти ко дну	[itʲ'ti kɑ 'dnu]

front (at war)	фронт (m)	[frɔnt]
rear (noun)	тыл (m)	[tɪl]
evacuation	эвакуация (f)	[ɛvɑku'atsɪja]
to evacuate (vt)	эвакуировать	[ɛvɑku'irɑvatʲ]

trench	окоп (m)	[ɑ'kɔp]
barbwire	колючая проволока (f)	[kɑ'lytʃaja 'prɔvɑlɑkə]
barrier	заграждение (n)	[zɑgrɑʒ'denie]
watchtower	вышка (f)	['vɪʃkə]

hospital	госпиталь (m)	['gɔspitɑʎ]
to wound (vi, vt)	ранить	['ranitʲ]
wound	рана (f)	['ranə]
wounded (noun)	раненый (m)	['ranenɪj]
to be injured	получить ранение	[pɑlu'tʃitʲ ra'nenie]
serious	тяжёлый	[ti'ʒɜlɪj]

185. War. Military actions. Part 2

captivity	плен (m)	[plen]
to take sb captive	взять в плен	[vzʲatʲ f 'plen]
to be in captivity	быть в плену	[bɪtʲ f ple'nu]
to be taken prisoner	попасть в плен	[pɑ'pastʲ f plen]

concentration camp	концлагерь (m)	[kants'lager']
prisoner of war	пленный (m)	['plennɪj]
to escape (vi)	бежать	[bi'ʒat']
to betray (vt)	предать	[pri'dat']
betrayer	предатель (m)	[pri'dateʌ]
betrayal	предательство (n)	[pri'dateʌstvə]
to execute (shoot)	расстрелять	[rastre'ʌat']
execution (shooting)	расстрел (m)	[rast'rel]
uniform	обмундирование (n)	[abmundira'vanie]
shoulder board	погон (m)	[pa'gon]
gas mask	противогаз (m)	[prativa'gas]
radio transmitter	рация (f)	['ratsɪja]
cipher, code	шифр (m)	[ʃɪfr]
conspiracy	конспирация (f)	[kanspi'ratsɪja]
password	пароль (m)	[pa'roʌ]
mine (explosive)	мина (f)	['minə]
to mine (road etc.)	заминировать	[zami'niravat']
minefield	минное поле (n)	['minnae 'pole]
air-raid warning	воздушная тревога (f)	[vaz'duʃnaja tri'vogə]
alarm (warning)	тревога (f)	[tri'vogə]
signal	сигнал (m)	[sig'nal]
signal flare	сигнальная ракета (f)	[sig'naʌnaja ra'ketə]
headquarters	штаб (m)	[ʃtap]
reconnaissance	разведка (f)	[raz'wetkə]
situation	обстановка (f)	[apsta'nofkə]
report	рапорт (m)	['rapart]
ambush	засада (f)	[za'sadə]
reinforcement (of army)	подкрепление (n)	[patkrep'lenie]
target	мишень (f)	[mi'ʃən]
shooting ground	полигон (m)	[pali'gon]
military exercise	манёвры (m pl)	[ma'nɜvrɪ]
panic	паника (f)	['panikə]
devastation	разруха (f)	[raz'ruhə]
destruction, ruins	разрушения (f)	[razru'ʃenija]
to destroy (vt)	разрушать	[razru'ʃʌt']
to survive (vi, vt)	выжить	['vɪʒɪt']
to disarm (vt)	обезоружить	[abiza'ruʒɪt']
to handle (e.g., ~ a gun)	обращаться	[abra'ɕatsə]
Attention!	Смирно!	['smirna]
At ease!	Вольно!	['voʌna]
feat (of courage)	подвиг (m)	['podwik]

| oath (vow) | клятва (f) | ['kʌatvə] |
| to swear (an oath) | клясться | ['kʌastsə] |

decoration (medal etc.)	награда (f)	[nag'radə]
to award (give medal to)	награждать	[nagraʒ'datʲ]
medal	медаль (f)	[mi'daʎ]
order (e.g., ~ of Merit)	орден (m)	['ɔrden]

victory	победа (f)	[pa'bedə]
defeat	поражение (n)	[para'ʒɛnie]
armistice	перемирие (n)	[pire'mirie]

banner (flag)	знамя (f)	['znamʲa]
glory (honor, fame)	слава (f)	['slavə]
parade	парад (m)	[pa'rat]
to march (on parade)	маршировать	[marʃira'vatʲ]

186. Weapons

weapons	оружие (n)	[a'ruʒie]
firearm	огнестрельное оружие (n)	[agnest'reʌnae a'ruʒie]
cold weapons (knives etc.)	холодное оружие (n)	[ha'lɔdnae a'ruʒie]

chemical weapons	химическое оружие (n)	[hi'mitʃeskae a'ruʒie]
nuclear	ядерный	['jadernɪj]
nuclear weapons	ядерное оружие (n)	['jadernae a'ruʒie]

| bomb | бомба (f) | ['bɔmbə] |
| atomic bomb | атомная бомба (f) | ['atamnaja 'bɔmbə] |

pistol (gun)	пистолет (m)	[pista'let]
rifle	ружьё (n)	[ru'ʒjo]
submachine gun	автомат (m)	[afta'mat]
machine gun	пулемёт (m)	[pule'mɜt]

muzzle	дуло (n)	['dulə]
barrel	ствол (m)	[stvɔl]
caliber	калибр (m)	[ka'libr]

trigger	курок (m)	[ku'rɔk]
sight (aiming device)	прицел (m)	[pri'tsel]
magazine	магазин (m)	[maga'zin]
butt (of rifle)	приклад (m)	[prik'lat]

| hand grenade | граната (f) | [gra'natə] |
| explosive | взрывчатка (f) | [vzrɪf'tʃatkə] |

| bullet | пуля (f) | ['puʌa] |
| cartridge | патрон (m) | [pat'rɔn] |

| charge | заряд (m) | [zɑˈrʲat] |
| ammunition | боеприпасы (pl) | [bɑipriˈpasɪ] |

bomber (aircraft)	бомбардировщик (m)	[bambardiˈrofɕik]
fighter	истребитель (m)	[istreˈbiteʎ]
helicopter	вертолёт (m)	[wirtɑˈlɔt]

anti-aircraft gun	зенитка (f)	[zeˈnitkə]
tank	танк (m)	[tank]
tank gun	пушка (f)	[ˈpuʃkə]

| artillery | артиллерия (f) | [artiˈlerija] |
| to take aim (at …) | навести на … | [nɑwesˈti na] |

shell (projectile)	снаряд (m)	[snɑˈrʲat]
mortar bomb	мина (f)	[ˈminə]
mortar	миномёт (m)	[minɑˈmɜt]
splinter (of shell)	осколок (m)	[asˈkɔlak]

submarine	подводная лодка (f)	[padˈvɔdnaja ˈlɔtkə]
torpedo	торпеда (f)	[tarˈpedə]
missile	ракета (f)	[rɑˈketə]

to load (gun)	заряжать	[zariˈʒatʲ]
to shoot (vi)	стрелять	[striˈʎatʲ]
to take aim (at …)	целиться	[ˈʦəliʦə]
bayonet	штык (m)	[ʃtɪk]

epee	шпага (f)	[ˈʃpagə]
saber (e.g., cavalry ~)	сабля (f)	[ˈsabʎa]
spear (weapon)	копьё (n)	[kɑˈpjo]
bow	лук (m)	[luk]
arrow	стрела (f)	[streˈla]
musket	мушкет (m)	[muʃˈket]
crossbow	арбалет (m)	[arbaˈlet]

187. Ancient people

primitive (prehistoric)	первобытный	[pirvɑˈbɪtnɪj]
prehistoric	доисторический	[daistɑˈritɕeskij]
ancient (civilization etc.)	древний	[ˈdrevnij]

Stone Age	Каменный Век (m)	[ˈkamenɪj wek]
Bronze Age	Бронзовый Век (m)	[ˈbrɔnzavɪj wek]
Ice Age	ледниковый период (m)	[ledniˈkɔvɪj piˈriat]

tribe	племя (f)	[ˈplemʲa]
cannibal	людоед (m)	[lʲydɑˈet]
hunter	охотник (m)	[aˈhɔtnik]
to hunt (vi, vt)	охотиться	[aˈhɔtiʦə]

mammoth	мамонт (m)	['mamənt]
cave	пещера (f)	[pi'ɕerə]
fire	огонь (m)	[a'gɔɲ]
campfire	костёр (m)	[kas'tɜr]
rock painting	наскальный рисунок (m)	[nas'kaʎnɪj ri'sʊnak]
tool (e.g., stone ax)	орудие (n) труда	[a'rʊdie trʊ'da]
spear	копьё (n)	[ka'pjo]
stone ax	каменный топор (m)	['kamenɪj ta'pɔr]
to be at war	воевать	[vai'vatʲ]
to domesticate (tame)	приручать	[prirʊ'ʧatʲ]
idol	идол (m)	['idal]
to worship (vt)	поклоняться	[pakla'ɲatsə]
superstition	суеверие (n)	[sʊi'werie]
evolution	эволюция (f)	[ɛva'lytsɪja]
development	развитие (n)	[raz'witie]
disappearance	исчезновение (n)	[iɕizna'wenie]
to adapt oneself	приспосабливаться	[prispa'sablivatsə]
archeology	археология (f)	[arhea'lɔgija]
archeologist	археолог (m)	[arhe'ɔlak]
archeological	археологический	[arheala'gitʃeskij]
excavation site	раскопки (pl)	[ras'kɔpki]
excavations	раскопки (pl)	[ras'kɔpki]
find (object)	находка (f)	[na'hɔtkə]
fragment	фрагмент (m)	[frag'ment]

188. Middle Ages

people (nation)	народ (m)	[na'rɔt]
peoples	народы (m pl)	[na'rɔdɪ]
tribe	племя (n)	['plemʲa]
tribes	племена (n pl)	[plime'na]
barbarians	варвары (m pl)	['varvarɪ]
Gauls	галлы (m pl)	['galɪ]
Goths	готы (m pl)	['gɔtɪ]
Slavs	славяне (pl)	[sla'vʲane]
Vikings	викинги (m pl)	['wikihgi]
Romans	римляне (pl)	['rimline]
Roman	римский	['rimskij]
Byzantines	византийцы (m pl)	[wizan'tijtsɪ]
Byzantium	Византия (f)	[wizan'tija]
Byzantine	византийский	[wizan'tijskij]
emperor	император (m)	[impe'ratar]

leader, chief	вождь (m)	[vɔʒtʲ]
powerful (e.g., ~ king)	могущественный	[maˈɡuɕestwenɪj]
king	король (m)	[kaˈrɔʎ]
ruler (sovereign)	правитель (m)	[praˈwiteʎ]
knight	рыцарь (m)	[ˈrɪtsarʲ]
knightly	рыцарский	[ˈrɪtsarskij]
feudal lord	феодал (m)	[fiaˈdal]
feudal (adj)	феодальный	[fiaˈdaʎnɪj]
vassal	вассал (m)	[vasˈsal]
duke	герцог (m)	[ˈɡertsak]
earl	граф (m)	[ɡraf]
baron	барон (m)	[baˈrɔn]
bishop	епископ (m)	[eˈpiskap]
armor	доспехи (pl)	[dasˈpehi]
shield	щит (m)	[ɕit]
sword	меч (m)	[metʃ]
visor	забрало (n)	[zabˈralə]
chain armor	кольчуга (f)	[kaʎˈtʃuɡə]
crusade	крестовый поход (m)	[krisˈtɔvɪj paˈhɔt]
crusader	крестоносец (m)	[krisˈtɔnasets]
territory	территория (f)	[tiriˈtɔrija]
to attack (invade)	нападать	[napaˈdatʲ]
to conquer (vt)	завоевать	[zavaiˈvatʲ]
to occupy (invade)	захватить	[zahvaˈtitʲ]
siege (to be under ~)	осада (f)	[aˈsadə]
besieged	осаждённый	[asaʒˈdɜnɪj]
to besiege (vt)	осаждать	[asaʒˈdatʲ]
inquisition	инквизиция (f)	[inkwiˈzitsɪja]
inquisitor	инквизитор (m)	[inkwiˈzitar]
torture	пытка (f)	[ˈpɪtkə]
cruel	жестокий	[ʒɪsˈtɔkij]
heretic	еретик (m)	[eriˈtik]
heresy	ересь (f)	[ˈeresʲ]
seafaring	мореплавание (n)	[marepˈlavanie]
pirate	пират (m)	[piˈrat]
piracy	пиратство (n)	[piˈratstvə]
boarding (attack)	абордаж (m)	[abarˈdaʃ]
loot	добыча (f)	[daˈbɪtʃə]
treasures	сокровища (pl)	[sakˈrɔwiɕə]
discovery	открытие (n)	[atkˈrɪtie]
to discover (new land etc.)	открыть	[atkˈrɪtʲ]
expedition (noun)	экспедиция (f)	[ɛkspeˈditsɪja]
musketeer	мушкетёр (m)	[muʃkeˈtɜr]

cardinal	кардинал (m)	[kardiˈnɑl]
heraldry	геральдика (f)	[giˈrɑʎdikə]
heraldic	геральдический	[girɑʎˈditʃeskij]

189. Leader. Chief. Authorities

king	король (m)	[kɑˈrɔʎ]
queen	королева (f)	[kɑrɑˈlevə]
royal	королевский	[kɑrɑˈlefskij]
kingdom	королевство (n)	[kɑrɑˈlefstvə]

| prince | принц (m) | [prints] |
| princess | принцесса (f) | [prinˈtsəsə] |

president	президент (m)	[priziˈdent]
vice-president	вице-президент (m)	[ˈwitsə preziˈdent]
senator	сенатор (m)	[siˈnɑtɑr]

monarch	монарх (m)	[mɑˈnɑrh]
ruler (sovereign)	правитель (m)	[prɑˈwiteʎ]
dictator	диктатор (m)	[dikˈtɑtɑr]
tyrant	тиран (m)	[tiˈrɑn]
magnate	магнат (m)	[mɑgˈnɑt]
director	директор (m)	[diˈrektɑr]
chief	шеф (m)	[ʃef]
manager (director)	управляющий (m)	[uprɑvˈʎɑjuɕij]
boss	босс (m)	[bɔs]
owner	хозяин (m)	[hɑˈzʲain]

head (~ of delegation)	глава (f)	[glaˈvɑ]
authorities	власти (pl)	[ˈvlasti]
management (of hotel etc.)	начальство (n)	[nɑˈtʃaʎstvə]

governor	губернатор (m)	[guberˈnɑtɑr]
consul	консул (m)	[ˈkɔnsul]
diplomat	дипломат (m)	[diplɑˈmat]
mayor	мэр (m)	[mɛr]
sheriff	шериф (m)	[ʃɪˈrif]

emperor	император (m)	[impeˈrɑtɑr]
tsar, czar	царь (m)	[tsarʲ]
Pharaoh	фараон (m)	[farɑˈɔn]
khan	хан (m)	[hɑn]

190. Road. Way. Directions

| road | дорога (f) | [dɑˈrɔgə] |
| way | путь (m) | [putʲ] |

freeway	шоссе (n)	[ʃʌsˈsɛ]
highway, freeway	автомагистраль (f)	[aftamagistˈraʎ]
interstate	национальная дорога (f)	[natsɪaˈnaʎnaja daˈrɔgə]

| main road | главная дорога (f) | [ˈglavnaja daˈrɔgə] |
| dirt road | просёлочная дорога (f) | [praˈsɜlatʃnaja daˈrɔgə] |

| pathway | тропа (f) | [traˈpa] |
| footpath | тропинка (f) | [traˈpinkə] |

Where?	Где?	[gde]
Where (to)?	Куда?	[kʊˈda]
Where … from?	Откуда?	[atˈkʊda]

| direction (way) | направление (n) | [napravˈlenie] |
| to point (e.g., ~ the way) | указать | [ukaˈzatʲ] |

to the left	налево	[naˈlevə]
to the right	направо	[napˈravə]
straight ahead	прямо	[ˈprʲamə]
back (e.g., to turn ~)	назад	[naˈzat]
turn, curve	поворот (m)	[pavaˈrot]
to turn (left, right etc.)	поворачивать	[pavaˈratʃivatʲ]
to make a U-turn	разворачиваться	[razvaˈratʃivatsə]

| to be visible | виднеться | [widˈnetsə] |
| to appear (come into view) | показаться | [pakaˈzatsə] |

stop, halt (in journey)	остановка (f)	[astaˈnofkə]
to rest, to halt (vi)	отдохнуть	[adah'nutʲ]
rest (pause)	отдых (m)	[ˈɔddɪh]

to lose one's way	заблудиться	[zabluˈditsə]
to lead to … (about road)	вести к …	[wisˈti k]
to reach … (arrive at)	выйти к …	[ˈvɪjti k]
stretch (of road)	отрезок (m)	[atˈrezak]

asphalt	асфальт (m)	[asˈfaʎt]
curb	бордюр (m)	[barˈdyr]
ditch	канава (f)	[kaˈnavə]
manhole	люк (m)	[lyk]
roadside	обочина (f)	[aˈbotʃinə]
pit, pothole	яма (f)	[ˈjamə]

| to go (on foot) | идти | [itʲˈti] |
| to pass (overtake) | обогнать | [abagˈnatʲ] |

step (footstep)	шаг (m)	[ʃʌk]
on foot	пешком	[piʃˈkɔm]
to block (road)	перегородить	[peregaraˈditʲ]
boom barrier	шлагбаум (m)	[ʃlagˈbaum]
dead end	тупик (m)	[tʊˈpik]

191. Breaking the law. Criminals. Part 1

bandit	**бандит** (m)	[banʹdit]
crime	**преступление** (n)	[pristʊpʹlenie]
criminal (person)	**преступник** (m)	[prisʹtʊpnik]
thief	**вор** (m)	[vɔr]
stealing	**воровство** (n)	[varafstʹvɔ]
theft	**кража** (f)	[ʹkraʒə]
to kidnap (vt)	**похитить**	[paʹhititʲ]
kidnapping	**похищение** (n)	[pahiʹɕenie]
kidnapper	**похититель** (m)	[pahiʹtiteʎ]
ransom	**выкуп** (m)	[ʹvɪkʊp]
to ask for ransom	**требовать выкуп**	[ʹtrebavatʲ ʹvɪkʊp]
to rob (vt)	**грабить**	[ʹgrabitʲ]
robber	**грабитель** (m)	[graʹbiteʎ]
to extort (vt)	**вымогать**	[vɪmaʹgatʲ]
extortionist	**вымогатель** (m)	[vɪmaʹgateʎ]
extortion	**вымогательство** (n)	[vɪmaʹgateʎstvə]
to murder, to kill	**убить**	[uʹbitʲ]
murder	**убийство** (n)	[uʹbijstvə]
murderer	**убийца** (f)	[uʹbijʦə]
gunshot	**выстрел** (m)	[ʹvɪstrel]
to fire a shot	**выстрелить**	[ʹvɪstrelitʲ]
to shoot down	**застрелить**	[zastreʹlitʲ]
to shoot (vi)	**стрелять**	[striʹʎatʲ]
shooting	**стрельба** (f)	[streʎʹba]
incident (fight etc.)	**происшествие** (n)	[praiʹʃɛstwie]
fight, brawl	**драка** (f)	[ʹdrakə]
victim	**жертва** (f)	[ʹʒertvə]
to damage (vt)	**повредить**	[pavreʹditʲ]
damage	**ущерб** (m)	[uʹɕerp]
dead body	**труп** (m)	[trʊp]
grave (e.g., ~ crime)	**тяжкий**	[ʹtʲaʃkij]
to attack (vi, vt)	**напасть**	[naʹpastʲ]
to beat (dog, person)	**бить**	[bitʲ]
to beat sb up	**избить**	[izʹbitʲ]
to take (snatch)	**отнять**	[atʹɲatʲ]
to stab to death	**зарезать**	[zaʹrezatʲ]
to maim (vt)	**изувечить**	[izuʹwetʃitʲ]
to wound (vi, vt)	**ранить**	[ʹranitʲ]
blackmail	**шантаж** (m)	[ʃʌnʹtaʃ]

| to blackmail (vt) | шантажировать | [ʃʌntaˈʒiravatʲ] |
| blackmailer | шантажист (m) | [ʃʌntaˈʒist] |

racketeering	рэкет (m)	[ˈrɛket]
racketeer	рэкетир (m)	[rɛkeˈtir]
gangster	гангстер (m)	[ˈgahgster]
mafia, Mob	мафия (f)	[ˈmafija]

pickpocket	карманный воришка (m)	[karˈmanɨj vaˈriʃkə]
burglar	взломщик (m)	[ˈvzlɔmɕik]
smuggling	контрабанда (f)	[kantraˈbandə]
smuggler	контрабандист (m)	[kantrabanˈdist]

forgery	подделка (f)	[paˈdelkə]
to forge (counterfeit)	подделывать	[paˈdelɨvatʲ]
fake, forged (adj)	фальшивый	[faʎˈʃivɨj]

192. Breaking the law. Criminals. Part 2

rape	изнасилование (n)	[iznaˈsilavanie]
to rape (vt)	изнасиловать	[iznaˈsilavatʲ]
rapist	насильник (m)	[naˈsiʎnik]
maniac	маньяк (m)	[maˈɲjak]

prostitute (woman)	проститутка (f)	[prastiˈtutkə]
prostitution	проституция (f)	[prastiˈtutsija]
pimp	сутенёр (m)	[suteˈnɜr]

drug addict	наркоман (m)	[narkaˈman]
drug dealer	торговец	[tarˈgoweʦ
	наркотиками (m)	narˈkɔtikami]

to blow up (bomb)	взорвать	[vzarˈvatʲ]
explosion	взрыв (m)	[fzrɨf]
to set fire	поджечь	[paˈdʒetʃ]
incendiary (arsonist)	поджигатель (m)	[padʒɨˈgateʎ]

terrorism	терроризм (m)	[tiraˈrizm]
terrorist	террорист (m)	[tiraˈrist]
hostage	заложник (m)	[zaˈlɔʒnik]

to swindle (vt)	обмануть	[abmaˈnutʲ]
swindle	обман (m)	[abˈman]
swindler	мошенник (m)	[maˈʃɛnnik]

to bribe (vt)	подкупить	[patkuˈpitʲ]
bribery	подкуп (m)	[ˈpɔtkup]
bribe	взятка (f)	[ˈvzʲatkə]
poison	яд (m)	[jat]
to poison (vt)	отравить	[atraˈwitʲ]

to poison oneself	отравиться	[atra'witsə]
suicide (act)	самоубийство (n)	[samau'bijstvə]
suicide (person)	самоубийца (m, f)	[samau'bijtsə]

to threaten (vt)	угрожать	[ugra'ʒatʲ]
threat	угроза (f)	[ug'rozə]
to make an attempt	покушаться	[paku'ʃʌtsə]
attempt (attack)	покушение (n)	[paku'ʃenie]

| to steal (a car) | угнать | [ug'natʲ] |
| to hijack (a plane) | угнать | [ug'natʲ] |

| revenge | месть (f) | [mestʲ] |
| to avenge (vt) | мстить | [mstitʲ] |

to torture (vt)	пытать	[pɪ'tatʲ]
torture	пытка (f)	['pɪtkə]
to abuse (treat cruelly)	мучить	['mutʃitʲ]

pirate	пират (m)	[pi'rat]
hooligan	хулиган (m)	[huli'gan]
armed	вооружённый	[vaaru'ʒʌnnɪj]
violence	насилие (n)	[na'silie]
illegal (unlawful)	нелегальный	[nile'gaʌnɪj]

| spying (noun) | шпионаж (m) | [ʃpia'naʃ] |
| to spy (vi) | шпионить | [ʃpi'ɔnitʲ] |

193. Police. Law. Part 1

| justice | правосудие (n) | [prava'sudie] |
| court (court room) | суд (m) | [sut] |

judge	судья (f)	[su'dja]
jurors	присяжные (pl)	[pri'sʲaʒnɪe]
jury trial	суд (m) присяжных	[sut pri'sʲaʒnɪh]
to judge (vt)	судить	[su'ditʲ]

lawyer, attorney	адвокат (m)	[adva'kat]
accused	подсудимый (m)	[patsu'dimɪj]
dock	скамья (f) подсудимых	[ska'mja patsu'dimɪh]

| charge | обвинение (n) | [abwi'nenie] |
| accused | обвиняемый (m) | [abwi'ɲaemɪj] |

| sentence | приговор (m) | [priga'vor] |
| to sentence (vt) | приговорить | [prigava'ritʲ] |

| guilty (e.g., ~ of murder) | виновник (m) | [wi'nɔvnik] |
| to punish (vt) | наказать | [naka'zatʲ] |

punishment	наказание (n)	[nakaˈzanie]
fine (penalty)	штраф (m)	[ʃtraf]
life imprisonment	пожизненное заключение (n)	[paˈʒiznenae zaklyˈtʃenie]

death penalty	смертная казнь (f)	[ˈsmertnaja kazɲ]
electric chair	электрический стул (m)	[ɛlektˈritʃeskij stʊl]
gallows	виселица (f)	[ˈwiselitsə]

| to execute (vt) | казнить | [kazˈnitʲ] |
| execution | казнь (f) | [kazɲ] |

| prison, jail | тюрьма (f) | [tyrʲˈma] |
| cell | камера (f) | [ˈkamerə] |

escort	конвой (m)	[kanˈvoj]
prison guard	надзиратель (m)	[nadziˈrateʎ]
prisoner	заключённый (m)	[zaklyˈtʃonnɪj]

| handcuffs | наручники (pl) | [naˈrʊtʃniki] |
| to handcuff (vt) | надеть наручники | [naˈdetʲ naˈrʊtʃniki] |

escape	побег (m)	[paˈbek]
to escape (vi, vt)	убежать	[ubeˈʒatʲ]
to disappear (vi)	исчезнуть	[iˈɕeznʊtʲ]
to release (from prison)	освободить	[asvabaˈditʲ]
amnesty	амнистия (f)	[amˈnistija]

police	полиция (f)	[paˈlitsɪja]
policeman	полицейский (m)	[paliˈtsejskij]
police station	полицейский участок (m)	[paliˈtsejskij uˈtʃastak]
billy club	резиновая дубинка (f)	[reˈzinavaja dʊˈbinkə]
loudspeaker	рупор (m)	[ˈrʊpar]

patrol car	патрульная машина (f)	[patˈrʊʎnaja maˈʃinə]
siren	сирена (f)	[siˈrenə]
to turn on the siren	включить сирену	[fklyˈtʃitʲ siˈrenʊ]
siren call	вой (m)	[voj]

scene of the crime	место (n) происшествия	[ˈmesta praiˈʃɛstwija]
witness	свидетель (m)	[swiˈdeteʎ]
freedom	свобода (f)	[svaˈbodə]
accomplice	сообщник (m)	[saˈopɕnik]
to flee	скрыться	[ˈskrɪtsə]
footprint	след (m)	[slet]

194. Police. Law. Part 2

search (for a criminal)	розыск (m)	[ˈrozɪsk]
to look for …	разыскивать …	[raˈzɪskivatʲ]
suspicion	подозрение (n)	[padazˈrenie]

suspicious (suspect)	**подозрительный**	[pɑdɑzʼritɛʎnɪj]
to stop (cause to halt)	**остановить**	[ɑstɑnɑʼwitʲ]
to detain (keep in custody)	**задержать**	[zɑderʼʒɑtʲ]
case (trial)	**дело** (n)	[ʼdelə]
investigation	**следствие** (n)	[ʼsletstwie]
detective	**детектив, сыщик** (m)	[dɛtɛkʼtif], [ʼsɪɕik]
investigator	**следователь** (m)	[ʼsledavateʎ]
version	**версия** (f)	[ʼwersija]
motive	**мотив** (m)	[mɑʼtif]
interrogation	**допрос** (m)	[dɑpʼrɔs]
to interrogate (vt)	**допрашивать**	[dɑpʼrɑʃivatʲ]
to question (interrogate)	**опрашивать**	[ɑpʼrɑʃivatʲ]
questioning	**опрос** (m)	[ɑpʼrɔs]
checking (police ~)	**проверка** (f)	[prɑʼwerkə]
round-up	**облава** (f)	[ɑbʼlavə]
search (by police)	**обыск** (m)	[ʼɔbɪsk]
chase (pursuit)	**погоня** (f)	[pɑʼgɔɲə]
to pursue, to chase	**преследовать**	[prisʼledavatʲ]
to track (a criminal)	**следить**	[sliʼditʲ]
arrest	**арест** (m)	[ɑʼrest]
to arrest (sb)	**арестовать**	[ɑristɑʼvatʲ]
to catch (thief etc.)	**поймать**	[pɑjʼmatʲ]
capture	**поимка** (f)	[pɑʼimkə]
document	**документ** (m)	[dɑkʊʼment]
proof (evidence)	**доказательство** (n)	[dɑkɑʼzatɛʎstvə]
to prove (vt)	**доказывать**	[dɑʼkazɪvatʲ]
footprint	**след** (m)	[slet]
fingerprints	**отпечатки** (m pl) **пальцев**	[ɑtpeʼʧatki ʼpaʎtsəf]
piece of evidence	**улика** (f)	[uʼlikə]
alibi	**алиби** (n)	[ʼɑlibi]
innocent (not guilty)	**невиновный**	[newiʼnɔvnɪj]
injustice (unjust act)	**несправедливость** (f)	[nisprawedʼlivastʲ]
unjust, unfair	**несправедливый**	[nisprawedʼlivɪj]
crime (e.g., ~ reporter)	**криминальный**	[krimiʼnaʎnɪj]
to confiscate (vt)	**конфисковать**	[kanfiskɑʼvatʲ]
drug (illegal substance)	**наркотик** (m)	[narʼkotik]
weapon, gun	**оружие** (n)	[ɑʼruʒie]
to disarm (vt)	**обезоружить**	[abizɑʼruʒɪtʲ]
to order (command)	**приказывать**	[priʼkazɪvatʲ]
to disappear (vi)	**исчезнуть**	[iʼɕeznutʲ]
law	**закон** (m)	[zɑʼkɔn]
legal	**законный**	[zɑʼkɔnnɪj]
illegal	**незаконный**	[nizɑʼkɔnnɪj]
responsibility	**ответственность** (f)	[atʼwetstwenastʲ]
responsible	**ответственный**	[atʼwetstwenɪj]

NATURE

The Earth. Part 1

195. Outer space

cosmos	космос (m)	['kosmas]
space (e.g., ~ flight)	космический	[kas'mitʃeskij]
outer space	космическое пространство	[kas'mitʃeskae prast'ranstve]
world	мир (m)	[mir]
galaxy	галактика (f)	[ga'laktike]
star	звезда (f)	[zwez'da]
constellation	созвездие (n)	[saz'wezdie]
planet	планета (f)	[pla'nete]
satellite	спутник (m)	['sputnik]
meteorite	метеорит (m)	[mitea'rit]
comet	комета (f)	[ka'mete]
asteroid	астероид (m)	[aste'roit]
orbit	орбита (f)	[ar'bite]
to rotate (vi)	вращаться	[vra'ɕatsə]
atmosphere	атмосфера (f)	[atmas'ferə]
the Sun	Солнце (n)	['sontse]
solar system	Солнечная система (f)	['solnetʃnaja sis'teme]
solar eclipse	солнечное затмение (n)	['solnetʃnae zat'menie]
the Earth	Земля (f)	[zem'ʎa]
the Moon	Луна (f)	['lunə]
Mars	Марс (m)	[mars]
Venus	Венера (f)	[wi'nerə]
Jupiter	Юпитер (m)	[ju'piter]
Saturn	Сатурн (m)	[sa'turn]
Mercury	Меркурий (m)	[mir'kurij]
Uranus	Уран (m)	[u'ran]
Neptune	Нептун (m)	[nip'tun]
Pluto	Плутон (m)	[plu'ton]
Milky Way	Млечный Путь (m)	['mletʃnij put']
Great Bear	Большая Медведица (f)	[baʎ'ʃʌja mid'weditsə]

Pole Star	Полярная Звезда (f)	[pɑ'ʌarnɑja zwez'dɑ]
Martian	марсианин (m)	[mɑrsi'ɑnin]
extraterrestrial	инопланетянин (m)	[inɑplɑne'tʲanin]
alien	пришелец (m)	[pri'ʃɕlɛts]
flying saucer	летающая тарелка (f)	[le'tɑjuɕeja tɑ'relkə]

| spaceship | космический корабль (m) | [kɑs'mitʃeskij kɑ'rabʌ] |

| space station | орбитальная станция (f) | [ɑrbi'tɑʌnaja 'stɑntsija] |
| blast-off | старт (m) | [start] |

engine	двигатель (m)	['dwigɑteʌ]
nozzle	сопло (n)	['soplə]
fuel	топливо (n)	['toplivə]

cockpit, flight deck	кабина (f)	[kɑ'binə]
antenna	антенна (f)	[ɑn'tɛnə]
porthole	иллюминатор (m)	[ilymi'nɑtar]
solar battery	солнечная батарея (f)	['solnetʃnaja bɑtɑ'reja]
spacesuit	скафандр (m)	[skɑ'fɑndr]

| weightlessness | невесомость (f) | [niwe'somɑstʲ] |
| oxygen | кислород (m) | [kislɑ'rot] |

| docking (in space) | стыковка (f) | [stɪ'kofkə] |
| to dock (vi, vt) | производить стыковку | [prɑizvɑ'ditʲ stɪ'kofkʊ] |

observatory	обсерватория (f)	[ɑpservɑ'torija]
telescope	телескоп (m)	[tiles'kop]
to observe (vt)	наблюдать	[nɑbly'dɑtʲ]
to explore (vt)	исследовать	[is'ledɑvatʲ]

196. The Earth

the Earth	Земля (f)	[zem'ʌa]
globe	земной шар (m)	[zem'noj ʃʌr]
planet	планета (f)	[plɑ'netə]

atmosphere	атмосфера (f)	[ɑtmɑs'ferə]
geography	география (f)	[giɑg'rɑfijə]
nature	природа (f)	[pri'rodə]

globe (model of Earth)	глобус (m)	['globʊs]
map	карта (f)	['kɑrtə]
atlas	атлас (m)	['ɑtlɑs]

Europe	Европа (f)	[ev'ropə]
Asia	Азия (f)	['ɑzijə]
Africa	Африка (f)	['ɑfrikə]
Australia	Австралия (f)	[ɑfst'rɑlijə]

America	Америка (f)	[ɑ'merikə]
North America	Северная Америка (f)	['sewernɑjɑ ɑ'merikə]
South America	Южная Америка (f)	['juʒnɑjɑ ɑ'merikə]

| Antarctica | Антарктида (f) | [ɑntɑrk'tidə] |
| the Arctic | Арктика (f) | ['ɑrktikə] |

197. Cardinal directions

north	север (m)	['sewer]
to the north	на север	[nɑ 'sewer]
in the north	на севере	[nɑ 'sewere]
northern	северный	['sewernɪj]

south	юг (m)	[juk]
to the south	на юг	[nɑ 'juk]
in the south	на юге	[nɑ 'juge]
southern	южный	['juʒnɪj]

west	запад (m)	['zɑpɑt]
to the west	на запад	[nɑ 'zɑpɑt]
in the west	на западе	[nɑ 'zɑpɑde]
western	западный	['zɑpɑdnɪj]

east	восток (m)	[vɑs'tɔk]
to the east	на восток	[nɑ vɑs'tɔk]
in the east	на востоке	[nɑ vɑs'tɔke]
eastern	восточный	[vɑs'tɔtʃnɪj]

198. Sea. Ocean

sea	море (n)	['mɔre]
ocean	океан (m)	[ɑki'ɑn]
gulf (bay)	залив (m)	[zɑ'lif]
straits	пролив (m)	[prɑ'lif]

| land | земля (f), суша (f) | [zem'ʎɑ], ['suʃə] |
| continent (mainland) | материк (m) | [mɑte'rik] |

island	остров (m)	['ɔstrɑf]
peninsula	полуостров (m)	[pɑlu'ɔstrɑf]
archipelago	архипелаг (m)	[ɑrhipe'lɑk]

bay	бухта (f)	['buhtə]
harbor	гавань (f)	['gɑvɑɲ]
lagoon	лагуна (f)	[lɑ'gunə]
cape	мыс (m)	[mɪs]
atoll	атолл (m)	[ɑ'tɔl]

reef	риф (m)	[rif]
coral	коралл (m)	[ka'ral]
coral reef	коралловый риф (m)	[ka'ralavıj rif]

deep	глубокий	[glu'bɔkij]
depth (deep water)	глубина (f)	[glubi'na]
abyss	бездна (f)	['beznə]
trench (e.g., Mariana ~)	впадина (f)	['fpadinə]

| current | течение (n) | [ti'ʧenie] |
| to surround (vt) | омывать | [ami'vatʲ] |

| shore | берег (m) | ['berek] |
| coast | побережье (n) | [pabe'reʒje] |

high tide	прилив (m)	[pri'lif]
low tide	отлив (m)	[at'lif]
sandbank	отмель (f)	['ɔtmeʎ]
bottom	дно (n)	[dnɔ]

wave	волна (f)	[val'na]
crest (~ of a wave)	гребень (m) волны	['grebeɲ val'nı]
foam	пена (f)	['penə]

hurricane	ураган (m)	[ura'gan]
tsunami	цунами (n)	[ʦu'nami]
calm	штиль (m)	[ʃtiʎ]
quiet (e.g., ~ ocean)	спокойный	[spa'kɔjnıj]

| pole | полюс (m) | ['pɔlys] |
| polar | полярный | [pa'ʎarnıj] |

latitude	широта (f)	[ʃıra'ta]
longitude	долгота (f)	[dalga'ta]
parallel	параллель (f)	[para'leʎ]
equator	экватор (m)	[ɛk'vatar]

sky	небо (n)	['nebə]
horizon	горизонт (m)	[gari'zɔnt]
air	воздух (m)	['vɔzduh]

lighthouse	маяк (m)	[ma'jak]
to dive (vi)	нырять	[nı'rʲatʲ]
to sink (about boat)	затонуть	[zata'nutʲ]
treasures	сокровища (pl)	[sak'rɔwiɕə]

199. Seas' and Oceans' names

| Atlantic Ocean | Атлантический океан (m) | [atlan'tiʧeskij aki'an] |
| Indian Ocean | Индийский океан (m) | [in'dijskij aki'an] |

Pacific Ocean	**Тихий океан** (m)	['tihij aki'an]
Arctic Ocean	**Северный Ледовитый океан** (m)	['sewernıj leda'witıj aki'an]
Black Sea	**Чёрное море** (n)	['tʃornae 'more]
Red Sea	**Красное море** (n)	['krasnae 'more]
Yellow Sea	**Желтое море** (n)	['ʒaltae 'more]
White Sea	**Белое море** (n)	['belae 'more]
Caspian Sea	**Каспийское море** (n)	[kas'pijskae 'more]
Dead Sea	**Мёртвое море** (n)	['mɜrtvae 'more]
Mediterranean Sea	**Средиземное море** (n)	[sredi'zemnae 'more]
Aegean Sea	**Эгейское море** (n)	[ɛ'gejskae 'more]
Adriatic Sea	**Адриатическое море** (n)	[adria'titʃeskae 'more]
Arabian Sea	**Аравийское море** (n)	[ara'wijskae 'more]
Sea of Japan	**Японское море** (n)	[ja'ponskae 'more]
Bering Sea	**Берингово море** (n)	['berihgava 'more]
South China Sea	**Южно-Китайское море** (n)	['juʒna ki'tajskae 'more]
Coral Sea	**Коралловое море** (n)	[ka'ralavae 'more]
Tasman Sea	**Тасманово море** (n)	[tas'manava 'more]
Caribbean Sea	**Карибское море** (n)	[ka'ripskae 'more]
Barents Sea	**Баренцево море** (n)	['barintseva 'more]
Kara Sea	**Карское море** (n)	['karskae 'more]
North Sea	**Северное море** (n)	['sewernae 'more]
Baltic Sea	**Балтийское море** (n)	[bal'tijskae 'more]
Norwegian Sea	**Норвежское море** (n)	[nar'weʃskae 'more]

200. Mountains

mountain	**гора** (f)	[ga'ra]
mountain range	**горная цепь** (f)	['gornaja tsep']
mountain ridge	**горный хребет** (m)	['gornıj hre'bet]
summit, top	**вершина** (f)	[wir'ʃinə]
peak	**пик** (m)	[pik]
foot (of mountain, hill)	**подножие** (n)	[pad'noʒıe]
slope (mountainside)	**склон** (m)	[sklɔn]
volcano	**вулкан** (m)	[vʊl'kan]
active volcano	**действующий вулкан** (m)	['dejstvʊɕij vʊl'kan]
dormant volcano	**потухший вулкан** (m)	[pa'tʊhʃij vʊl'kan]
eruption	**извержение** (n)	[izwer'ʒɛnie]
crater	**кратер** (m)	['krater]

magma	**магма** (f)	['magmə]
lava	**лава** (f)	['lavə]
molten (~ lava)	**раскалённый**	[raska'lɛnnɪj]
canyon	**каньон** (m)	[ka'ɲjon]
gorge	**ущелье** (n)	[u'ɕeʎje]
crevice	**расщелина** (f)	[ra'ɕelinə]
pass, col	**перевал** (m)	[pere'val]
plateau	**плато** (n)	[pla'tɔ]
cliff	**скала** (f)	[ska'la]
hill	**холм** (m)	[hɔlm]
glacier	**ледник** (m)	[lid'nik]
waterfall	**водопад** (m)	[vada'pat]
geyser	**гейзер** (m)	['gejzer]
lake	**озеро** (n)	['ɔzerə]
plain	**равнина** (f)	[rav'ninə]
landscape	**пейзаж** (m)	[pij'zaʃ]
echo	**эхо** (n)	['ɛhə]
alpinist	**альпинист** (m)	[aʎpi'nist]
rock climber	**скалолаз** (m)	[skala'las]
conquer (in climbing)	**покорять**	[paka'rʲatʲ]
climb (e.g., an easy ~)	**восхождение** (n)	[vashaʒ'denie]

201. Mountains names

Alps	**Альпы** (pl)	['aʎpɪ]
Mont Blanc	**Монблан** (m)	[manb'lan]
Pyrenees	**Пиренеи** (pl)	[pire'nei]
Carpathians	**Карпаты** (pl)	[kar'patɪ]
Ural Mountains	**Уральские горы** (pl)	[u'raʎskie 'gorɪ]
Caucasus	**Кавказ** (m)	[kaf'kas]
Elbrus	**Эльбрус** (m)	[ɛʎb'rʊs]
Altai	**Алтай** (m)	[al'taj]
Tien Shan	**Тянь-Шань** (f)	[tʲaɲ 'ʃʌɲ]
Pamir Mountains	**Памир** (m)	[pa'mir]
Himalayas	**Гималаи** (pl)	[gima'lai]
Everest	**Эверест** (m)	[ɛwi'rest]
Andes	**Анды** (pl)	['andɪ]
Cordilleras	**Кордильеры** (pl)	[kardi'ʎjerɪ]
Kilimanjaro	**Килиманджаро** (f)	[kiliman'ʒarə]

202. Rivers

river	**река** (f)	[ri'ka]
spring (natural source)	**источник** (m)	[is'totʃnik]
bed (of the river)	**русло** (n)	['rʊslə]
basin	**бассейн** (m)	[ba'sɛjn]
to flow into …	**впадать в …**	[fpa'datⁱ v]
tributary	**приток** (m)	[pri'tɔk]
bank (of river)	**берег** (m)	['berek]
current, stream	**течение** (n)	[ti'tʃenie]
downstream	**вниз по течению**	[vnis pa ti'tʃeniju]
upstream	**вверх по течению**	[werh pa ti'tʃeniju]
flood	**наводнение** (n)	[navad'nenie]
flooding	**половодье** (n)	[pala'vodje]
to overflow (vi)	**разливаться**	[razli'vatsə]
to flood (vt)	**затоплять**	[zatap'ʎatⁱ]
shallows (shoal)	**мель** (f)	[meʎ]
rapids	**порог** (m)	[pa'rɔk]
dam	**плотина** (f)	[pla'tinə]
canal	**канал** (m)	[ka'nal]
reservoir, artificial lake	**водохранилище** (n)	[vadahra'niliɕe]
sluice, lock	**шлюз** (m)	[ʃlys]
reservoir (water body)	**водоём** (m)	[vadaзm]
marsh, swamp	**болото** (n)	[ba'lotə]
bog	**трясина** (f)	[tri'sinə]
whirlpool	**водоворот** (m)	[vadava'rɔt]
stream (brook)	**ручей** (m)	[rʊ'tʃej]
drinking (about water)	**питьевой**	[pitje'vɔj]
fresh (not salt)	**пресный**	['presnıj]
ice	**лёд** (m)	['lзt]
to ice over	**замёрзнуть**	[za'mзrznʊtⁱ]

203. Rivers' names

Seine	**Сена** (f)	['senə]
Loire	**Луара** (f)	[lu'arə]
Thames	**Темза** (f)	['tɛmzə]
Rhine	**Рейн** (m)	[rɛjn]
Danube	**Дунай** (m)	[dʊ'naj]
Volga	**Волга** (f)	['vɔlgə]

Don	**Дон** (m)	[dɔn]
Lena	**Лена** (f)	[ˈlenə]
Yellow River	**Хуанхэ** (f)	[hʊanˈhɛ]
Yangtze	**Янцзы** (f)	[janˈzi]
Mekong	**Меконг** (m)	[miˈkɔnk]
Ganges	**Ганг** (m)	[gɑnk]
Nile River	**Нил** (m)	[nil]
Congo	**Конго** (f)	[ˈkɔhgə]
Okavango	**Окаванго** (f)	[akaˈvahgə]
Zambezi	**Замбези** (f)	[zamˈbezi]
Limpopo	**Лимпопо** (f)	[limˈpopɔ]
Mississippi River	**Миссисипи** (f)	[misiˈsipi]

204. Forest

forest	**лес** (m)	[les]
forest (attr)	**лесной**	[lisˈnɔj]
thick forest	**чаща** (f)	[ˈʧaɕə]
grove	**роща** (f)	[ˈrɔɕə]
clearing	**поляна** (f)	[paˈʎanə]
thicket	**заросли** (pl)	[ˈzarɑsli]
scrubland	**кустарник** (m)	[kʊsˈtarnik]
pathway	**тропа** (f)	[traˈpa]
footpath	**тропинка** (f)	[traˈpinkə]
gully	**овраг** (m)	[avˈrak]
tree	**дерево** (n)	[ˈderevə]
leaf	**лист** (m)	[list]
leaves	**листва** (f)	[listˈva]
falling leaves	**листопад** (m)	[listaˈpat]
to fall (about leaves)	**опадать**	[apaˈdatʲ]
top (of the tree)	**верхушка** (f)	[wirˈhʊʃkə]
branch	**ветка** (f)	[ˈwetkə]
bough	**сук** (m)	[sʊk]
bud (on shrub, tree)	**почка** (f)	[ˈpɔʧkə]
needle (of pine tree)	**игла** (f)	[igˈla]
cone (of pine, fir)	**шишка** (f)	[ˈʃiʃkə]
hollow (in a tree)	**дупло** (n)	[dʊpˈlɔ]
nest	**гнездо** (n)	[gnizˈdɔ]
burrow, animal hole	**нора** (f)	[naˈra]
trunk (of a tree)	**ствол** (m)	[stvɔl]
root	**корень** (m)	[ˈkɔreɲ]

| bark (of a tree) | кора (f) | [ka'ra] |
| moss | мох (m) | [mɔh] |

to uproot (vt)	корчевать	[kartʃe'vatʲ]
to chop down	рубить	[rʊ'bitʲ]
to deforest (vt)	вырубать	[vɪrʊ'batʲ]
tree stump	пень (m)	[peɲ]

campfire	костёр (m)	[kas'tɜr]
forest fire	пожар (m)	[pa'ʒar]
to extinguish (vt)	тушить	[tʊ'ʃitʲ]

forest ranger	лесник (m)	[lis'nik]
protection	охрана (f)	[ah'ranə]
to protect (e.g., ~ nature)	охранять	[ahra'ɲatʲ]
poacher	браконьер (m)	[braka'ɲjer]
trap (e.g., bear ~)	капкан (m)	[kap'kan]

to pick (mushrooms)	собирать	[sabi'ratʲ]
to pick (berries)	собирать	[sabi'ratʲ]
to lose one's way	заблудиться	[zablu'ditsə]

205. Natural resources

| natural resources | природные ресурсы (m pl) | [pri'rɔdnɪe re'sʊrsɪ] |
| minerals | полезные ископаемые (n pl) | [pa'leznɪe iska'paemɪe] |

| deposit (e.g., coal ~) | залежи (pl) | ['zaleʒɪ] |
| field (e.g., oilfield) | месторождение (n) | [mistaraʒ'denie] |

to mine (extract)	добывать	[dabɪ'vatʲ]
mining (extraction)	добыча (f)	[da'bɪtʃə]
ore	руда (f)	[rʊ'da]
mine (e.g., for coal)	рудник (m)	[rʊd'nik]
mine shaft, pit	шахта (f)	['ʃʌhtə]
miner	шахтёр (m)	[ʃʌh'tɜr]

| gas | газ (m) | [gas] |
| gas pipeline | газопровод (m) | [gazapra'vɔt] |

oil (petroleum)	нефть (f)	[neftʲ]
oil pipeline	нефтепровод (m)	[neftepra'vɔt]
oil rig	нефтяная вышка (f)	[neftʲa'naja 'vɪʃkə]
derrick	буровая вышка (f)	[bʊra'vaja 'vɪʃkə]
tanker	танкер (m)	['tanker]

sand	песок (m)	[pi'sɔk]
limestone	известняк (m)	[izves'ɲak]
gravel	гравий (m)	['grawij]

peat	**торф** (m)	[tɔrf]
clay	**глина** (f)	[ˈglinə]
coal	**уголь** (m)	[ˈugaʎ]
iron	**железо** (n)	[ʒɪˈlezə]
gold	**золото** (n)	[ˈzɔlɐtə]
silver	**серебро** (n)	[sirib'rɔ]
nickel	**никель** (m)	[ˈnikeʎ]
copper	**медь** (f)	[metʲ]
zinc	**цинк** (m)	[tsɪnk]
manganese	**марганец** (m)	[ˈmarganets]
mercury	**ртуть** (f)	[rtʊtʲ]
lead	**свинец** (m)	[swiˈnets]
mineral	**минерал** (m)	[mineˈral]
crystal	**кристалл** (m)	[krisˈtal]
marble	**мрамор** (m)	[ˈmramar]
uranium	**уран** (m)	[uˈran]
diamond (stone)	**алмаз** (m)	[alˈmas]

The Earth. Part 2

206. Weather

weather	**погода** (f)	[pa'godə]
weather forecast	**прогноз** (m) **погоды**	[prag'nɔs pa'gɔdɪ]
temperature	**температура** (f)	[timpera'turə]
thermometer	**термометр** (m)	[tir'mɔmetr]
barometer	**барометр** (m)	[ba'rɔmetr]
humid	**влажный**	['vlaʒnɪj]
humidity	**влажность** (f)	['vlaʒnəstʲ]
heat (of summer)	**жара** (f)	[ʒa'ra]
hot (torrid)	**жаркий**	['ʒarkij]
it's hot	**жарко**	['ʒarkə]
it's warm	**тепло**	[tip'lɔ]
warm (moderately hot)	**тёплый**	['tɵplɪj]
it's cold	**холодно**	['hɔladnə]
cold	**холодный**	[ha'lɔdnɪj]
sun	**солнце** (n)	['sɔntse]
to shine	**светить**	[swi'titʲ]
sunny (day)	**солнечный**	['sɔlnetʃnɪj]
to come up (vi)	**взойти**	[vzaj'ti]
to set (vi)	**сесть**	[sestʲ]
cloud	**облако** (n)	['ɔblakə]
cloudy	**облачный**	['ɔblatʃnɪj]
rain cloud	**туча** (f)	['tutʃə]
somber (gloomy)	**пасмурный**	['pasmurnɪj]
rain	**дождь** (m)	[dɔʒtʲ]
it's raining	**идёт дождь**	[i'dɛt 'dɔʒtʲ]
rainy (day)	**дождливый**	[daʒd'livɪj]
to drizzle (vi)	**моросить**	[mara'sitʲ]
pouring rain	**проливной дождь** (m)	[praliv'nɔj dɔʒtʲ]
downpour	**ливень** (m)	['liweɲ]
heavy (e.g., ~ rain)	**сильный**	['siʎnɪj]
puddle	**лужа** (f)	['luʒə]
to get wet (in rain)	**промокнуть**	[pra'mɔknutʲ]
mist (fog)	**туман** (m)	[tu'man]
misty	**туманный**	[tu'mannɪj]

| snow | снег (m) | [snek] |
| it's snowing | идет снег | [i'dɜt 'snek] |

207. Severe weather. Natural disasters

thunderstorm	гроза (f)	[gra'za]
lightning (~ strike)	молния (f)	['mɔlnija]
to flash (vi)	сверкать	[swir'katʲ]

thunder	гром (m)	[grɔm]
to thunder (vi)	греметь	[gri'metʲ]
it's thundering	гремит гром	[gri'mit grɔm]

| hail | град (m) | [grat] |
| it's hailing | идёт град | [i'dɜt 'grat] |

| to flood (vt) | затопить | [zata'pitʲ] |
| flood | наводнение (n) | [navad'nenie] |

earthquake	землетрясение (n)	[zemletri'senie]
tremor, quake	толчок (m)	[tal'tʃɔk]
epicenter	эпицентр (m)	[ɛpi'tsentr]

| eruption | извержение (n) | [izwer'ʒɛnie] |
| lava | лава (f) | ['lavə] |

| tornado | торнадо (m) | [tar'nadə] |
| typhoon | тайфун (m) | [taj'fʊn] |

hurricane	ураган (m)	[ura'gan]
storm	буря (f)	['bʊrʲa]
tsunami	цунами (n)	[tsu'nami]

cyclone (e.g., tropical ~)	циклон (m)	[tsɪk'lɔn]
bad weather	непогода (f)	[nipa'gɔdə]
fire (e.g., house on ~)	пожар (m)	[pa'ʒar]
disaster	катастрофа (f)	[katast'rɔfə]
meteorite	метеорит (m)	[mitea'rit]

avalanche	лавина (f)	[la'winə]
snowslide	обвал (m)	[ab'val]
blizzard	метель (f)	[mi'teʎ]
snowstorm	вьюга (f)	['vjygə]

208. Noises. Sounds

| quiet, silence | тишина (f) | [tiʃɪ'na] |
| sound | звук (m) | [zvʊk] |

noise	шум (m)	[ʃʊm]
to make noise	шуметь	[ʃʊˈmetʲ]
noisy	шумный	[ˈʃʊmnɪj]

loudly (to speak etc.)	громко	[ˈɡrɔmkə]
loud (voice etc.)	громкий	[ˈɡrɔmkij]
constant (continuous)	постоянный	[pəstaˈjannɪj]

shout (noun)	крик (m)	[krik]
to shout (vi)	кричать	[kriˈʧatʲ]
whisper	шёпот (m)	[ˈʃɔpət]
to whisper (vi, vt)	шептать	[ʃɛpˈtatʲ]

| barking (of dog) | лай (m) | [lɑj] |
| to bark (vi) | лаять | [ˈlɑitʲ] |

groan (of pain)	стон (m)	[stɔn]
to groan (vi)	стонать	[ˈstɔnatʲ]
cough	кашель (m)	[ˈkɑʃəʎ]
to cough (vi)	кашлять	[ˈkɑʃlitʲ]

whistle	свист (m)	[swist]
to whistle (vi)	свистеть	[swisˈtetʲ]
knock (at the door)	стук (m)	[stʊk]
to knock (vi)	стучать	[stʊˈʧatʲ]

| to crackle (vi) | трещать | [triˈɕatʲ] |
| crackle | треск (m) | [tresk] |

siren	сирена (f)	[siˈrenə]
whistle (factory's ~)	гудок (m)	[ɡʊˈdɔk]
to whistle (ship, train)	гудеть	[ɡʊˈdetʲ]
honk (signal)	сигнал (m)	[siɡˈnɑl]
to honk (about car)	сигналить	[siɡˈnɑlitʲ]

209. Winter

winter (noun)	зима (f)	[ziˈmɑ]
winter (attr)	зимний	[ˈzimnij]
in the winter	зимой	[ziˈmɔj]

snow	снег (m)	[snek]
it's snowing	идёт снег	[iˈdɔt ˈsnek]
snowfall	снегопад (m)	[sniɡaˈpɑt]
snowdrift	сугроб (m)	[sʊɡˈrɔp]

snowflake	снежинка (f)	[sniˈʒinkə]
snowball	снежок (m)	[sniˈʒɔk]
snowman	снеговик (m)	[sniɡaˈwik]
icicle	сосулька (f)	[saˈsʊʎkə]

December	декабрь (m)	[di'kabrʲ]
January	январь (m)	[en'varʲ]
February	февраль (m)	[fiv'raʎ]
New Year	Новый год (m)	['novɪj gɔt]
Christmas tree	Рождественская ёлка (f)	[raʒ'destwenskaja ɜlkə]
Christmas	Рождество (n)	[raʒdest'vɔ]
heavy frost	мороз (m)	[ma'rɔs]
frosty (weather, air)	морозный	[ma'rɔznɪj]
below zero	ниже нуля	['niʒɛ nʊ'ʎa]
light frost	заморозки (pl)	['zamaraski]
hoarfrost	иней (m)	['inej]
cold (cold weather)	холод (m)	['hɔlat]
it's cold	холодно	['hɔladnə]
fur coat	шуба (f)	['ʃubə]
mittens	варежки (f pl)	['variʃki]
to get sick	заболеть	[zaba'letʲ]
cold (illness)	простуда (f)	[pras'tʊdə]
to catch a cold	простудиться	[prastʊ'ditsə]
ice	лёд (m)	['lɜt]
black ice	гололёд (m)	[gala'lɜt]
to ice over	замёрзнуть	[za'mɜrznʊtʲ]
ice floe	льдина (f)	['ʎdinə]
skis	лыжи (f pl)	['lɪʒɪ]
skier	лыжник (m)	['lɪʒnik]
to ski (vi)	кататься на лыжах	[ka'tatsa na 'lɪʒah]
to skate (vi)	кататься на коньках	[ka'tatsa na kaɲ'kah]

Fauna

210. Mammals. Predators

predator	хищник (m)	['hiɕnik]
tiger	тигр (m)	[tigr]
lion	лев (m)	[lef]
wolf	волк (m)	[vɔlk]
fox	лиса (f)	['lisə]
jaguar	ягуар (m)	[jagu'ar]
leopard	леопард (m)	[lia'part]
cheetah	гепард (m)	[gi'part]
black panther	пантера (f)	[pan'tɛrə]
puma	пума (f)	['pʊmə]
snow leopard	снежный барс (m)	['snɛʒnıj bars]
lynx	рысь (m)	[rısʲ]
coyote	койот (m)	[ka'jot]
jackal	шакал (m)	[ʃʌ'kal]
hyena	гиена (f)	[gi'enə]

211. Wild animals

animal	животное (n)	[ʒı'vɔtnɑe]
beast (animal)	зверь (m)	[zwerʲ]
squirrel	белка (f)	['belkə]
hedgehog	ёж (m)	[ʒʃ]
hare	заяц (m)	['zaits]
rabbit	кролик (m)	['krɔlik]
badger	барсук (m)	[bar'sʊk]
raccoon	енот (m)	[e'not]
hamster	хомяк (m)	[ha'mʲak]
marmot	сурок (m)	[sʊ'rɔk]
mole	крот (m)	[krɔt]
mouse	мышь (f)	[mıʃ]
rat	крыса (f)	['krısə]
bat	летучая мышь (f)	[le'tʊtʃija mıʃ]
ermine	горностай (m)	[garnɑs'taj]
sable	соболь (m)	['sɔbaʎ]

marten	куница (f)	[kʊ'nitsə]
weasel	ласка (f)	['laskə]
mink	норка (f)	['nɔrkə]

| beaver | бобр (m) | [bɔbr] |
| otter | выдра (f) | ['vɪdrə] |

horse	лошадь (f)	['lɔʃʌtʲ]
moose	лось (m)	[lɔsʲ]
deer	олень (m)	[ɑ'leɲ]
camel	верблюд (m)	[wirb'lyt]

bison	бизон (m)	[bi'zɔn]
aurochs	зубр (m)	[zubr]
buffalo	буйвол (m)	['bʊjval]

zebra	зебра (f)	['zebrə]
antelope	антилопа (f)	[anti'lɔpə]
roe deer	косуля (f)	[ka'sʊʎə]
fallow deer	лань (f)	[laɲ]
chamois	серна (f)	['sernə]
wild boar	кабан (m)	[ka'ban]

whale	кит (m)	[kit]
seal	тюлень (m)	[ty'leɲ]
walrus	морж (m)	[mɔrʃ]
fur seal	котик (m)	['kɔtik]
dolphin	дельфин (m)	[diʎ'fin]

bear	медведь (m)	[mid'wetʲ]
polar bear	белый медведь (m)	['belɪj mid'wetʲ]
panda	панда (f)	['pandə]

monkey	обезьяна (f)	[abi'zjanə]
chimpanzee	шимпанзе (n)	[ʃɪmpan'ze]
orangutan	орангутанг (m)	[arahgu'tank]
gorilla	горилла (f)	[ga'rilə]
macaque	макака (f)	[ma'kakə]
gibbon	гиббон (m)	[gi'bɔn]

elephant	слон (m)	[slɔn]
rhinoceros	носорог (m)	[nasa'rɔk]
giraffe	жираф (m)	[ʒɪ'raf]
hippopotamus	бегемот (m)	[bige'mɔt]

| kangaroo | кенгуру (m) | [kihgu'rʊ] |
| koala (bear) | коала (f) | [ka'alə] |

mongoose	мангуст (m)	[ma'ŋust]
chinchilla	шиншилла (f)	[ʃɪn'ʃilə]
skunk	скунс (m)	[skʊns]
porcupine	дикобраз (m)	[dikab'ras]

212. Domestic animals

cat	кошка (f)	[ˈkɔʃkə]
tomcat	кот (m)	[kɔt]
horse	лошадь (m)	[ˈlɔʃʌtⁱ]
stallion	жеребец (m)	[ʒɪreˈbets]
mare	кобыла (f)	[kɑˈbɪlə]
cow	корова (f)	[kɑˈrɔvə]
bull	бык (m)	[bɪk]
ox	вол (m)	[vɔl]
sheep	овца (f)	[ɑvˈtsa]
ram	баран (m)	[bɑˈran]
goat	коза (f)	[kɑˈza]
billy goat, he-goat	козёл (m)	[kɑˈzɜl]
donkey	осёл (m)	[ɑˈsɜl]
mule	мул (m)	[mʊl]
pig	свинья (f)	[swiˈɲja]
piglet	поросёнок (m)	[pɑrɑˈsɔnɑk]
rabbit	кролик (m)	[ˈkrɔlik]
hen (chicken)	курица (f)	[ˈkʊritsə]
rooster	петух (m)	[piˈtʊh]
duck	утка (f)	[ˈutkə]
drake	селезень (m)	[ˈselezeɲ]
goose	гусь (m)	[gʊsⁱ]
turkey cock	индюк (m)	[inˈdyk]
turkey (hen)	индюшка (f)	[inˈdyʃkə]
domestic animals	домашние животные (n pl)	[dɑˈmaʃnie ʒɪˈvɔtnɪe]
tame (e.g., ~ hamster)	ручной	[rʊʧˈnɔj]
to tame (vt)	приручать	[priruˈʧatⁱ]
to breed (vt)	выращивать	[vɪˈraɕivatⁱ]
farm	ферма (f)	[ˈfermə]
poultry	домашняя птица (f)	[dɑˈmaʃnaja ˈptitsə]
cattle	скот (m)	[skɔt]
herd (of cattle, goats)	стадо (n)	[ˈstadə]
stable	конюшня (f)	[kɑˈnyʃɲa]
pigpen	свинарник (m)	[swiˈnarnik]
cowshed	коровник (m)	[kɑˈrɔvnik]
rabbit hutch	крольчатник (m)	[krɑʎˈʧatnik]
hen house	курятник (m)	[kʊˈrⁱatnik]

213. Dogs. Dog breeds

dog	собака (f)	[sɑˈbakə]
sheepdog	овчарка (f)	[afˈʧarkə]
German shepherd dog	немецкая овчарка (f)	[niˈmetskaja avˈʧarkə]
poodle	пудель (m)	[ˈpudeʎ]
dachshund	такса (f)	[ˈtaksə]

bulldog	бульдог (m)	[buʎˈdɔk]
boxer	боксёр (m)	[bakˈsɜr]
mastiff	мастиф (m)	[masˈtif]
rottweiler	ротвейлер (m)	[ratˈwejler]
Doberman	доберман (m)	[daberˈman]

basset	бассет (m)	[ˈbasɛt]
bobtail	бобтейл (m)	[bapˈtejl]
Dalmatian	далматинец (m)	[dalmaˈtinets]
cocker spaniel	кокер-спаниель (m)	[ˈkɔker spaniˈeʎ]

| Newfoundland | ньюфаундленд (m) | [ɲjyˈfaundlent] |
| Saint Bernard | сенбернар (m) | [senberˈnar] |

husky	хаски (m)	[ˈhaski]
chow-chow	чау-чау (m)	[ˈʧau ˈʧau]
spitz	шпиц (m)	[ʃpits]
pug	мопс (m)	[mɔps]

214. Sounds made by animals

barking (noun)	лай (m)	[laj]
to bark (vi)	лаять	[ˈlaitʲ]
to meow (vi)	мяукать	[miˈukatʲ]
to purr (vi)	мурлыкать	[murˈlɪkatʲ]

to moo (vi)	мычать	[mɪˈʧatʲ]
to bellow (bull)	реветь	[riˈwetʲ]
to growl (vi)	рычать	[rɪˈʧatʲ]

howl (noun)	вой (m)	[vɔj]
to howl (vi)	выть	[vɪtʲ]
to whine (vi)	скулить	[skuˈlitʲ]

to bleat (sheep)	блеять	[ˈbleitʲ]
to oink, to grunt (pig)	хрюкать	[ˈhrykatʲ]
to squeal (vi)	визжать	[wiˈʐatʲ]

to croak (frog)	квакать	[ˈkvakatʲ]
to buzz (insect)	жужжать	[ʒuˈʐatʲ]
to stridulate (vi)	стрекотать	[strekaˈtatʲ]

215. Young animals

cub	**детёныш** (m)	[di'tɜnɪʃ]
kitten	**котёнок** (m)	[kɑ'tɜnɑk]
baby mouse	**мышонок** (m)	[mɪ'ʃonɑk]
pup, puppy	**щенок** (m)	[ɕi'nɔk]
leveret	**зайчонок** (m)	[zɑj'ʧonɑk]
baby rabbit	**крольчонок** (m)	[krɑʎ'ʧonɑk]
wolf cub	**волчонок** (m)	[vɑl'ʧonɑk]
fox cub	**лисёнок** (m)	[li'sɜnɑk]
bear cub	**медвежонок** (m)	[midwe'ʒonɑk]
lion cub	**львёнок** (m)	['ʎwɜnɑk]
tiger cub	**тигрёнок** (m)	[tig'rɜnɑk]
elephant calf	**слонёнок** (m)	[slɑ'nɜnɑk]
piglet	**поросёнок** (m)	[pɑrɑ'sɜnɑk]
calf (young cow, bull)	**телёнок** (m)	[ti'lɜnɑk]
kid (young goat)	**козлёнок** (m)	[kɑz'lɜnɑk]
lamb	**ягнёнок** (m)	[jag'nɜnɑk]
fawn (deer)	**оленёнок** (m)	[ɑli'nɜnɑk]
young camel	**верблюжонок** (m)	[wirbly'ʒonɑk]
baby snake	**змеёныш** (m)	[zmiɜnɪʃ]
baby frog	**лягушонок** (m)	[ligʊ'ʃonɑk]
nestling	**птенец** (m)	[pti'nets]
chick (of chicken)	**цыплёнок** (m)	[tsɪp'lɜnɑk]
duckling	**утёнок** (m)	[u'tɜnɑk]

216. Birds

bird	**птица** (f)	['ptitsə]
pigeon	**голубь** (m)	['gɔlupʲ]
sparrow	**воробей** (m)	[vɑrɑ'bej]
tit	**синица** (f)	[si'nitsə]
magpie	**сорока** (f)	[sɑ'rɔkə]
raven	**ворон** (m)	['vɔrɑn]
hooded crow	**ворона** (f)	[vɑ'rɔnə]
jackdaw	**галка** (f)	['gɑlkə]
rook	**грач** (m)	[grɑʧ]
duck	**утка** (f)	['utkə]
goose	**гусь** (m)	[gʊsʲ]
pheasant	**фазан** (m)	[fɑ'zɑn]
eagle	**орёл** (m)	[ɑ'rɜl]
hawk	**ястреб** (m)	['jɑstrep]

falcon	сокол (m)	[ˈsɔkal]
vulture	гриф (m)	[grif]
condor	кондор (m)	[ˈkɔndɑr]
swan	лебедь (m)	[ˈlebetʲ]
crane	журавль (m)	[ʒuˈrɑvʎ]
stork	аист (m)	[ˈɑist]
parrot	попугай (m)	[pɑpʊˈgɑj]
hummingbird	колибри (f)	[kɑˈlibri]
peacock	павлин (m)	[pɑvˈlin]
ostrich	страус (m)	[ˈstrɑus]
heron	цапля (f)	[ˈʦapʎa]
flamingo	фламинго (n)	[flaˈmihgə]
pelican	пеликан (m)	[piliˈkan]
nightingale	соловей (m)	[sɑlaˈwej]
swallow	ласточка (f)	[ˈlɑstaʧkə]
fieldfare	дрозд (m)	[drɔzt]
song thrush	певчий дрозд (m)	[ˈpevʧij drɔzt]
blackbird	чёрный дрозд (m)	[ˈʧɔrnıj drɔzt]
swift	стриж (m)	[striʃ]
lark	жаворонок (m)	[ˈʒavarɑnak]
quail	перепел (m)	[ˈperepel]
woodpecker	дятел (m)	[ˈdʲatel]
cuckoo	кукушка (f)	[kʊˈkʊʃkə]
owl	сова (f)	[sɑˈva]
eagle owl	филин (m)	[ˈfilin]
wood grouse	глухарь (m)	[gluˈharʲ]
black grouse	тетерев (m)	[ˈteteref]
partridge	куропатка (f)	[kʊrɑˈpatkə]
starling	скворец (m)	[skvaˈreʦ]
canary	канарейка (f)	[kanaˈrejkə]
hazel grouse	рябчик (m)	[ˈrʲabʧik]
chaffinch	зяблик (m)	[ˈzʲablik]
bullfinch	снегирь (m)	[sniˈgirʲ]
gull (seagull)	чайка (f)	[ˈʧajkə]
albatross	альбатрос (m)	[aʎbatˈrɔs]
penguin	пингвин (m)	[pihgˈwin]

217. Birds. Singing and sounds

| to sing (vi) | петь | [petʲ] |
| to call (shout) | кричать | [kriˈʧatʲ] |

| to crow (rooster) | кукарекать | [kʊkɑˈrekɑtʲ] |
| cock-a-doodle-doo | кукареку (n) | [kʊkɑreˈkʊ] |

to cluck (hen)	кудахтать	[kʊˈdɑhtɑtʲ]
to caw (vi)	каркать	[ˈkɑrkɑtʲ]
to quack (duck)	крякать	[ˈkrʲakɑtʲ]
to cheep (vi)	пищать	[piˈɕatʲ]
to chirp, to twitter	чирикать	[ʧʲiˈrikɑtʲ]

218. Fish. Marine animals

bream	лещ (m)	[leɕ]
carp	карп (m)	[kɑrp]
perch	окунь (m)	[ˈɔkʊɲ]
catfish	сом (m)	[sɔm]
pike	щука (f)	[ˈɕukə]

| salmon | лосось (m) | [lɑˈsɔsʲ] |
| sturgeon | осётр (m) | [ɑˈsɜtr] |

herring	сельдь (f)	[seʌtʲ]
Atlantic salmon	сёмга (f)	[ˈsɜmgə]
mackerel	скумбрия (f)	[ˈskumbrijə]
flatfish	камбала (f)	[ˈkɑmbalə]

zander, pike perch	судак (m)	[sʊˈdak]
cod	треска (f)	[trisˈkɑ]
tuna	тунец (m)	[tʊˈnets]
trout	форель (f)	[fɑˈreʌ]
eel	угорь (m)	[ˈugarʲ]
electric ray	электрический скат (m)	[ɛlektˈriʧeskij skat]
moray eel	мурена (f)	[mʊˈrenə]
piranha	пиранья (f)	[piˈraɲjə]

shark	акула (f)	[ɑˈkʊlə]
dolphin	дельфин (m)	[diʌˈfin]
whale	кит (m)	[kit]

crab	краб (m)	[krɑp]
jellyfish	медуза (f)	[miˈdʊzə]
octopus	осьминог (m)	[asʲmiˈnɔk]

starfish	морская звезда (f)	[marsˈkaja zwezˈda]
sea urchin	морской ёж (m)	[marsˈkɔj ɜʃ]
seahorse	морской конёк (m)	[marsˈkɔj kɑˈnɜk]

oyster	устрица (f)	[ˈustritsə]
shrimp	креветка (f)	[kriˈwetkə]
lobster	омар (m)	[ɑˈmar]
spiny lobster	лангуст (m)	[lɑˈŋust]

219. Amphibians. Reptiles

| snake | змея (f) | [zmi'ja] |
| poisonous | ядовитый | [jadɑ'witıj] |

viper	гадюка (f)	[gɑ'dykə]
cobra	кобра (f)	['kobrə]
python	питон (m)	[pi'tɔn]
boa	удав (m)	[u'dɑf]

grass snake	уж (m)	[uʃ]
rattle snake	гремучая змея (f)	[gri'mʊtʃaja zme'ja]
anaconda	анаконда (f)	[anɑ'kɔndə]

lizard	ящерица (f)	['jaɕiritsə]
iguana	игуана (f)	[igʊ'anə]
monitor lizard	варан (m)	[va'ran]
salamander	саламандра (f)	[salɑ'mandrə]
chameleon	хамелеон (m)	[hamele'ɔn]
scorpion	скорпион (m)	[skɑrpi'ɔn]

turtle	черепаха (f)	[tʃire'pahə]
frog	лягушка (f)	[li'gʊʃkə]
toad	жаба (f)	['ʒabə]
crocodile	крокодил (m)	[krɑkɑ'dil]

220. Insects

insect, bug	насекомое (n)	[nase'kɔmae]
butterfly	бабочка (f)	['babatʃkə]
ant	муравей (m)	[mʊrɑ'wej]
fly	муха (f)	['mʊhə]
mosquito	комар (m)	[kɑ'mar]
beetle	жук (m)	[ʒuk]

wasp	оса (f)	[ɑ'sa]
bee	пчела (f)	[ptʃi'la]
bumblebee	шмель (m)	[ʃmeʎ]
gadfly	овод (m)	['ɔvat]

| spider | паук (m) | [pɑ'uk] |
| spider's web | паутина (f) | [pau'tinə] |

dragonfly	стрекоза (f)	[strekɑ'za]
grasshopper	кузнечик (m)	[kʊz'netʃik]
moth (night butterfly)	мотылёк (m)	[mɑtı'lɜk]

| cockroach | таракан (m) | [tarɑ'kan] |
| tick | клещ (m) | [kleɕ] |

| flea | блоха (f) | [bla'ha] |
| midge | мошка (f) | ['moʃkə] |

locust	саранча (f)	[saraɲ'ʧa]
snail	улитка (f)	[u'litkə]
cricket	сверчок (m)	[swir'ʧok]

lightning bug	светлячок (m)	[switli'ʧok]
ladybug	божья коровка (f)	['boʒja ka'rofkə]
cockchafer	майский жук (m)	['majskij ʒuk]

leech	пиявка (f)	[pi'jafkə]
caterpillar	гусеница (f)	['gusenitsə]
worm	червь (m)	['ʧerfʲ]
larva	личинка	[li'ʧinka]

221. Animals. Body parts

beak	клюв (m)	[klyf]
wings	крылья (f)	['krɪʎja]
foot (of bird)	лапа (f)	['lapə]
feathering	оперение (n)	[api'renie]

| feather | перо (n) | [pi'ro] |
| crest | хохолок (m) | [haha'lok] |

gill	жабры (pl)	['ʒabrɪ]
spawn	икра (f)	[ik'ra]
larva	личинка (f)	[li'ʧinkə]

| fin | плавник (m) | [plav'nik] |
| scales (of fish, reptile) | чешуя (f) | [ʧi'ʃuja] |

fang (of wolf etc.)	клык (m)	[klɪk]
paw (e.g., cat's ~)	лапа (f)	['lapə]
muzzle	морда (f)	['mordə]
mouth (of cat, dog)	пасть (f)	[pastʲ]

| tail | хвост (m) | [hvost] |
| whiskers | усы (m pl) | [u'sɪ] |

| hoof | копыто (n) | [ka'pɪtə] |
| horn | рог (m) | [rok] |

carapace	панцирь (m)	['pantsirʲ]
shell (of mollusk)	ракушка (f)	[ra'kuʃkə]
shell (of egg)	скорлупа (f)	[skarlu'pa]

| hair (e.g., dog's ~) | шерсть (f) | [ʃerstʲ] |
| skin (of animal) | шкура (f) | ['ʃkurə] |

222. Actions of animals

to fly (bird, insect)	летать	[li'tat^j]
to make circles	кружить	[kru'ʒit^j]
to fly away	улететь	[uli'tet^j]
to flap (~ the wings)	махать	[ma'hat^j]
to peck (vi)	клевать	[kli'vat^j]
to incubate (vt)	высиживать яйца	[vɪ'siʒɪvat^j 'jajtsə]
to hatch out (vi)	вылупляться	[vɪlup'ʎatsə]
to build (nest)	вить	[wit^j]
to slither, to crawl	ползать	['polzat^j]
to sting, to bite (insect)	жалить	['ʒalit^j]
to bite (about animal)	кусать	[ku'sat^j]
to sniff (vt)	нюхать	['nyhat^j]
to bark (vi)	лаять	['lait^j]
to hiss (snake)	шипеть	[ʃɪ'pet^j]
to scare (vt)	пугать	[pu'gat^j]
to attack (vt)	нападать	[napa'dat^j]
to gnaw (bone etc.)	грызть	['grɪs^jt^j]
to scratch (with claws)	царапать	[tsa'rapat^j]
to hide (vi)	прятаться	['pr^jatatsə]
to play (kittens etc.)	играть	[ig'rat^j]
to hunt (vi, vt)	охотиться	[a'hotitsə]
to hibernate (vi)	быть в спячке	[bɪt^j f 'sp^jatʃke]
to become extinct	вымереть	['vɪmeret^j]

223. Animals. Habitats

habitat	среда (f) обитания	[sre'da abi'tanija]
migration	миграция (f)	[mig'ratsɪja]
mountain	гора (f)	[ga'ra]
reef	риф (m)	[rif]
cliff	скала (f)	[ska'la]
forest	лес (m)	[les]
jungle	джунгли (pl)	['dʒuhgli]
savanna	саванна (f)	[sa'vannə]
tundra	тундра (f)	['tundrə]
steppe	степь (f)	[step^j]
desert	пустыня (f)	[pus'tɪɲa]
oasis	оазис (m)	[a'azis]
sea	море (n)	['more]

lake	озеро (n)	[ˈɔzerə]
ocean	океан (m)	[ɑkiˈɑn]
wetland	болото (n)	[bɑˈlɔtə]
freshwater	пресноводный	[prisnɑˈvɔdnɪj]
pond	пруд (m)	[prʊt]
river	река (f)	[riˈkɑ]
den	берлога (f)	[birˈlɔgə]
nest	гнездо (n)	[gnizˈdɔ]
hollow (in tree)	дупло (n)	[dʊpˈlɔ]
burrow (animal hole)	нора (f)	[nɑˈrɑ]
anthill	муравейник (m)	[mʊrɑˈwejnik]

224. Animal care

zoo	зоопарк (m)	[zɑɑˈpɑrk]
nature preserve	заповедник (m)	[zɑpɑˈwednik]
breeder, breed club	питомник (m)	[piˈtɔmnik]
open-air cage	вольер (m)	[vɑˈʎjer]
cage	клетка (f)	[ˈkletkə]
doghouse	конура (f)	[kɑnʊˈrɑ]
dovecot	голубятня (f)	[gɑluˈbʲatɲa]
aquarium	аквариум (m)	[ɑkˈvɑrium]
dolphinarium	дельфинарий (m)	[diʎfiˈnɑrij]
to breed (animals)	разводить	[rɑzvɑˈditʲ]
brood, litter	потомство (n)	[pɑˈtɔmstvə]
to tame (vt)	приручать	[prirʊˈtʃatʲ]
feed (for animal)	корм (m)	[kɔrm]
to feed (vt)	кормить	[kɑrˈmitʲ]
to train (animals)	дрессировать	[drisirɑˈvatʲ]
pet store	зоомагазин (m)	[zɔɔmɑgɑˈzin]
muzzle (for dog)	намордник (m)	[nɑˈmɔrdnik]
collar (for animal)	ошейник (m)	[ɑˈʃejnik]
name (of animal)	кличка (f)	[ˈklitʃkə]
pedigree (of dog)	родословная (f)	[rɑdɑsˈlɔvnɑja]

225. Animals. Miscellaneous

pack (wolves)	стая (f)	[ˈstɑja]
flock (birds)	стая (f)	[ˈstɑja]
shoal (fish)	стая, косяк	[ˈstɑja], [kɑˈsʲak]
herd	табун (m)	[tɑˈbʊn]
male (noun)	самец (m)	[sɑˈmets]

female (noun)	самка (f)	['samkə]
hungry	голодный	[ga'lɔdnɪj]
wild	дикий	['dikij]
dangerous	опасный	[a'pasnɪj]

226. Horses

breed (race)	порода (f)	[pa'rɔdə]
foal (of horse)	жеребёнок (m)	[ʒɪre'bɜnak]
mare	кобыла (f)	[ka'bɪlə]

mustang	мустанг (m)	[mʊs'tank]
pony (small horse)	пони (m)	['pɔni]
draft horse	тяжеловоз (m)	[tɪʒɪla'vɔs]

| mane | грива (f) | ['grivə] |
| tail | хвост (m) | [hvɔst] |

hoof	копыто (n)	[ka'pɪtə]
horseshoe	подкова (f)	[pat'kɔvə]
to shoe (vt)	подковать	[patka'vatʲ]
blacksmith	кузнец (m)	[kʊz'nets]

saddle	седло (n)	[sid'lɔ]
stirrup	стремя (f)	['stremʲa]
bridle	уздечка (f)	[uz'detʃkə]
reins	вожжи (pl)	['vɔʒɪ]
whip (for riding)	плётка (f)	['plɜtkə]

rider	наездник (m)	[na'eznik]
to break in (horse)	объезжать	[abʲi'ʒatʲ]
to saddle (vt)	оседлать	[asid'latʲ]
to mount (a horse)	сесть в седло	[sestʲ f sed'lɔ]

gallop	галоп (m)	[ga'lɔp]
to gallop (vi)	скакать галопом	[ska'katʲ ga'lɔpam]
trot (noun)	рысь (f)	[rɪsʲ]
at a trot	рысью	['rɪsjy]
to go at a trot	скакать рысью	[ska'katʲ 'rɪsjy]

| racehorse | скаковая лошадь (f) | [skaka'vaja 'lɔʃʌtʲ] |
| races | скачки (pl) | ['skatʃki] |

stable	конюшня (f)	[ka'nyʃna]
to feed (vt)	кормить	[kar'mitʲ]
hay	сено (n)	['senə]
to water (animals)	поить	[pa'itʲ]
to wash (horse)	чистить	['tʃistitʲ]
to hobble (vt)	стреножить	[stre'nɔʒitʲ]
horse-drawn cart	воз, повозка (f)	[vɔs], [pa'vɔskə]

horse-drawn wagon	повозка (f)	[pɑ'vɔskə]
to graze (vi)	пастись	[pɑs'tisʲ]
to neigh (vi)	ржать	[rʒatʲ]
to kick (horse)	лягнуть	[lig'nutʲ]

Flora

227. Trees

tree	дерево (n)	['derevə]
deciduous	лиственное	['listwenɑe]
coniferous	хвойное	['hvɔjnɑe]
evergreen	вечнозеленое	[wetʃnɑze'lɜnɑe]
apple tree	яблоня (f)	['jablɑɲa]
pear tree	груша (f)	['grʊʃə]
cherry tree (sweet)	черешня (f)	[tʃi'reʃɲa]
cherry tree (sour)	вишня (f)	['wiʃɲa]
plum tree	слива (f)	['slivə]
birch	берёза (f)	[bi'rɜzə]
oak	дуб (m)	[dʊp]
linden tree	липа (f)	['lipə]
aspen	осина (f)	[ɑ'sinə]
maple	клён (m)	['klɜn]
fir tree	ель (f)	[eʎ]
pine	сосна (f)	[sɑs'nɑ]
larch	лиственница (f)	['listwenitsə]
silver fir	пихта (f)	['pihtə]
cedar	кедр (m)	[kedr]
poplar	тополь (m)	['tɔpɑʎ]
rowan	рябина (f)	[ri'binə]
willow	ива (f)	['ivə]
alder	ольха (f)	[ɑʎ'hɑ]
beech	бук (m)	[bʊk]
elm	вяз (m)	[vʲas]
ash (tree)	ясень (m)	['jaseɲ]
chestnut	каштан (m)	[kɑʃ'tan]
magnolia	магнолия (f)	[mɑg'nɔlija]
palm tree	пальма (f)	['pɑʎmə]
cypress	кипарис (m)	['kiparis]
mangrove	мангровое дерево (n)	['mɑhgrɑvɑe 'derevə]
baobab	баобаб (m)	[bɑɑ'bɑp]
eucalyptus	эвкалипт (m)	[ɛfkɑ'lipt]
redwood	секвойя (f)	[sik'vɔja]

228. Shrubs

bush	**куст** (m)	[kʊst]
shrub	**кустарник** (m)	[kʊsˈtarnik]
grapevine	**виноград** (m)	[winagˈrat]
vineyard	**виноградник** (m)	[winagˈradnik]
raspberry bush	**малина** (f)	[maˈlinə]
blackcurrant bush	**чёрная смородина** (f)	[ˈtʃɔrnaja smaˈrɔdinə]
redcurrant bush	**красная смородина** (f)	[ˈkrasnaja smaˈrɔdinə]
gooseberry bush	**крыжовник** (m)	[krɪˈʒɔvnik]
acacia	**акация** (f)	[aˈkatsɪja]
barberry	**барбарис** (m)	[barbaˈris]
jasmine	**жасмин** (m)	[ʒasˈmin]
juniper	**можжевельник** (m)	[maʒɛˈweʎnik]
rosebush	**розовый куст** (m)	[ˈrɔzavɪj kʊst]
dog rose	**шиповник** (m)	[ʃɪˈpɔvnik]

229. Mushrooms

mushroom	**гриб** (m)	[grip]
edible mushroom	**съедобный гриб** (m)	[sʰeˈdɔbnɪj grip]
toadstool	**ядовитый гриб** (m)	[jadaˈwitɪj grip]
cap (of mushroom)	**шляпка** (f)	[ˈʃʎapkə]
foot (of mushroom)	**ножка** (f)	[ˈnɔʃkə]
boletus	**белый гриб** (m)	[ˈbelɪj grip]
orange-cap boletus	**подосиновик** (m)	[padaˈsinawik]
brown-cap boletus	**подберёзовик** (m)	[padbeˈrzzawik]
chanterelle	**лисичка** (f)	[liˈsitʃkə]
russula	**сыроежка** (f)	[sɪraˈeʃkə]
morel	**сморчок** (m)	[smarˈtʃɔk]
fly agaric	**мухомор** (m)	[mʊhaˈmor]
death cap	**поганка** (f)	[paˈgankə]

230. Fruits. Berries

apple	**яблоко** (n)	[ˈjablakə]
pear	**груша** (f)	[ˈgrʊʃə]
plum	**слива** (f)	[ˈslivə]
strawberry	**клубника** (f)	[klubˈnikə]
cherry (sour cherry)	**вишня** (f)	[ˈwiʃna]

| cherry (sweet cherry) | черешня (f) | [ʧi'reʃnə] |
| grapes | виноград (m) | [winag'rat] |

raspberry	малина (f)	[ma'linə]
blackcurrant	чёрная смородина (f)	['ʧɔrnaja sma'rɔdinə]
redcurrant	красная смородина (f)	['krasnaja sma'rɔdinə]
gooseberry	крыжовник (m)	[krɪ'ʒɔvnik]
cranberry	клюква (f)	['klykvə]

orange	апельсин (m)	[apiʎ'sin]
mandarin	мандарин (m)	[manda'rin]
pineapple	ананас (m)	[ana'nas]
banana	банан (m)	[ba'nan]
date	финик (m)	['finik]

lemon	лимон (m)	[li'mɔn]
apricot	абрикос (m)	[abri'kɔs]
peach	персик (m)	['persik]
kiwi	киви (m)	['kiwi]
grapefruit	грейпфрут (m)	[gripf'rʊt]

berry	ягода (f)	['jagadə]
berries	ягоды (f pl)	['jagadɪ]
cowberry	брусника (f)	[brʊs'nikə]
field strawberry	земляника (f)	[zemli'nikə]
bilberry	черника (f)	[ʧir'nikə]

231. Flowers. Plants

| flower | цветок (m) | [ʦwi'tɔk] |
| bouquet (of flowers) | букет (m) | [bʊ'ket] |

rose (flower)	роза (f)	['rɔzə]
tulip	тюльпан (m)	[tyʎ'pan]
carnation	гвоздика (f)	[gvaz'dikə]
gladiolus	гладиолус (m)	[gladi'ɔlus]

cornflower	василёк (m)	[vasi'lɜk]
bluebell	колокольчик (m)	[kala'kɔʎʧik]
dandelion	одуванчик (m)	[adʊ'vanʧik]
camomile	ромашка (f)	[ra'maʃkə]

aloe	алоэ (n)	[a'lɔɛ]
cactus	кактус (m)	['kaktʊs]
rubber plant	фикус (m)	['fikʊs]

lily	лилия (f)	['lilija]
geranium	герань (f)	[gi'raɲ]
hyacinth	гиацинт (m)	[gia'ʦɪnt]
mimosa	мимоза (f)	[mi'mɔzə]

| narcissus | нарцисс (m) | [nar'tsɪs] |
| nasturtium | настурция (f) | [nas'turtsija] |

orchid	орхидея (f)	[arhi'deja]
peony	пион (m)	[pi'ɔn]
violet	фиалка (f)	[fi'alkə]

pansy	анютины глазки (pl)	[a'nytɪnɪ 'glaski]
forget-me-not	незабудка (f)	[niza'butkə]
daisy	маргаритка (f)	[marga'ritkə]

poppy	мак (m)	[mak]
hemp	конопля (f)	[kanap'ʎa]
mint	мята (f)	['mʲatə]

| lily of the valley | ландыш (m) | ['landɪʃ] |
| snowdrop | подснежник (m) | [pats'neʒnik] |

nettle	крапива (f)	[kra'pivə]
sorrel	щавель (m)	['ɕaveʎ]
water lily	кувшинка (f)	[kuf'ʃinkə]
fern	папоротник (m)	['paparatnik]
lichen	лишайник (m)	[li'ʃʌjnik]

greenhouse (tropical ~)	оранжерея (f)	[aranʒɪ'reja]
lawn	газон (m)	[ga'zɔn]
flowerbed	клумба (f)	['klumbə]

plant	растение (n)	[ras'tenie]
grass	трава (f)	[tra'va]
blade (of grass)	травинка (f)	[tra'winkə]

leaf	лист (m)	[list]
petal (of flower)	лепесток (m)	[lipes'tɔk]
stem (of plant)	стебель (m)	['stebeʎ]
tuber	клубень (m)	['klubeɲ]

| young plant (shoot) | росток (m) | [ras'tɔk] |
| thorn | шип (m) | [ʃɪp] |

to blossom (vi)	цвести	[tswis'ti]
to fade, to wither	вянуть	['vʲanutʲ]
smell (odor)	запах (m)	['zapah]
to cut (flowers)	срезать	['srezatʲ]
to pick (a flower)	сорвать	[sar'vatʲ]

232. Cereals, grains

| grain | зерно (n) | [zer'nɔ] |
| cereals | зерновые растения (n pl) | [zerna'vɪe ras'tenija] |

ear (of grain)	колос (m)	['kɔləs]
wheat	пшеница (f)	[pʃɪ'nitsə]
rye	рожь (f)	[rɔʃ]
oats	овёс (m)	[a'wɜs]
millet	просо (n)	['prɔsə]
barley	ячмень (m)	[itʃ'meɲ]

corn	кукуруза (f)	[kuku'ruzə]
rice	рис (m)	[ris]
buckwheat	гречиха (f)	[gri'tʃihə]

pea	горох (m)	[ga'rɔh]
kidney beans	фасоль (f)	[fa'sɔʎ]
soy beans	соя (f)	['sɔja]
lentil	чечевица (f)	[tʃitʃe'witsə]
beans	бобы (pl)	[ba'bɪ]

233. Vegetables. Greens

| vegetables | овощи (m pl) | ['ɔvaɕi] |
| greens | зелень (f) | ['zeleɲ] |

tomato	помидор (m)	[pami'dɔr]
cucumber	огурец (m)	[agu'rets]
carrot	морковь (f)	[mar'kɔfʲ]
potato	картофель (m)	[kar'tɔfeʎ]
onion	лук (m)	[luk]
garlic	чеснок (m)	[tʃis'nɔk]

cabbage	капуста (f)	[ka'pustə]
cauliflower	цветная капуста (f)	[tsvet'naja ka'pustə]
Brussels sprouts	брюссельская капуста (f)	[bry'seʎskaja ka'pustə]
broccoli	капуста брокколи (f)	[ka'pusta 'brɔkali]

beetroot	свёкла (f)	['swɜklə]
eggplant	баклажан (m)	[bakla'ʒan]
zucchini	кабачок (m)	[kaba'tʃɔk]
pumpkin	тыква (f)	['tɪkvə]
turnip	репа (f)	['repə]

parsley	петрушка (f)	[pit'ruʃkə]
dill	укроп (m)	[uk'rɔp]
lettuce	салат (m)	[sa'lat]
celery	сельдерей (m)	[siʎde'rej]
asparagus	спаржа (f)	['sparʒə]
spinach	шпинат (m)	[ʃpi'nat]

| pea | горох (m) | [ga'rɔh] |
| beans | бобы (pl) | [ba'bɪ] |

| corn (maize) | **кукуруза** (f) | [kʊkʊˈrʊzə] |
| kidney beans | **фасоль** (f) | [faˈsɔʎ] |

bell pepper	**перец** (m)	[ˈperets]
radish	**редис** (m)	[riˈdis]
artichoke	**артишок** (m)	[artiˈʃok]

REGIONAL GEOGRAPHY

Countries. Nationalities

234. Western Europe

Europe	**Европа** (f)	[ev'rɔpə]
European Union	**Европейский Союз** (m)	[evrɑ'pejskij sɑ'jus]
European (noun)	**европеец** (m)	[evrɑ'peets]
European (adj)	**европейский**	[evrɑ'pejskij]
Austria	**Австрия** (f)	['ɑfstrijɑ]
Austrian (man)	**австриец** (m)	[ɑfst'riets]
Austrian (woman)	**австрийка** (f)	[ɑfst'rijkə]
Austrian (adj)	**австрийский**	[ɑfst'rijskij]
Great Britain	**Великобритания** (f)	[wilikɑbri'tɑnijɑ]
England	**Англия** (f)	['ɑhglijɑ]
British (man)	**англичанин** (m)	[ɑhgli'tʃɑnin]
British (woman)	**англичанка** (f)	[ɑhgli'tʃɑnkə]
English, British (adj)	**английский**	[ɑhg'lijskij]
Belgium	**Бельгия** (f)	['beʎgijɑ]
Belgian (man)	**бельгиец** (m)	[biʎ'giets]
Belgian (woman)	**бельгийка** (f)	[biʎ'gijkə]
Belgian (adj)	**бельгийский**	[biʎ'gijskij]
Germany	**Германия** (f)	[gir'mɑnijɑ]
German (man)	**немец** (m)	['nemets]
German (woman)	**немка** (f)	['nemkə]
German (adj)	**немецкий**	[ni'metskij]
Netherlands	**Нидерланды** (pl)	[nider'lɑndɪ]
Holland	**Голландия** (f)	[gɑ'lɑndijɑ]
Dutchman	**голландец** (m)	[gɑ'lɑndets]
Dutchwoman	**голландка** (f)	[gɑ'lɑntkə]
Dutch (adj)	**голландский**	[gɑ'lɑntskij]
Greece	**Греция** (f)	['gretsɪjɑ]
Greek (man)	**грек** (m)	[grek]
Greek (woman)	**гречанка** (f)	[gri'tʃɑnkə]
Greek (adj)	**греческий**	['gretʃiskij]
Denmark	**Дания** (f)	['dɑnijɑ]
Dane (man)	**датчанин** (m)	[dɑ'tʃɑnin]

| Dane (woman) | датчанка (f) | [dɑ'tʃankə] |
| Danish (adj) | датский | ['dɑtskij] |

Ireland	Ирландия (f)	[ir'landija]
Irishman	ирландец (m)	[ir'landets]
Irishwoman	ирландка (f)	[ir'lantkə]
Irish (adj)	ирландский	[ir'lantskij]

Iceland	Исландия (f)	[is'landija]
Icelander (man)	исландец (m)	[is'landets]
Icelander (woman)	исландка (f)	[is'lantkə]
Icelandic (adj)	исландский	[is'lantskij]

Spain	Испания (f)	[is'panija]
Spaniard (man)	испанец (m)	[is'panets]
Spaniard (woman)	испанка (f)	[is'pankə]
Spanish (adj)	испанский	[is'panskij]

Italy	Италия (f)	[i'talija]
Italian (man)	итальянец (m)	[ita'ʎjanets]
Italian (woman)	итальянка (f)	[ita'ʎjankə]
Italian (adj)	итальянский	[ita'ʎjanskij]

Cyprus	Кипр (m)	[kipr]
Cypriot (man)	киприот (m)	[kipri'ɔt]
Cypriot (woman)	киприотка (f)	[kipri'ɔtkə]
Cypriot (adj)	кипрский	['kiprskij]

Malta	Мальта (f)	['maʎtə]
Maltese (man)	мальтиец (m)	[maʎ'tiets]
Maltese (woman)	мальтийка (f)	[maʎ'tijkə]
Maltese (adj)	мальтийский	[maʎ'tijskij]

Norway	Норвегия (f)	[nar'wegija]
Norwegian (man)	норвежец (m)	[nar'weʒɛts]
Norwegian (woman)	норвежка (f)	[nar'weʃkə]
Norwegian (adj)	норвежский	[nar'weʃskij]

Portugal	Португалия (f)	[partʊ'galija]
Portuguese (man)	португалец (m)	[partʊ'galets]
Portuguese (woman)	португалка (f)	[partʊ'galkə]
Portuguese (adj)	португальский	[partʊ'gaʎskij]

Finland	Финляндия (f)	[fin'ʎandija]
Finn (man)	финн (m)	[fin]
Finn (woman)	финка (f)	['finkə]
Finnish (adj)	финский	['finskij]

France	Франция (f)	['frantsija]
Frenchman	француз (m)	[fran'tsus]
Frenchwoman	француженка (f)	[fran'tsuʒɛnkə]
French (adj)	французский	[fran'tsuskij]

Sweden	Швеция (f)	['ʃwetsɪja]
Swede (man)	швед (m)	[ʃwet]
Swede (woman)	шведка (f)	['ʃwetkə]
Swedish (adj)	шведский	['ʃwetskij]

Switzerland	Швейцария (f)	[ʃwi'tsarija]
Swiss (man)	швейцарец (m)	[ʃwi'tsarets]
Swiss (woman)	швейцарка (f)	[ʃwi'tsarkə]
Swiss (adj)	швейцарский	[ʃwi'tsarskij]

Scotland	Шотландия (f)	[ʃʌt'landija]
Scottish (man)	шотландец (m)	[ʃʌt'landets]
Scottish (woman)	шотландка (f)	[ʃʌt'lantkə]
Scottish (adj)	шотландский	[ʃʌt'lantskij]

Vatican	Ватикан (m)	[vati'kan]
Liechtenstein	Лихтенштейн (m)	[lihtɛnʃ'tɛjn]
Luxembourg	Люксембург (m)	[lyksem'burk]
Monaco	Монако (n)	[ma'nakə]

235. Central and Eastern Europe

Albania	Албания (f)	[al'banija]
Albanian (man)	албанец (m)	[al'banets]
Albanian (woman)	албанка (f)	[al'bankə]
Albanian (adj)	албанский	[al'banskij]

Bulgaria	Болгария (f)	[bal'garija]
Bulgarian (man)	болгарин (m)	[bal'garin]
Bulgarian (woman)	болгарка (f)	[bal'garkə]
Bulgarian (adj)	болгарский	[bal'garskij]

Hungary	Венгрия (f)	['wehgrija]
Hungarian (man)	венгр (m)	[wehgr]
Hungarian (woman)	венгерка (f)	[wi'ŋerkə]
Hungarian (adj)	венгерский	[wi'ŋerskij]

Latvia	Латвия (f)	['latwija]
Latvian (man)	латыш (m)	[la'tɪʃ]
Latvian (woman)	латышка (f)	[la'tɪʃkə]
Latvian (adj)	латышский	[la'tɪʃskij]

Lithuania	Литва (f)	[lit'va]
Lithuanian (man)	литовец (m)	[li'towets]
Lithuanian (woman)	литовка (f)	[li'tɔfkə]
Lithuanian (adj)	литовский	[li'tɔfskij]

Poland	Польша (f)	['pɔʎʃə]
Pole (man)	поляк (m)	[pa'ʎak]
Pole (woman)	полька (f)	['pɔʎkə]

Polish (adj)	польский	['poʎskij]
Romania	Румыния (f)	[rʊ'mɨnija]
Romanian (man)	румын (m)	[rʊ'mɨn]
Romanian (woman)	румынка (f)	[rʊ'mɨnkə]
Romanian (adj)	румынский	[rʊ'mɨnskij]

Serbia	Сербия (f)	['serbija]
Serbian (man)	серб (m)	[serp]
Serbian (woman)	сербка (f)	['serpkə]
Serbian (adj)	сербский	['serpskij]

Slovakia	Словакия (f)	[sla'vakija]
Slovak (man)	словак (m)	[sla'vak]
Slovak (woman)	словачка (f)	[sla'vatʃkə]
Slovak (adj)	словацкий	[sla'vatskij]

Croatia	Хорватия (f)	[har'vatija]
Croatian (man)	хорват (m)	[har'vat]
Croatian (woman)	хорватка (f)	[har'vatkə]
Croatian (adj)	хорватский	[har'vatskij]

The Czech Republic	Чехия (f)	['tʃehija]
Czech (man)	чех (m)	[tʃeh]
Czech (woman)	чешка (f)	['tʃeʃkə]
Czech (adj)	чешский	['tʃeʃskij]

Estonia	Эстония (f)	[ɛs'tonija]
Estonian (man)	эстонец (m)	[ɛs'tonets]
Estonian (woman)	эстонка (f)	[ɛs'tonkə]
Estonian (adj)	эстонский	[ɛs'tonskij]

| Bosnia-Herzegovina | Босния и Герцеговина (f) | ['bosnia i girtsega'winə] |

Macedonia	Македония (f)	[make'donija]
Slovenia	Словения (f)	[sla'wenija]
Montenegro	Черногория (f)	[tʃirna'gorija]

236. Former USSR countries

Azerbaijan	Азербайджан (m)	[azirbaj'dʒan]
Azerbaijani (man)	азербайджанец (m)	[azirbaj'dʒanets]
Azerbaijani (woman)	азербайджанка (f)	[azirbaj'dʒankə]
Azerbaijani (adj)	азербайджанский	[azirbaj'dʒanskij]

Armenia	Армения (f)	[ar'menija]
Armenian (man)	армянин (m)	[armi'nin]
Armenian (woman)	армянка (f)	[ar'mʲankə]
Armenian (adj)	армянский	[ar'mʲanskij]
Belarus	Беларусь (f)	[bila'rusʲ]
Belarusian (man)	белорус (m)	[bila'rus]

| Belarusian (woman) | белоруска (f) | [bilɑ'ruskə] |
| Belarusian (adj) | белорусский | [bilɑ'ruskij] |

Georgia	Грузия (f)	['gruzija]
Georgian (man)	грузин (m)	[gru'zin]
Georgian (woman)	грузинка (f)	[gru'zinkə]
Georgian (adj)	грузинский	[gru'zinskij]

Kazakhstan	Казахстан (m)	[kazahs'tan]
Kazakh (man)	казах (m)	[ka'zah]
Kazakh (woman)	казашка (f)	[ka'zaʃkə]
Kazakh (adj)	казахский	[ka'zahskij]
Kirghizia	Кыргызстан (m)	[kırgıs'tan]
Kirghiz (man)	киргиз (m)	[kir'gis]
Kirghiz (woman)	киргизка (f)	[kir'giskə]
Kirghiz (adj)	киргизский	[kir'giskij]

Moldavia	Молдова (f)	[mal'dovə]
Moldavian (man)	молдаванин (m)	[malda'vanin]
Moldavian (woman)	молдаванка (f)	[malda'vankə]
Moldavian (adj)	молдавский	[mal'dafskij]

Russia	Россия (f)	[ra'sija]
Russian (man)	русский (m)	['ruskij]
Russian (woman)	русская (f)	['ruskaja]
Russian (adj)	русский	['ruskij]
Tajikistan	Таджикистан (m)	[tadʒıkis'tan]
Tajik (man)	таджик (m)	[ta'dʒik]
Tajik (woman)	таджичка (f)	[ta'dʒiʧkə]
Tajik (adj)	таджикский	[ta'dʒikskij]

Turkmenistan	Туркменистан (m)	[turkmenis'tan]
Turkmen (man)	туркмен (m)	[turk'men]
Turkmen (woman)	туркменка (f)	[turk'menkə]
Turkmenian (adj)	туркменский	[turk'menskij]

Uzbekistan	Узбекистан (m)	[uzbekis'tan]
Uzbek (man)	узбек (m)	[uz'bek]
Uzbek (woman)	узбечка (f)	[uz'beʧkə]
Uzbek (adj)	узбекский	[uz'bekskij]

Ukraine	Украина (f)	[ukra'inə]
Ukrainian (man)	украинец (m)	[ukra'inets]
Ukrainian (woman)	украинка (f)	[ukra'inkə]
Ukrainian (adj)	украинский	[ukra'inskij]

237. Asia

| Asia | Азия (f) | ['azija] |
| Asian | азиатский | [azi'atskij] |

Vietnam	Вьетнам (m)	[vjet′nam]
Vietnamese (man)	вьетнамец (m)	[vjet′namets]
Vietnamese (woman)	вьетнамка (f)	[vjet′namkə]
Vietnamese (adj)	вьетнамский	[vjet′namskij]

India	Индия (f)	[′indija]
Indian (man)	индус (m)	[in′dus]
Indian (woman)	индуска (f)	[in′duskə]
Indian (adj)	индийский	[in′dijskij]

Israel	Израиль (m)	[iz′raiʎ]
Israeli (man)	израильтянин (m)	[izraiʎ′t′anin]
Israeli (woman)	израильтянка (f)	[izraiʎ′t′ankə]
Israeli (adj)	израильский	[iz′raiʎskij]

Jew (noun)	еврей (m)	[ev′rej]
Jewess (noun)	еврейка (f)	[ev′rejkə]
Jewish (adj)	еврейский	[ev′rejskij]

China	Китай (m)	[ki′taj]
Chinese (man)	китаец (m)	[ki′taets]
Chinese (woman)	китаянка (f)	[kita′jankə]
Chinese (adj)	китайский	[ki′tajskij]

Korean (man)	кореец (m)	[ka′reets]
Korean (woman)	кореянка (f)	[kare′jankə]
Korean (adj)	корейский	[ka′rejskij]

Lebanon	Ливан (m)	[li′van]
Lebanese (man)	ливанец (m)	[li′vanets]
Lebanese (woman)	ливанка (f)	[li′vankə]
Lebanese (adj)	ливанский	[li′vanskij]

Mongolia	Монголия (f)	[ma′ŋolija]
Mongolian (man)	монгол (m)	[ma′ŋol]
Mongolian (woman)	монголка (f)	[ma′ŋolkə]
Mongolian (adj)	монгольский	[ma′ŋoʎskij]

Malaysia	Малайзия (f)	[ma′lajzija]
Malaysian (man)	малаец (m)	[ma′laets]
Malaysian (woman)	малайка (f)	[ma′lajkə]
Malaysian (adj)	малайский	[ma′lajskij]

Pakistan	Пакистан (m)	[pakis′tan]
Pakistani (man)	пакистанец (m)	[pakis′tanets]
Pakistani (woman)	пакистанка (f)	[pakis′tankə]
Pakistani (adj)	пакистанский	[pakis′tanskij]

Saudi Arabia	Саудовская Аравия (f)	[sa′udafskaja a′rawija]
Arab (man)	араб (m)	[a′rap]
Arab (woman)	арабка (f)	[a′rapkə]
Arabian (adj)	арабский	[a′rapskij]

Thailand	Таиланд (m)	[tai'lant]
Thai (man)	таец (m)	['taɛʦ]
Thai (woman)	тайка (f)	['tajkə]
Thai (adj)	тайский	['tajskij]
Taiwan	Тайвань (m)	[taj'vaɲ]
Taiwanese (man)	тайванец (m)	[taj'vanɛʦ]
Taiwanese (woman)	тайванка (f)	[taj'vankə]
Taiwanese (adj)	тайванский	[taj'vanskij]
Turkey	Турция (f)	['turʦija]
Turk (man)	турок (m)	['turak]
Turk (woman)	турчанка (f)	[tur'ʧankə]
Turkish (adj)	турецкий	[tu'retskij]
Japan	Япония (f)	[ja'pɔnija]
Japanese (man)	японец (m)	[ja'pɔnɛʦ]
Japanese (woman)	японка (f)	[ja'pɔnkə]
Japanese (adj)	японский	[ja'pɔnskij]
Afghanistan	Афганистан (m)	[afganis'tan]
Bangladesh	Бангладеш (m)	[bahgla'deʃ]
Indonesia	Индонезия (f)	[inda'nɛzija]
Jordan	Иордания (f)	[iar'danija]
Iraq	Ирак (m)	[i'rak]
Iran	Иран (m)	[i'ran]
Cambodia	Камбоджа (f)	[kam'bɔdʒə]
Kuwait	Кувейт (m)	[ku'wejt]
Laos	Лаос (m)	[la'ɔs]
Myanmar	Мьянма (f)	['mjanmə]
Nepal	Непал (m)	[ni'pal]
United Arab Emirates	Объединённые Арабские Эмираты (pl)	[abjedinɜnnɪe a'rapskie ɛmi'ratɪ]
Syria	Сирия (f)	['sirija]
Palestine	Палестина (f)	[pales'tinə]
South Korea	Южная Корея (f)	['juznaja ka'reja]
North Korea	Северная Корея (f)	['sewernaja ka'reja]

238. North America

United States of America	Соединённые Штаты (pl) Америки	[saedinɜnnɪe ʃ'tatɪ a'meriki]
American (man)	американец (m)	[amiri'kanɛʦ]
American (woman)	американка (f)	[amiri'kankə]
American (adj)	американский	[amiri'kanskij]
Canada	Канада (f)	[ka'nadə]
Canadian (man)	канадец (m)	[ka'nadɛʦ]

| Canadian (woman) | **канадка** (f) | [kɑ'nɑtkə] |
| Canadian (adj) | **канадский** | [kɑ'nɑtskij] |

Mexico	**Мексика** (f)	['meksikə]
Mexican (man)	**мексиканец** (m)	[miksi'kɑnets]
Mexican (woman)	**мексиканка** (f)	[miksi'kɑnkə]
Mexican (adj)	**мексиканский**	[miksi'kɑnskij]

239. Central and South America

Argentina	**Аргентина** (f)	[ɑrgen'tinə]
Argentinian (man)	**аргентинец** (m)	[ɑrgen'tinets]
Argentinian (woman)	**аргентинка** (f)	[ɑrgen'tinkə]
Argentinian (adj)	**аргентинский**	[ɑrgen'tinskij]

Brazil	**Бразилия** (f)	[brɑ'zilija]
Brazilian (man)	**бразилец** (m)	[brɑ'zilets]
Brazilian (woman)	**бразильянка** (f)	[brɑzi'ʎjankə]
Brazilian (adj)	**бразильский**	[brɑ'ziʎskij]

Colombia	**Колумбия** (f)	[kɑ'lumbija]
Colombian (man)	**колумбиец** (m)	[kɑlum'biets]
Colombian (woman)	**колумбийка** (f)	[kɑlum'bijkə]
Colombian (adj)	**колумбийский**	[kɑlum'bijskij]

Cuba	**Куба** (f)	['kʊbə]
Cuban (man)	**кубинец** (m)	[kʊ'binets]
Cuban (woman)	**кубинка** (f)	[kʊ'binkə]
Cuban (adj)	**кубинский**	[kʊ'binskij]

Chile	**Чили** (f)	['ʧili]
Chilean (man)	**чилиец** (m)	[ʧi'liets]
Chilean (woman)	**чилийка** (f)	[ʧi'lijkə]
Chilean (adj)	**чилийский**	[ʧi'lijskij]

Bolivia	**Боливия** (f)	[bɑ'liwija]
Venezuela	**Венесуэла** (f)	[winesʊ'ɛlə]
Paraguay	**Парагвай** (m)	[pɑrɑg'vaj]
Peru	**Перу** (n)	[pi'rʊ]

Surinam	**Суринам** (m)	[sʊri'nɑm]
Uruguay	**Уругвай** (m)	[urʊg'vaj]
Ecuador	**Эквадор** (m)	[ɛkvɑ'dɔr]

Bahamas	**Багамские острова** (f)	[bɑ'gamskie astra'va]
Haiti	**Гаити** (m)	[gɑ'iti]
Dominican Republic	**Доминиканская республика** (f)	[damini'kanskaja res'pʊblikə]
Panama	**Панама** (f)	[pɑ'namə]
Jamaica	**Ямайка** (f)	[ja'majkə]

240. Africa

Egypt	Египет (m)	[e'gipet]
Egyptian (man)	египтянин (m)	[egip't'anin]
Egyptian (woman)	египтянка (f)	[egip't'anke]
Egyptian (adj)	египетский	[e'gipetskij]

Morocco	Марокко (n)	[ma'rɔkke]
Moroccan (man)	марокканец (m)	[mara'kanets]
Moroccan (woman)	марокканка (f)	[mara'kanke]
Moroccan (adj)	марокканский	[mara'kanskij]

Tunisia	Тунис (m)	[tu'nis]
Tunisian (man)	тунисец (m)	[tu'nisets]
Tunisian (woman)	туниска (f)	[tu'niske]
Tunisian (adj)	тунисский	[tu'niskij]

Ghana	Гана (f)	['gane]
Zanzibar	Занзибар (m)	[zanzi'bar]
Kenya	Кения (f)	['kenija]
Libya	Ливия (f)	['liwija]
Madagascar	Мадагаскар (m)	[madagas'kar]

Namibia	Намибия (f)	[na'mibija]
Senegal	Сенегал (m)	[sine'gal]
Tanzania	Танзания (f)	[tan'zanija]
South Africa	ЮАР (m)	[ju'ar]

African (man)	африканец (m)	[afri'kanets]
African (woman)	африканка (f)	[afri'kanke]
African (adj)	африканский	[afri'kanskij]

241. Australia. Oceania

| Australia | Австралия (f) | [afst'ralija] |
| Australian (man) | австралиец (m) | [afstra'liets] |

| Australian (woman) | австралийка (f) | [afstra'lijke] |
| Australian (adj) | австралийский | [afstra'lijskij] |

| New Zealand | Новая Зеландия (f) | ['nɔvaja ze'landija] |
| New Zealander (man) | новозеландец (m) | [navaze'landets] |

| New Zealander (woman) | новозеландка (f) | [navaze'lantke] |
| New Zealand (attr) | новозеландский | [navaze'lantskij] |

| Tasmania | Тасмания (f) | [tas'manija] |
| French Polynesia | Французская Полинезия (f) | [fran'tsuskaja pali'nezija] |

242. Cities

Amsterdam	**Амстердам** (m)	[amster'dam]
Ankara	**Анкара** (f)	[anka'ra]
Athens	**Афины** (pl)	[a'finɪ]
Baghdad	**Багдад** (m)	[bag'dat]
Bangkok	**Бангкок** (m)	[ba'ŋkɔk]
Barcelona	**Барселона** (f)	[barsi'lɔnə]
Beijing	**Пекин** (m)	[pi'kin]
Beirut	**Бейрут** (m)	[bij'rʊt]
Berlin	**Берлин** (m)	[bir'lin]
Bombay	**Бомбей** (m)	[bam'bej]
Bonn	**Бонн** (m)	[bɔn]
Bordeaux	**Бордо** (m)	[bar'dɔ]
Bratislava	**Братислава** (f)	[bratis'lavə]
Brussels	**Брюссель** (m)	[bry'seʎ]
Bucharest	**Бухарест** (m)	[bʊha'rest]
Budapest	**Будапешт** (m)	[bʊda'peʃt]
Cairo	**Каир** (m)	[ka'ir]
Calcutta	**Калькутта** (f)	[kaʎ'kʊtə]
Chicago	**Чикаго** (m)	[ʧi'kagə]
Copenhagen	**Копенгаген** (m)	[kape'ŋagen]
Dar-es-Salaam	**Дар-эс-Салам** (m)	[dar ɛssa'lam]
Delhi	**Дели** (m)	['dɛli]
Dubai	**Дубай** (m)	[dʊ'baj]
Dublin	**Дублин** (m)	['dʊblin]
Düsseldorf	**Дюссельдорф** (m)	[dyseʎ'dɔrf]
Florence	**Флоренция** (f)	[fla'rentsija]
Frankfurt	**Франкфурт** (m)	['frankfʊrt]
Geneva	**Женева** (f)	[ʒɪ'nevə]
Hamburg	**Гамбург** (m)	['gambʊrk]
Hanoi	**Ханой** (m)	[ha'nɔj]
Havana	**Гавана** (f)	[ga'vanə]
Helsinki	**Хельсинки** (m)	['heʎsinki]
Hiroshima	**Хиросима** (f)	[hira'simə]
Hong Kong	**Гонконг** (m)	[ga'ŋkɔnk]
Istanbul	**Стамбул** (m)	[stam'bʊl]
Jerusalem	**Иерусалим** (m)	[iirʊsa'lim]
Kiev	**Киев** (m)	['kief]
Kuala Lumpur	**Куала-Лумпур** (m)	[kʊ'ala 'lumpʊr]
Lisbon	**Лиссабон** (m)	[lisa'bɔn]
London	**Лондон** (m)	['lɔndan]
Los Angeles	**Лос-Анджелес** (m)	[lɔs 'anʒɪles]
Lyons	**Лион** (m)	[li'ɔn]

Madrid	**Мадрид** (m)	[mɑd'rit]
Marseille	**Марсель** (m)	[mɑr'seʎ]
Mexico	**Мехико** (m)	['mehikə]
Miami	**Майями** (m)	[mɑ'jami]
Montréal	**Монреаль** (m)	[mɑnre'aʎ]
Moscow	**Москва** (f)	[mɑsk'vɑ]
Munich	**Мюнхен** (m)	['mynhen]

Nairobi	**Найроби** (m)	[nɑj'rɔbi]
Naples	**Неаполь** (m)	[ni'ɑpoʎ]
New York	**Нью-Йорк** (m)	[ɲjy 'jork]
Nice	**Ницца** (f)	['nitsə]
Oslo	**Осло** (m)	['ɔslə]
Ottawa	**Оттава** (f)	[ɑt'tɑvə]

Paris	**Париж** (m)	[pɑ'riʃ]
Prague	**Прага** (f)	['prɑgə]
Rio de Janeiro	**Рио-де-Жанейро** (m)	[riɑ de ʒɑ'nejrə]
Rome	**Рим** (m)	[rim]

Saint Petersburg	**Санкт-Петербург** (m)	[sɑnkt peter'bʊrk]
Seoul	**Сеул** (m)	[si'ul]
Shanghai	**Шанхай** (m)	[ʃʌn'hɑj]
Singapore	**Сингапур** (m)	[sihgɑ'pʊr]
Stockholm	**Стокгольм** (m)	[stɑk'gɔʎm]
Sydney	**Сидней** (m)	['sidnej]

Taipei	**Тайпей** (m)	[tɑj'pej]
The Hague	**Гаага** (f)	[gɑ'ɑgə]
Tokyo	**Токио** (m)	['tɔkiə]
Toronto	**Торонто** (m)	[tɑ'rɔntə]

Venice	**Венеция** (f)	[wi'netsɪjɑ]
Vienna	**Вена** (f)	['wenə]
Warsaw	**Варшава** (f)	[vɑr'ʃʌvə]
Washington	**Вашингтон** (m)	[vɑʃɪnk'tɔn]

243. Politics. Government. Part 1

politics	**политика** (f)	[pɑ'litikə]
political	**политический**	[pɑli'titʃeskij]
politician	**политик** (m)	[pɑ'litik]

state (country)	**государство** (n)	[gɑsʊ'dɑrstvə]
citizen	**гражданин** (m)	[grɑʒdɑ'nin]
citizenship	**гражданство** (n)	[grɑʒ'dɑnstvə]

national emblem	**национальный герб** (m)	[nɑtsɪɑ'nɑʎnɪj gerp]
national anthem	**государственный гимн** (m)	[gɑsʊ'dɑrstwenɪj gimn]

government	**правительство** (n)	[prɑ'witeʎstvə]
head of state	**руководитель** (m) **страны**	[rʊkavɑ'diteʎ strɑ'nɪ]
parliament	**парламент** (m)	[par'lament]
party	**партия** (f)	['partija]
capitalism	**капитализм** (m)	[kapitɑ'lizm]
capitalist (adj)	**капиталистический**	[kapitalis'titʃeskij]
socialism	**социализм** (m)	[sɑtsıɑ'lizm]
socialist (adj)	**социалистический**	[sɑtsıalis'titʃeskij]
communism	**коммунизм** (m)	[kamʊ'nizm]
communist (adj)	**коммунистический**	[kamʊnis'titʃeskij]
communist (noun)	**коммунист** (m)	[kamʊ'nist]
democracy	**демократия** (f)	[dimak'ratija]
democrat	**демократ** (m)	[dimak'rat]
democratic (adj)	**демократический**	[dimakrɑ'titʃeskij]
Democratic party	**демократическая партия** (f)	[dimakrɑ'titʃiskaja 'partija]
liberal (noun)	**либерал** (m)	[libe'ral]
liberal (adj)	**либеральный**	[libe'raʎnıj]
conservative (noun)	**консерватор** (m)	[kanser'vatar]
conservative (adj)	**консервативный**	[kanservɑ'tivnıj]
republic (noun)	**республика** (f)	[ris'pʊblikə]
republican (noun)	**республиканец** (m)	[rispʊbli'kanets]
Republican party	**республиканская партия** (f)	[rispʊbli'kanskaja 'partija]
poll, elections	**выборы** (pl)	['vıbarı]
to elect (vt)	**выбирать**	[vıbi'ratʲ]
elector, voter	**избиратель** (m)	[izbi'rateʎ]
election campaign	**избирательная кампания** (f)	[izbi'rateʎnaja kam'panija]
voting (noun)	**голосование** (n)	[galasɑ'vanie]
to vote (vi, vt)	**голосовать**	[galasɑ'vatʲ]
suffrage, right to vote	**право** (n) **голоса**	['prava 'golasə]
candidate	**кандидат** (m)	[kandi'dat]
to be a candidate	**баллотироваться**	[balɑ'tiravatsə]
campaign	**кампания** (f)	[kam'panija]
opposition (attr)	**оппозиционный**	[apazitsı'ɔnnıj]
opposition (noun)	**оппозиция** (f)	[apɑ'zitsıja]
visit	**визит** (m)	[wi'zit]
official visit	**официальный визит** (m)	[afitsı'aʎnıj wi'zit]
international	**международный**	[miʒdʊna'rɔdnıj]

negotiations	**переговоры** (pl)	[pirega'vɔrɪ]
to negotiate (vi)	**вести переговоры**	[wis'ti perega'vɔrɪ]

244. Politics. Government. Part 2

society	**общество** (n)	['ɔpɕestvə]
constitution	**конституция** (f)	[kɑnsti'tutsɪja]
power (political control)	**власть** (f)	[vlɑstʲ]
corruption	**коррупция** (f)	[kɑ'ruptsɪja]
law (justice)	**закон** (m)	[zɑ'kɔn]
legal (legitimate)	**законный**	[zɑ'kɔnnɪj]
justice (fairness)	**справедливость** (f)	[sprawed'livɑstʲ]
just (fair)	**справедливый**	[sprawed'livɪj]
committee	**комитет** (m)	[kami'tet]
bill (draft of law)	**законопроект** (m)	[zakɔnaprɑ'ekt]
budget	**бюджет** (m)	[by'dʒet]
policy	**политика** (f)	[pɑ'litikə]
reform	**реформа** (f)	[ri'fɔrmə]
radical (adj)	**радикальный**	[radi'kaʎnɪj]
power (strength, force)	**сила** (f)	['silə]
powerful	**сильный**	['siʎnɪj]
supporter (follower)	**сторонник** (m)	[stɑ'rɔnnik]
influence	**влияние** (n)	[vli'janie]
regime (e.g., military ~)	**режим** (m)	[ri'ʒim]
conflict	**конфликт** (m)	[kɑnf'likt]
conspiracy (plot)	**заговор** (m)	['zagavar]
provocation	**провокация** (f)	[prava'katsɪja]
to overthrow (regime etc.)	**свергнуть**	['swergnutʲ]
overthrow (of government)	**свержение** (n)	[swir'ʒenie]
revolution	**революция** (f)	[riva'lytsɪja]
coup d'état	**переворот** (m)	[pireva'rɔt]
military coup	**военный переворот** (m)	[va'ennɪj pireva'rɔt]
crisis	**кризис** (m)	['krizis]
economic recession	**экономический спад** (m)	[ɛkana'mitʃeskij spat]
demonstrator (protester)	**демонстрант** (m)	[dimanst'rant]
demonstration	**демонстрация** (f)	[dimanst'ratsɪja]
martial law	**военное положение** (n)	[va'ennae pala'ʒenie]
military base	**база** (f)	['bazə]
stability	**стабильность** (f)	[stɑ'biʎnastʲ]
stable	**стабильный**	[stɑ'biʎnɪj]
exploitation	**эксплуатация** (f)	[iksplua'tatsɪja]

to exploit (workers)	эксплуатировать	[iksplua'tiravat']
racism	расизм (m)	[ra'sizm]
racist	расист (m)	[ra'sist]
fascism	фашизм (m)	[fa'ʃizm]
fascist	фашист (m)	[fa'ʃist]

245. Countries. Miscellaneous

foreigner	иностранец (m)	[inast'ranets]
foreign (adj)	иностранный	[inast'rannij]
abroad (overseas)	за границей	[za gra'nitsəj]
emigrant	эмигрант (m)	[ɛmig'rant]
emigration	эмиграция (f)	[ɛmig'ratsija]
to emigrate (vi)	эмигрировать	[ɛmig'riravat']
the West	Запад (m)	['zapat]
the East	Восток (m)	[vas'tok]
the Far East	Дальний Восток (m)	['daʎnij vas'tok]
civilization	цивилизация (f)	[tsıwili'zatsija]
humanity (mankind)	человечество (n)	[tʃila'wetʃestvə]
world (earth)	мир (m)	[mir]
peace	мир (m)	[mir]
worldwide (adj)	мировой	[mira'voj]
homeland (native country)	родина (f)	['rodinə]
people	народ (m)	[na'rot]
population	население (n)	[nasi'lenie]
people (e.g., a lot of ~)	люди (m pl)	['lydi]
nation (people)	нация (f)	['natsija]
generation	поколение (n)	[paka'lenie]
territory (area)	территория (f)	[tiri'torija]
region	регион (m)	[rigi'on]
state (part of a country)	штат (m)	[ʃtat]
tradition	традиция (f)	[tra'ditsija]
custom (tradition)	обычай (m)	[a'bıtʃej]
ecology	экология (f)	[ɛka'logija]
Indian (Native American)	индеец (m)	[in'deits]
Gipsy (man)	цыган (m)	[tsı'gan]
Gipsy (woman)	цыганка (f)	[tsı'gankə]
Gipsy (adj)	цыганский	[tsı'ganskij]
empire	империя (f)	[im'perija]
colony	колония (f)	[ka'lonija]
slavery	рабство (n)	['rapstvə]
invasion	нашествие (n)	[na'ʃɛstwie]
famine	голод (m)	['golat]

246. Major religious groups. Confessions

religion	религия (f)	[ri'ligija]
religious	религиозный	[riligi'ɔznıj]
belief (in God)	верование (n)	['weravanie]
to believe (vi)	верить	['weritʲ]
believer	верующий (m)	['werʊjuɕij]
atheism	атеизм (m)	[atɛ'izm]
atheist	атеист (m)	[atɛ'ist]
Christianity	христианство (n)	[hristi'anstvə]
Christian (noun)	христианин (m)	[hristia'nin]
Christian (adj)	христианский	[hristi'anskij]
Catholicism	Католицизм (m)	[katali'ʦızm]
Catholic (noun)	католик (m)	[ka'tɔlik]
Catholic (adj)	католический	[kata'litʃeskij]
Protestantism	Протестантство (n)	[prates'tanstvə]
Protestant Church	Протестантская церковь (f)	[prates'tanskaja 'ʦerkavʲ]
Protestant	протестант (m)	[prates'tant]
Orthodoxy	Православие (n)	[pravas'lawie]
Orthodox Church	Православная церковь (f)	[pravas'lavnaja 'ʦerkafʲ]
Orthodox	православный (m)	[pravas'lavnıj]
Presbyterianism	Пресвитерианство (n)	[priswiteri'anstvə]
Presbyterian Church	Пресвитерианская церковь (f)	[preswiteri'anskaja 'ʦerkafʲ]
Presbyterian (noun)	пресвитерианин (m)	[priswiteri'anin]
Lutheranism	Лютеранская церковь (f)	[lyte'ranskaja 'ʦerkafʲ]
Lutheran	лютеранин (m)	[lyte'ranin]
Baptist Church	Баптизм (m)	[bap'tizm]
Baptist	баптист (m)	[bap'tist]
Anglican Church	Англиканская церковь (f)	[ahgli'kanskaja 'ʦerkafʲ]
Anglican	англиканин (m)	[ahgli'kanin]
Mormonism	Мормонство (n)	[mar'mɔnstvə]
Mormon	мормон (m)	[mar'mɔn]
Judaism	Иудаизм (m)	[iuda'izm]
Jew	иудей (m)	[iu'dej]
Buddhism	Буддизм (m)	[bʊ'dizm]
Buddhist	буддист (m)	[bʊ'dist]

| Hinduism | Индуизм (m) | [indʊ'izm] |
| Hindu | индуист (m) | [indʊ'ist] |

Islam	Ислам (m)	[is'lam]
Muslim (noun)	мусульманин (m)	[mʊsʊʎ'manin]
Muslim (adj)	мусульманский	[mʊsʊʎ'manskij]

Shiism	Шиизм (m)	[ʃi'izm]
Shiite (noun)	шиит (m)	[ʃi'it]
Sunni (religion)	Суннизм (m)	[sʊ'ɲizm]
Sunnite (noun)	суннит (m)	[sʊ'ɲit]

247. Religions. Priests

| priest | священник (m) | [swi'çennik] |
| the Pope | Папа Римский (m) | ['papa 'rimskij] |

monk, friar	монах (m)	[ma'nah]
nun	монахиня (f)	[ma'nahiɲa]
pastor	пастор (m)	['pastar]

abbot	аббат (m)	[a'bat]
vicar	викарий (m)	[wi'karij]
bishop	епископ (m)	[e'piskap]
cardinal	кардинал (m)	[kardi'nal]
pope (orthodox priest)	поп (m)	[pɔp]

preacher	проповедник (m)	[prapa'wednik]
preaching	проповедь (f)	['propawetʲ]
parishioners	прихожане (pl)	[priha'ʒane]

| believer | верующий (m) | ['werʊjʊçij] |
| atheist | атеист (m) | [atɛ'ist] |

248. Faith. Christianity. Islam

| Adam | Адам (m) | [a'dam] |
| Eve | Ева (f) | ['evə] |

God	Бог (m)	[bɔk]
the Lord	Господь (m)	[gas'pɔtʲ]
the Almighty	Всемогущий (m)	[fsima'gʊçij]

sin	грех (m)	[greh]
to sin (vi)	грешить	[gri'ʃitʲ]
sinner (man)	грешник (m)	['greʃnik]
sinner (woman)	грешница (f)	['greʃnitsə]
hell	ад (m)	[at]

paradise	**рай** (m)	[raj]
Jesus	**Иисус** (m)	[ii'sus]
Jesus Christ	**Иисус Христос** (m)	[ii'sus hris'tos]
Christ	**Христос** (m)	[hris'tos]
the Holy Spirit	**Святой Дух** (m)	[swi'toj duh]
the Savior	**Спаситель** (m)	[spa'siteʎ]
the Virgin Mary	**Богородица** (f)	[baga'roditsə]
the Devil	**Дьявол** (m)	['djaval]
devil's	**дьявольский**	['djavaʎskij]
Satan	**Сатана** (f)	[sata'na]
Satan's	**сатанинский**	[sata'ninskij]
angel	**ангел** (m)	['ahgel]
guardian angel	**ангел-хранитель** (m)	['ahgel hra'niteʎ]
angelic	**ангельский**	['ahgeʎskij]
apostle	**апостол** (m)	[a'postal]
archangel	**архангел** (m)	[ar'hahgel]
the Antichrist	**антихрист** (m)	[an'tihrist]
the Church	**Церковь** (f)	['tsɛrkafʲ]
Bible	**библия** (f)	['biblija]
biblical	**библейский**	[bib'lejskij]
Old Testament	**Ветхий Завет** (m)	['wethij za'wet]
New Testament	**Новый Завет** (m)	['novij za'wet]
Gospel	**Евангелие** (n)	[e'vahgelie]
Holy Scripture	**Священное Писание** (n)	[swi'cennae pi'sanie]
Heaven	**Царство** (n) **Небесное**	['tsarstva ne'besnae]
Commandment	**заповедь** (f)	['zapawetʲ]
prophet	**пророк** (m)	[pra'rok]
prophecy	**пророчество** (n)	[pra'rotʃestvə]
Allah	**Аллах** (m)	[a'lah]
Mohammed	**Мухаммед** (m)	[mu'hamet]
the Koran	**Коран** (m)	[ka'ran]
mosque	**мечеть** (f)	[mi'tʃetʲ]
mullah	**мулла** (f)	[mul'la]
prayer	**молитва** (f)	[ma'litvə]
to pray (vi, vt)	**молиться**	[ma'litsə]
pilgrimage	**паломничество** (n)	[pa'lomnitʃestvə]
pilgrim	**паломник** (m)	[pa'lomnik]
Mecca	**Мекка** (f)	['mekkə]
church	**церковь** (f)	['tsɛrkafʲ]
temple	**храм** (m)	[hram]
cathedral	**собор** (m)	[sa'bor]

Gothic	готический	[ga'titʃeskij]
synagogue	синагога (f)	[sina'gogə]
mosque	мечеть (f)	[mi'tʃetʲ]

chapel	часовня (f)	[tʃi'sovɲa]
abbey	аббатство (n)	[a'batstvə]
convent	монастырь (m)	[manas'tɪrʲ]
monastery	монастырь (m)	[manas'tɪrʲ]

bell (in church)	колокол (m)	['kɔlakal]
bell tower	колокольня (f)	[kala'kɔʎɲa]
to ring (about bells)	звонить	[zva'nitʲ]

cross	крест (m)	[krest]
cupola (roof)	купол (m)	['kupal]
icon	икона (f)	[i'kɔnə]

soul	душа (f)	[du'ʃʌ]
fate (destiny)	судьба (f)	[sud'ba]
evil (noun)	зло (n)	[zlɔ]
good (noun)	добро (n)	[dab'rɔ]

vampire	вампир (m)	[vam'pir]
witch (sorceress)	ведьма (f)	['wedʲmə]
demon	демон (m)	['deman]
devil	чёрт (m)	['tʃɔrt]
spirit	дух (m)	[duh]

| redemption | искупление (n) | [iskup'lenie] |
| to redeem (vt) | искупить | [isku'pitʲ] |

church service, mass	служба (f)	['sluʒbə]
to say mass	служить	[slu'ʒitʲ]
confession	исповедь (f)	['ispawetʲ]
to confess (vi)	исповедоваться	[ispa'wedavatsə]

saint (noun)	святой (m)	[swi'tɔj]
sacred (holy)	священный	[swi'ɕennɪj]
holy water	святая вода (f)	[swi'taja va'da]

ritual (noun)	ритуал (m)	[ritu'al]
ritual (adj)	ритуальный	[ritu'aʎnɪj]
sacrifice (offering)	жертвоприношение (n)	[ʒertvaprina'ʃenie]

superstition	суеверие (n)	[sui'werie]
superstitious	суеверный	[sui'wernɪj]
afterlife	загробная жизнь (f)	[zag'robnaja ʒɪzɲ]
eternal life	вечная жизнь (f)	['wetʃnaja ʒɪzɲ]

MISCELLANEOUS

249. Various useful words

background (green ~)	фон (m)	[fɔn]
balance (of situation)	баланс (m)	[baˈlans]
barrier (obstacle)	преграда (f)	[prigˈradə]
base (basis)	база (f)	[ˈbazə]
beginning	начало (n)	[naˈtʃalə]
category	категория (f)	[kateˈgɔrija]
cause (reason)	причина (f)	[priˈtʃinə]
choice	выбор (m)	[ˈvɪbar]
coincidence	совпадение (n)	[safpaˈdenie]
comfortable (~ chair)	удобный	[uˈdɔbnɪj]
comparison	сравнение (n)	[sravˈnenie]
compensation	компенсация (f)	[kampenˈsatsɪja]
degree (extent, amount)	степень (f)	[ˈstepeɲ]
development	развитие (n)	[razˈwitie]
difference	различие (n)	[razˈlitʃie]
effect (e.g., of drug)	эффект (m)	[ɛˈfekt]
effort (exertion)	усилие (n)	[uˈsilie]
element	элемент (m)	[ɛliˈment]
end (finish)	окончание (n)	[akaɲˈtʃanie]
example (illustration)	пример (m)	[priˈmer]
fact	факт (m)	[fakt]
frequent	частый	[ˈtʃastɪj]
growth (development)	рост (m)	[rɔst]
help	помощь (f)	[ˈpɔmaɕ]
ideal	идеал (m)	[idiˈal]
kind (sort, type)	вид (m)	[wit]
labyrinth	лабиринт (m)	[labiˈrint]
mistake	ошибка (f)	[aˈʃipkə]
moment	момент (m)	[maˈment]
object (thing)	объект (m)	[abʰˈekt]
obstacle	препятствие (n)	[priˈpʲatstwie]
original (original copy)	оригинал (m)	[arigiˈnal]
part (~ of sth)	часть (f)	[tʃastʲ]
particle, small part	частица (f)	[tʃisˈtitsə]
pause (break)	пауза (f)	[ˈpauzə]

position	позиция (f)	[pɑ'zitsija]
principle	принцип (m)	['printsip]
problem (is there any ~?)	проблема (f)	[prɑb'lemə]

process	процесс (m)	[prɑ'tses]
progress	прогресс (m)	[prɑg'res]
property (quality)	свойство (n)	['svɔjstvə]
reaction	реакция (f)	[ri'ɑktsija]
risk	риск (m)	[risk]

secret	тайна (f)	['tajnə]
section (sector)	секция (f)	['sektsija]
series	серия (f)	['serija]
shape (outer form)	форма (f)	['fɔrmə]
situation	ситуация (f)	[situ'atsija]

solution	решение (n)	[ri'ʃənie]
standard (adj)	стандартный	[stan'dartnij]
standard (level of quality)	стандарт (m)	[stan'dart]
stop (pause)	остановка (f)	[asta'nɔfkə]
style	стиль (m)	[stiʎ]
system	система (f)	[sis'temə]

table (chart)	таблица (f)	[tab'litsə]
tempo, rate	темп (m)	[tɛmp]
term (word, expression)	термин (m)	['termin]
thing (object)	предмет (m)	[prid'met]
thing (object, item)	вещь (f)	[weɕ]
truth	истина (f)	['istinə]
turn (please, wait your ~)	очередь (f)	['ɔtʃiretʲ]
type (sort, kind)	тип (m)	[tip]

urgent	срочный	['srɔtʃnij]
urgently	срочно	['srɔtʃnə]
use (usefulness)	польза (f)	['pɔʎzə]

variant	вариант (m)	[vari'ɑnt]
way (means, method)	способ (m)	['spɔsɑp]
zone	зона (f)	['zɔnə]

250. Modifiers. Adjectives. Part 1

additional	дополнительный	[dapal'niteʎnij]
ancient (civilization etc.)	древний	['drevnij]
artificial	искусственный	[is'kustwennij]

back, rear	задний	['zadnij]
bad	плохой	[plɑ'hɔj]
beautiful	красивый	[kra'sivij]
beautiful (e.g., ~ palace)	прекрасный	[prik'rasnij]

big (in size)	**большой**	[bɐʌ'ʃoj]
bitter (taste)	**горький**	['gorʲkij]
blind (sightless)	**слепой**	[sli'poj]
calm	**тихий**	['tihij]
calm, quiet	**спокойный**	[spɐ'kojnɪj]
careless (negligent)	**небрежный**	[nib'reʒnɪj]
caring (kindly)	**заботливый**	[zɐ'botlivɪj]
central (in location)	**центральный**	[tsɪnt'raʌnɪj]
cheap (inexpensive)	**дешёвый**	[di'ʃovɪj]
children's	**детский**	['detskij]
civil (of community)	**гражданский**	[grɐʒ'danskij]
clandestine (secret)	**подпольный**	[pɐt'poʌnɪj]
clean (free from dirt)	**чистый**	['ʧistɪj]
clear (thinking, argument)	**понятный**	[pɐ'ɲatnɪj]
clever (smart)	**умный**	['umnɪj]
close (near in space)	**близкий**	['bliskij]
closed	**закрытый**	[zɑk'rɪtɪj]
cloudless (sky)	**безоблачный**	[bi'zoblaʧnɪj]
cold (drink, weather)	**холодный**	[hɐ'lodnɪj]
compatible	**совместимый**	[sɐvmes'timɪj]
contented	**довольный**	[dɐ'voʌnɪj]
continuous	**продолжительный**	[prɐdɐ'ʒiteʌnɪj]
continuous (uninterrupted)	**непрерывный**	[nipre'rɪvnɪj]
cool (weather)	**прохладный**	[prɐh'ladnɪj]
dangerous	**опасный**	[ɐ'pɑsnɪj]
dark (room)	**тёмный**	['tɜmnɪj]
dead (not alive)	**мёртвый**	['mɜrtvɪj]
dense (fog, smoke)	**плотный**	['plotnɪj]
different (from each other)	**разный**	['rɑznɪj]
different (various)	**различный**	[raz'liʧnɪj]
difficult (decision)	**трудный**	['trʊdnɪj]
difficult (problem, task)	**сложный**	['sloʒnɪj]
dim, faint (light)	**тусклый**	['tʊsklɪj]
dirty (not clean)	**грязный**	['grʲaznɪj]
distant (faraway)	**дальний**	['dɑʌnɪj]
dry (climate, clothing)	**сухой**	[sʊ'hoj]
easy (not difficult)	**лёгкий**	['lɜɦkij]
empty (glass, room)	**пустой**	[pʊs'toj]
exact (amount)	**точный**	['toʧnɪj]
excellent	**отличный**	[ɐt'liʧnɪj]
excessive (demand)	**чрезмерный**	[ʧrez'mernɪj]
expensive	**дорогой**	[dɐrɐ'goj]
exterior	**внешний**	['vneʃnij]
far (distant in space)	**далёкий**	[dɐ'lɜkij]

fast (quick)	быстрый	[ˈbɪstrɪj]
fatty (food)	жирный	[ˈʒɪrnɪj]
fertile (land, soil)	плодородный	[plada'rodnɪj]
flat (e.g., ~ panel display)	плоский	[ˈploskɪj]
flat (e.g., ~ surface)	ровный	[ˈrovnɪj]
foreign (country, language)	иностранный	[inast'rannɪj]
fragile (china, glass)	хрупкий	[ˈhrupkɪj]
free (at no cost)	бесплатный	[bisp'latnɪj]
free (unrestricted)	свободный	[sva'bodnɪj]
fresh (~ water)	пресный	[ˈpresnɪj]
fresh (e.g., ~ bred)	свежий	[ˈsweʒɪj]
frozen (food)	замороженный	[zama'roʒɪnɪj]
full (completely filled)	полный	[ˈpolnɪj]
good (book etc.)	хороший	[ha'roʃɪj]
good, kind	добрый	[ˈdobrɪj]
grateful	благодарный	[blaga'darnɪj]
happy	счастливый	[ɕis'livɪj]
hard (not soft)	твёрдый	[ˈtwɜrdɪj]
heavy (in weight)	тяжёлый	[ti'ʒɜlɪj]
hostile	враждебный	[vraʒ'debnɪj]
hot (high in temperature)	горячий	[ga'ratʃɪj]
huge	огромный	[ag'romnɪj]
humid	влажный	[ˈvlaʒnɪj]
hungry	голодный	[ga'lodnɪj]
ill (sick, unwell)	больной	[baʎ'noj]
illegible	непонятный	[nipa'ɲatnɪj]
immobile	неподвижный	[nipad'wiʒnɪj]
important	важный	[ˈvaʒnɪj]
impossible (not possible)	невозможный	[nivaz'moʒnɪj]
indispensable	необходимый	[niabha'dimɪj]
inexperienced	неопытный	[ni'opɪtnɪj]
insignificant (unimportant)	незначительный	[nizna'tʃiteʎnɪj]
interior	внутренний	[ˈvnutrenɪj]
joint (~ decision)	совместный	[sav'mesnɪj]
last (e.g., ~ week)	прошлый	[ˈproʃlɪj]
last (final)	последний	[pas'lednɪj]
left (e.g., ~ side)	левый	[ˈlevɪj]
legal (legitimate)	законный	[za'konnɪj]
light (in weight)	лёгкий	[ˈlɜɦkɪj]
light (pale color)	светлый	[ˈswetlɪj]
limited (restricted)	ограниченный	[agra'nitʃenɪj]
liquid (fluid)	жидкий	[ˈʒitkɪj]
long (e.g., ~ way)	длинный	[ˈdlinnɪj]
loud (voice etc.)	громкий	[ˈgromkɪj]
low (voice)	тихий	[ˈtiɦɪj]

251. Modifiers. Adjectives. Part 2

main (principal)	главный	['glavnɪj]
matt	матовый	['matavɪj]
merry, cheerful	весёлый	[wi'sɜlɪj]
meticulous (job)	аккуратный	[aku'ratnɪj]
mysterious	загадочный	[za'gadatʃnɪj]
narrow (street, passage)	узкий	['uskij]
native (of country)	родной	[rad'nɔj]
near (in space)	ближний	['blɪʒnɪj]
near-sighted	близорукий	[blɪza'rʊkij]
necessary (indispensable)	нужный	['nʊʒnɪj]
negative	отрицательный	[atri'tsateʌnɪj]
neighboring	соседний	[sa'sednɪj]
nervous	нервный	['nervnɪj]
new	новый	['nɔvɪj]
next (e.g., ~ week)	следующий	['sleduɕij]
nice (kind)	милый	['mɪlɪj]
nice (voice)	приятный	[pri'jatnɪj]
normal (common, typical)	нормальный	[nar'maʌnɪj]
not big	небольшой	[nibaʌ'ʃɔj]
not clear	неясный	[ni'jasnɪj]
not difficult	нетрудный	[nit'rʊdnɪj]
obligatory	обязательный	[abi'zateʌnɪj]
old (house)	старый	['starɪj]
open	открытый	[atk'rɪtɪj]
opposite	противоположный	[prativapa'lɔʒnɪj]
ordinary (usual, normal)	обыкновенный	[abɪkna'wennɪj]
original (unusual)	оригинальный	[arigi'naʌnɪj]
past (recent)	прошедший	[pra'ʃetʃij]
permanent	постоянный	[pasta'jannɪj]
personal (message, letter)	персональный	[pirsa'naʌnɪj]
polite	вежливый	['weʒlivɪj]
poor (not rich)	бедный	['bednɪj]
possible	возможный	[vaz'mɔʒnɪj]
poverty-stricken	нищий	['niɕij]
present (in time)	настоящий	[nasta'jaɕij]
principal (main)	основной	[asnav'nɔj]
private (not for the public)	частный	['tʃasnɪj]
private (personal)	личный	['lɪtʃnɪj]
probable (likely)	вероятный	[wira'jatnɪj]
public (open to all)	общественный	[ap'ɕestwenɪj]
punctual (person)	пунктуальный	[pʊnktu'aʌnɪj]
rare (uncommon)	редкий	['retkij]

raw (uncooked)	**сырой**	[sɪˈrɔj]
right	**правый**	[ˈpravɪj]
right, correct	**правильный**	[ˈprawiʎnɪj]
ripe (fruit)	**зрелый**	[ˈzrelɪj]
risky	**рискованный**	[risˈkɔvanɪj]
sad (depressing)	**грустный**	[ˈgrʊsnɪj]
sad (unhappy)	**печальный**	[piˈtʃaʎnɪj]
safe (not dangerous)	**безопасный**	[bizaˈpasnɪj]
salty (food)	**солёный**	[saˈlɔnɪj]
satisfied (customer)	**удовлетворённый**	[udavletvaˈrɜnnɪj]
second hand	**бывший**	[ˈbɪʃʃɪj
	в употреблении	v upatrebˈlenii]
shallow (water)	**мелкий**	[ˈmelkij]
sharp (blade, scissors)	**острый**	[ˈɔstrɪj]
short (in length)	**короткий**	[kaˈrɔtkij]
short, short-lived	**кратковременный**	[kratkavˈreminnɪj]
significant (notable)	**значительный**	[znaˈtʃiteʎnɪj]
similar	**похожий**	[paˈhɔʒɪj]
simple (easy)	**простой**	[prasˈtɔj]
skinny (too thin)	**тощий**	[ˈtɔɕij]
slim (person)	**худой**	[hʊˈdɔj]
smooth (surface)	**гладкий**	[ˈglatkij]
soft (to touch)	**мягкий**	[ˈmʲaɦkij]
somber, gloomy	**мрачный**	[ˈmratʃnɪj]
sour (flavor, taste)	**кислый**	[ˈkislɪj]
spacious (house, room)	**просторный**	[prasˈtɔrnɪj]
special	**специальный**	[spitsɪˈaʎnɪj]
straight (line, road)	**прямой**	[priˈmɔj]
strong (construction)	**прочный**	[ˈprɔtʃnɪj]
strong (person)	**сильный**	[ˈsiʎnɪj]
stupid (foolish)	**глупый**	[ˈglupɪj]
suitable	**пригодный**	[priˈgɔdnɪj]
sunny (day)	**солнечный**	[ˈsɔlnetʃnɪj]
superb, perfect	**превосходный**	[privasˈhɔdnɪj]
swarthy	**смуглый**	[ˈsmuglɪj]
sweet (in taste)	**сладкий**	[ˈslatkij]
tan	**загорелый**	[zagaˈrelɪj]
tasty	**вкусный**	[ˈfkʊsnɪj]
tender (affectionate)	**нежный**	[ˈneʒnɪj]
the highest	**высший**	[ˈvɪʃɪj]
the most important	**самый важный**	[ˈsamɪj ˈvaʒnɪj]
the nearest	**ближайший**	[bliˈʒajʃɪj]
the same, equal	**одинаковый**	[adiˈnakavɪj]
thick (e.g., ~ fog)	**густой**	[gʊsˈtɔj]

256

thick (wall, slice)	толстый	['tolstɪj]
tight (e.g., ~ shoes)	тесный	['tesnɪj]
tired (exhausted)	усталый	[us'talɪj]
tiring	утомительный	[uta'miteʎnɪj]
transparent	прозрачный	[praz'ratʃnɪj]
unique (exceptional)	уникальный	[uni'kaʎnɪj]
warm (moderately hot)	тёплый	['tɜplɪj]
wet (e.g., ~ clothes)	мокрый	['mɔkrɪj]
whole (entire, complete)	целый	['ʦelɪj]
wide (e.g., ~ road)	широкий	[ʃɪ'rɔkij]
young	молодой	[mala'dɔj]

MAIN 500 VERBS

252. Verbs A-C

to accompany (vt)	сопровождать	[saprava3'dat']
to accuse (vt)	обвинять	[abwi'ɲat']
to act (take action)	действовать	['dejstvavat']
to add (put together)	добавлять	[dabav'ʎat']
to address (speak to)	обращаться	[abra'ɕatsə]
to admire (vi)	восхищаться	[vashi'ɕatsə]
to advertise (vt)	рекламировать	[rikla'miravat']
to advise (give advice to)	советовать	[sa'wetavat']
to affirm (vt)	утверждать	[utwer3'dat']
to agree (say yes)	соглашаться	[sagla'ʃʌtsə]
to allow (sb to do sth)	позволять	[pazva'ʎat']
to amputate (vt)	ампутировать	[ampʊ'tiravat']
to anger (vt)	сердить	[sir'dit']
to answer (vi, vt)	отвечать	[atwe'ʨat']
to apologize (vi)	извиняться	[izwi'ɲatsə]
to appear (come into view)	появляться	[paiv'ʎatsə]
to applaud (vi, vt)	аплодировать	[apla'diravat']
to appoint (assign)	назначать	[nazna'ʨat']
to approach (come nearer)	подходить	[padha'dit']
to arrive (about train)	прибывать	[pribɪ'vat']
to ask (~ sb to do sth)	просить	[pra'sit']
to aspire (vi)	стремиться	[stri'mitsə]
to assist (help)	ассистировать	[asis'tiravat']
to attack (military)	атаковать	[ataka'vat']
to attain (objectives)	достигать	[dasti'gat']
to avenge (vt)	мстить	[mstit']
to avoid (danger, task)	избегать	[izbe'gat']
to award (give medal to)	наградить	[nagra'dit']
to bathe (~ one's baby)	купать	[kʊ'pat']
to battle (vi)	сражаться	[sra'3atsə]
to be (condition)	быть	[bɪt']
to be (constantly)	быть	[bɪt']
to be (on the table etc.)	лежать	[li'3at']
to be able to ...	мочь	[moʨ]

to be afraid (of …)	бояться	[ba'jatsə]
to be angry (with …)	сердиться	[sir'ditsə]
to be at war	воевать	[vai'vatʲ]
to be based (on …)	базироваться	[ba'ziravatsə]
to be bored	скучать	[sku'ʧatʲ]
to be convinced	убеждаться	[ubeʒ'datsə]
to be enough	хватать	[hva'tatʲ]
to be envious	завидовать	[za'widavatʲ]
to be in a hurry	торопиться	[tara'pitsə]
to be indignant	возмущаться	[vazmu'ɕatsə]
to be interested in …	интересоваться …	[interesa'vatsa]
to be needed	требоваться	['trebavatsə]
to be perplexed	недоумевать	[nidaume'vatʲ]
to be preserved	сохраниться	[sahra'nitsə]
to be required	требоваться	['trebavatsə]
to be surprised	удивляться	[udiv'ʎatsə]
to be worried	беспокоиться	[bispa'koitsə]
to beat (dog, person)	бить	[bitʲ]
to become (e.g., ~ old)	становиться	[stana'witsə]
to become pensive	задуматься	[za'dumatsə]
to behave (vi)	вести себя	[wis'ti se'bʲa]
to believe (think)	верить	['weritʲ]
to belong to …	принадлежать …	[prinadle'ʒatʲ]
to berth (moor)	причаливать	[pri'ʧalivatʲ]
to blind (of flash of light)	ослеплять	[aslep'ʎatʲ]
to blow (wind)	дуть	[dutʲ]
to blush (vi)	краснеть	[kras'netʲ]
to boast (vi)	хвастаться	['hvastatsə]
to borrow (money)	занимать	[zani'matʲ]
to break (branch, toy etc.)	ломать	[la'matʲ]
to breathe (vi)	дышать	[dɪ'ʃʌtʲ]
to bring sth	привозить	[priva'zitʲ]
to burn (paper, logs)	жечь	[ʒɛʧ]
to burst (vi)	разорваться	[razar'vatsə]
to buy (purchase)	покупать	[paku'patʲ]
to call (for help)	звать	[zvatʲ]
to call (with one's voice)	позвать	[paz'vatʲ]
to calm down (vt)	успокаивать	[uspa'kaivatʲ]
to cancel (call off)	отменить	[atme'nitʲ]
to cast off	отчаливать	[a'ʧalivatʲ]
to catch (e.g., ~ a ball)	ловить	[la'witʲ]
to catch sight (of …)	увидеть	[u'widetʲ]
to cause …	быть причиной …	[bɪtʲ pri'ʧinaj]
to change (~ one's opinion)	изменить	[izme'nitʲ]

| to change (exchange) | менять | [mi'nat^j] |
| to charm (please, delight) | очаровывать | [atʃe'rovıvat^j] |

to choose (select)	выбирать	[vıbi'rat^j]
to chop off (vt)	отрубить	[atru'bit^j]
to clean (from dirt)	чистить	['tʃistit^j]
to clean (shoes etc.)	очищать	[atʃi'ɕat^j]
to clean (tidy)	убирать	[ubi'rat^j]

to close (window, shop)	закрывать	[zakrı'vat^j]
to comb hair	причёсываться	[pri'tʃɔsıvatsə]
to come down (the stairs)	спускаться	[spus'katsə]
to come in (enter)	войти	[vaj'ti]
to come out (book)	выйти	['vıjti]

to compare (vt)	сравнивать	['sravnivat^j]
to compensate (vt)	компенсировать	[kampen'siravat^j]
to compete (vi)	конкурировать	[kanku'riravat^j]

to compile, to make (a list)	составлять	[sastav'ʎat^j]
to complain (vi, vt)	жаловаться	['ʒalavatsə]
to complicate (vt)	осложнить	[aslaʒ'nit^j]
to compose (music etc.)	сочинить	[satʃi'nit^j]

to compromise (vt)	компрометировать	[kamprame'tiravat^j]
to concentrate (vi)	концентрироваться	[kantsınt'riravatsə]
to confess (criminal)	признаваться	[prizna'vatsə]
to congratulate (vt)	поздравлять	[pazdrav'ʎat^j]
to consult (doctor, expert)	консультироваться с	[kansuʎ'tiravattsa c]
to continue (~ to do sth)	продолжать	[prada'ʒat^j]

to control (verify)	контролировать	[kantra'liravat^j]
to convince (vt)	убеждать	[ubeʒ'dat^j]
to cooperate (with)	сотрудничать	[sat'rudnitʃet^j]
to coordinate (vt)	координировать	[kaardi'niravat^j]
to correct (rectify)	исправлять	[isprav'ʎat^j]

to cost (vt)	стоить	['stoit^j]
to count (add up)	считать	[ɕi'tat^j]
to count on …	рассчитывать на …	[ra'ɕitıvat^j na]

to crack (ab. ceiling, wall)	трескаться	['treskatsə]
to create (vt)	создать	[saz'dat^j]
to cry (weep)	плакать	['plakat^j]
to cut off (vt)	отрезать	[at'rezat^j]

253. Verbs D-G

| to dare (e.g., ~ to do sth) | осмеливаться | [as'melivatsə] |
| to date from | датироваться | [da'tiravatsə] |

to deceive (vi, vt)	обманывать	[ab'manıvatʲ]
to decide (e.g., ~ to do sth)	решать	[ri'ʃʌtʲ]
to decorate (tree, street)	украшать	[ukra'ʃʌtʲ]
to dedicate (book etc.)	посвящать	[pɔswi'ɕatʲ]
to defend (a country etc.)	защищать	[zaɕi'ɕatʲ]
to defend oneself	защищаться	[zaɕi'ɕatsə]
to demand (request firmly)	требовать	['trebavatʲ]
to denounce (vt)	доносить	[dana'sitʲ]
to deny (declare untrue)	отрицать	[atri'tsatʲ]
to depend on ...	зависеть	[za'wisetʲ]
to deprive (vt)	лишать	[li'ʃʌtʲ]
to deserve (vt)	заслуживать	[zas'luʒıvatʲ]
to design (machine etc.)	проектировать	[praek'tiravatʲ]
to desire (want, wish)	желать	[ʒı'latʲ]
to despise (vt)	презирать	[prizi'ratʲ]
to destroy (documents etc)	уничтожать	[unitʃta'ʒatʲ]
to differ (from sth)	отличаться	[atli'tʃatsə]
to dig (tunnel etc.)	рыть	[rɪtʲ]
to direct (point the way)	направлять	[naprav'ʎatʲ]
to disappear (vi)	исчезнуть	[i'ɕeznutʲ]
to discover (new land etc.)	открывать	[atkrı'vatʲ]
to discuss (talk about)	обсуждать	[apsuʒ'datʲ]
to dismiss (from job)	освобождать	[asvabaʒ'datʲ]
to distribute (leaflets etc.)	распространять	[rasprastra'ɲatʲ]
to disturb (vt)	беспокоить	[bispa'kɔitʲ]
to dive (vi)	нырять	[nı'ratʲ]
to divide (math)	делить	[di'litʲ]
to do (vt)	делать	['delatʲ]
to do the laundry	стирать	[sti'ratʲ]
to double (increase)	удваивать	[ud'vaivatʲ]
to doubt (have doubts)	сомневаться	[samne'vatsə]
to draw a conclusion	делать заключение	[delatʲ zaklytʃenie]
to dream (daydream)	мечтать	[mitʃ'tatʲ]
to dream (in sleep)	видеть сны	['widetʲ snı]
to drink (vi, vt)	пить	[pitʲ]
to drive (a car)	вести машину	[wis'ti ma'ʃınu]
to drive sb away	прогнать	[prag'natʲ]
to drop (let fall)	ронять	[ra'ɲatʲ]
to drown (ab. person)	тонуть	[ta'nutʲ]
to dry (clothes, hair)	сушить	[su'ʃitʲ]
to eat (vi, vt)	кушать, есть	['kuʃʌtʲ], [estʲ]
to eavesdrop (vi)	подслушивать	[pats'luʃıvatʲ]
to emit (smell)	распространять	[rasprastra'ɲatʲ]

to enter (on list)	вписывать	[ˈfpisɪvatʲ]
to entertain (amuse)	развлекать	[razvleˈkatʲ]
to equip (fit out)	оборудовать	[abaˈrudavatʲ]
to examine (proposal)	рассмотреть	[rassmatˈretʲ]
to exchange sth	обмениваться	[abˈmenivatsə]
to exclude, to expel	исключать	[isklyˈʧatʲ]
to excuse (forgive)	извинять	[izwiˈɲatʲ]
to exist (vi)	существовать	[suɕestvaˈvatʲ]
to expect (anticipate)	ожидать	[aʒɪˈdatʲ]
to expect (foresee)	предвидеть	[pridˈwidetʲ]
to explain (vi, vt)	объяснять	[abʰesˈɲatʲ]
to express (vt)	выразить	[ˈvɪrazitʲ]
to extinguish (a fire)	тушить	[tuˈʃitʲ]
to fall in love (with …)	влюбиться	[vlyˈbitsə]
to feed (provide food)	кормить	[karˈmitʲ]
to feel (fear, regret)	чувствовать	[ˈʧustvavatʲ]
to fight (against the enemy)	бороться	[baˈrotsə]
to fight (vi)	драться	[ˈdratsə]
to fill (glass, bottle)	наполнять	[napalˈɲatʲ]
to find (~ lost items)	находить	[nahaˈditʲ]
to find out (make enquiries)	узнавать	[uznaˈvatʲ]
to finish (vt)	заканчивать	[zaˈkanʧivatʲ]
to fish (with a line)	ловить рыбу	[laˈwitʲ ˈrɪbu]
to fit (about dress etc.)	подходить	[padhaˈditʲ]
to flatter (vi, vt)	льстить	[ˈʎstitʲ]
to fly (bird, plane)	летать	[liˈtatʲ]
to follow … (come after)	следовать	[ˈsledavatʲ]
to forbid (not allow)	запрещать	[zapreˈɕatʲ]
to force (compel)	принуждать	[prinuʒˈdatʲ]
to forget (vi, vt)	забыть	[zaˈbɪtʲ]
to forgive (pardon)	прощать	[praˈɕatʲ]
to form (constitute)	образовывать	[abraˈzɔvɪvatʲ]
to get dirty (vi)	испачкаться	[isˈpaʧkatsə]
to get infected (with …)	заразиться	[zaraˈzitsə]
to get irritated	раздражаться	[razdraˈʒatsə]
to get married	жениться	[ʒɪˈnitsə]
to get rid of …	избавиться от …	[izˈbawitsa at]
to get tired	уставать	[ustaˈvatʲ]
to get up (arise from bed)	вставать	[fstaˈvatʲ]
to give a hug, to hug (vt)	обнимать	[abniˈmatʲ]
to give in (yield to)	уступать	[ustuˈpatʲ]
to go (by car, train etc.)	ехать	[ˈehatʲ]
to go (to walk)	идти	[itʲˈti]

to go for a swim	купаться	[kʊ'patsə]
to go out (for dinner etc.)	выйти	['vɪjti]
to go to bed	ложиться спать	[la'ʒitsa spatʲ]

to greet (vt)	приветствовать	[pri'wetstvavatʲ]
to grow (plants)	растить	[ras'titʲ]
to guarantee (assure)	гарантировать	[garan'tiravatʲ]
to guess right	отгадать	[atga'datʲ]

254. Verbs H-M

to hand out (distribute)	раздать	[raz'datʲ]
to hang (curtains etc.)	вешать	['weʃʌtʲ]
to have (vt)	иметь	[i'metʲ]

to have a try	попытаться	[papɪ'tatsə]
to have breakfast	завтракать	['zaftrakatʲ]
to have dinner	ужинать	['uʒɪnatʲ]
to have fun	веселиться	[wise'litsə]
to have lunch	обедать	[a'bedatʲ]

to head (group etc.)	возглавлять	[vazglav'ʎatʲ]
to hear (vi, vt)	слышать	['slɪʃʌtʲ]
to heat (vt)	нагревать	[nagre'vatʲ]
to help (assist, aid)	помогать	[pama'gatʲ]
to hide (e.g., ~ something)	прятать	['prʲatatʲ]

to hint (vi)	намекать	[name'katʲ]
to hire (e.g., ~ a boat)	нанимать	[nani'matʲ]
to hire (staff)	нанимать	[nani'matʲ]
to hope (vi, vt)	надеяться	[na'deitsə]
to hunt (for food, sport)	охотиться	[a'hotitsə]
to hurry sb	торопить	[tara'pitʲ]

to imagine (to picture)	представлять себе	[pritstav'ʎatʲ si'be]
to imitate (vt)	имитировать	[imi'tiravatʲ]
to implore (vt)	умолять	[uma'ʎatʲ]
to import (vt)	импортировать	[impar'tiravatʲ]
to increase (vi)	увеличиваться	[uwe'litʃivatsə]
to increase (vt)	увеличивать	[uwe'litʃivatʲ]

to infect (vt)	заражать	[zara'ʒatʲ]
to influence (vt)	влиять	[vli'jatʲ]
to inform (~ sb about ...)	сообщать	[saap'çatʲ]
to inform (vi, vt)	информировать	[infar'miravatʲ]
to inherit (property, right)	наследовать	[nas'ledavatʲ]

to insist (vi, vt)	настаивать	[nas'taivatʲ]
to inspire (vt)	воодушевлять	[vaaduʃəv'ʎatʲ]
to instruct (teach)	инструктировать	[instrʊk'tiravatʲ]

to insult (offend)	оскорблять	[askarb'ʎatʲ]
to interest (vt)	интересовать	[interesa'vatʲ]
to intervene (vi)	вмешиваться	['vmeʃivatsə]
to introduce (present)	знакомить	[zna'komitʲ]
to invent (machine etc.)	изобретать	[izabre'tatʲ]
to invite (ask to come)	приглашать	[prigla'ʃʌtʲ]
to iron (laundry)	гладить	['gladitʲ]
to irritate (annoy)	раздражать	[razdra'ʒatʲ]
to isolate (vt)	изолировать	[iza'liravatʲ]
to join (political party etc.)	присоединяться	[prisaedi'ɲatsə]
to joke (be kidding)	шутить	[ʃu'titʲ]
to keep (old letters etc.)	хранить	[hra'nitʲ]
to keep silent	молчать	[mal'tʃatʲ]
to kill (vt)	убивать	[ubi'vatʲ]
to knock (at the door)	стучать	[stu'tʃatʲ]
to know (sb)	знать	[znatʲ]
to know (sth)	знать	[znatʲ]
to laugh (at the joke)	смеяться	[smi'jatsə]
to launch (start up)	запускать	[zapus'katʲ]
to leave (abandon)	бросать	[bra'satʲ]
to leave (e.g., ~ for Mexico)	уезжать	[ui'zatʲ]
to leave (forget)	оставлять	[astav'ʎatʲ]
to liberate (vt)	освобождать	[asvabaʒ'datʲ]
to lie (be in lying position)	лежать	[li'ʒatʲ]
to lie (tell untruth)	врать	[vratʲ]
to light (e.g., a campfire)	зажечь	[za'ʒɛtʃ]
to light up (illuminate)	освещать	[aswe'ɕatʲ]
to like (e.g., I like ...)	нравиться	['nrawitsə]
to like (enjoy)	любить	[lʲy'bitʲ]
to limit (vt)	ограничивать	[agra'nitʃivatʲ]
to listen (vi)	слушать	['sluʃʌtʲ]
to live (e.g., ~ in France)	жить	[ʒitʲ]
to live (exist)	жить	[ʒitʲ]
to load (gun)	заряжать	[zari'ʒatʲ]
to load (vehicle etc.)	грузить	[gru'zitʲ]
to look (out of the window)	смотреть	[smat'retʲ]
to look for ... (search)	искать ...	[is'katʲ]
to look like (resemble)	быть похожим	[bitʲ pa'hoʒim]
to lose (umbrella etc.)	терять	[ti'rʲatʲ]
to love (sb)	любить	[lʲy'bitʲ]
to lower (blind, head)	опускать	[apus'katʲ]
to make (e.g., ~ dinner)	готовить	[ga'towitʲ]
to make a mistake	ошибаться	[aʃi'batsə]

to make copies	размножить	[razm'noʒitʲ]
to make easier	облегчить	[ablek'tʃitʲ]
to make use (of …)	пользоваться	['poʎzavatsə]

to manage (business)	руководить	[rukava'ditʲ]
to mark (make a mark)	отметить	[at'metitʲ]
to mean (signify)	значить	['znatʃitʲ]
to meet (get acquainted)	знакомиться	[zna'komitsə]
to memorize (vt)	запомнить	[za'pomnitʲ]
to mention (talk about)	упоминать	[upami'natʲ]

to miss (school etc.)	пропускать	[prapus'katʲ]
to mix (combine, blend)	смешивать	['smeʃivatʲ]
to mix up (confuse)	путать	['putatʲ]

to mock (deride)	насмехаться	[nasme'hatsə]
to move (wardrobe etc.)	передвигать	[piredwi'gatʲ]
to multiply (math)	умножать	[umna'ʒatʲ]
must	быть должным	[bɪtʲ 'doʒnɪm]

255. Verbs N-S

to name, to call (vt)	называть	[nazɪ'vatʲ]
to negotiate (vi)	вести переговоры	[wis'ti perega'vorɪ]
to note (write down)	пометить	[pa'metitʲ]
to notice (see)	замечать	[zame'tʃatʲ]

to obey (vi, vt)	подчиняться	[patʃi'ɲatsə]
to object (vi, vt)	возражать	[vazra'ʒatʲ]
to observe (see)	наблюдать	[nably'datʲ]
to offend (person)	обижать	[abi'ʒatʲ]
to omit (word, phrase)	опускать	[apus'katʲ]

to open (vt)	открывать	[atkrɪ'vatʲ]
to order (in restaurant)	заказывать	[za'kazɪvatʲ]
to order (military)	приказывать	[pri'kazɪvatʲ]

to organize (concert, party)	устраивать	[ust'raivatʲ]
to overestimate (vt)	переоценивать	[pirea'tsenivatʲ]
to own (possess)	владеть	[vla'detʲ]

to participate (vi)	участвовать	[u'tʃastvavatʲ]
to pass (go beyond)	проезжать	[prai'zatʲ]
to pay (vi, vt)	платить	[pla'titʲ]

to peep, spy on	подсматривать	[pats'matrivatʲ]
to penetrate (vi)	проникать	[prani'katʲ]
to permit (allow)	разрешать	[razre'ʃʌtʲ]
to pick (flowers)	рвать	[rvatʲ]
to place (put, set)	располагать	[raspala'gatʲ]

to plan (~ to do sth)	планировать	[plɑ'nirɑvatʲ]
to play (actor)	играть	[ig'ratʲ]
to play (children)	играть	[ig'ratʲ]
to point (e.g., ~ the way)	указать	[ukɑ'zatʲ]
to pour (liquid)	наливать	[nɑli'vatʲ]
to pray (vi, vt)	молиться	[mɑ'litsə]
to predominate (vi)	преобладать	[priɑblɑ'datʲ]
to prefer (like better)	предпочитать	[pritpɑtʃi'tatʲ]
to prepare (~ a plan)	подготовить	[pɑdgɑ'towitʲ]
to present (sb to sb)	представлять	[pritstav'ʎatʲ]
to preserve (peace, life)	сохранять	[sɑhrɑ'ɲatʲ]
to progress (move forward)	продвигаться	[prɑdwi'gatsə]
to promise (vt)	обещать	[abi'ɕatʲ]
to pronounce (say)	произносить	[praiznɑ'sitʲ]
to propose (vt)	предлагать	[pridlɑ'gatʲ]
to protect (e.g., ~ nature)	охранять	[ahrɑ'ɲatʲ]
to protest (vi)	протестовать	[pratestɑ'vatʲ]
to prove (vt)	доказывать	[dɑ'kazıvatʲ]
to provoke (vt)	провоцировать	[pravɑ'ʦıravatʲ]
to pull (e.g., ~ the rope)	тянуть	[ti'nutʲ]
to punish (vt)	наказывать	[nɑ'kazıvatʲ]
to push (e.g., ~ the door)	толкать	['tɔlkatʲ]
to put away (vt)	убирать	[ubi'ratʲ]
to put in (insert, include)	вставлять	[fstav'ʎatʲ]
to put in order	приводить в порядок	[priva'ditʲ f pa'rʲadak]
to put, to place	класть, положить	[klastʲ], [pala'ʒitʲ]
to quote (cite)	цитировать	[ʦı'tiravatʲ]
to reach (arrive at)	достигать	[dosti'gatʲ]
to read (vi, vt)	читать	[tʃi'tatʲ]
to realize (achieve)	осуществлять	[asuɕestv'ʎatʲ]
to recall (~ one's name)	вспоминать	[fspami'natʲ]
to recognize (admit)	признавать	[prizna'vatʲ]
to recognize (identify sb)	узнавать	[uzna'vatʲ]
to recommend (vt)	рекомендовать	[rikamenda'vatʲ]
to recover (~ from flu)	выздоравливать	[vızda'ravlivatʲ]
to redo (vt)	переделывать	[pire'delıvatʲ]
to reduce (speed etc.)	уменьшать	[umiɲ'ʃʌtʲ]
to refuse (~ sb)	отказывать	[at'kazıvatʲ]
to regret (be sorry)	сожалеть	[saʒi'letʲ]
to reinforce (position)	укреплять	[ukrip'ʎatʲ]
to remember (not forget)	помнить	['pɔmnitʲ]
to remind (vt)	напоминать	[napami'natʲ]
to remove (~ an obstacle)	устранять	[ustra'ɲatʲ]

to remove (e.g., ~ a stain)	удалять	[uda'ʎatʲ]
to rent (of a tenant)	снимать	[sni'matʲ]
to repair (mend)	исправлять	[isprav'ʎatʲ]
to repeat (say again)	повторять	[pafta'rʲatʲ]
to report (make a report)	докладывать	[dak'ladɪvatʲ]
to reproach (vt)	упрекать	[upre'katʲ]
to reserve, to book	бронировать	[bra'niravatʲ]
to restrain (hold back)	удерживать	[u'derʒɪvatʲ]
to return (come back)	возвращаться	[vazvra'ɕatsə]
to risk, to take a risk	рисковать	[riska'vatʲ]
to rub off (erase)	стереть	[sti'retʲ]
to run (move fast)	бежать	[bi'ʒatʲ]
to satisfy (please)	удовлетворять	[udavletva'rʲatʲ]
to save (rescue)	спасать	[spa'satʲ]
to say (e.g., ~ thank you)	сказать	[ska'zatʲ]
to scold (vt)	ругать	[rʊ'gatʲ]
to scratch (with claws)	царапать	[tsa'rapatʲ]
to select (to pick)	отобрать	[atab'ratʲ]
to sell (goods)	продавать	[prada'vatʲ]
to send (a letter)	отправлять	[atprav'ʎatʲ]
to send back (vt)	отправить обратно	[atp'rawitʲ ab'ratnə]
to sentence (vt)	приговаривать	[priga'varivatʲ]
to serve (in restaurant)	обслуживать	[aps'luʒɪvatʲ]
to settle (a conflict)	улаживать	[u'laʒɪvatʲ]
to shake (vt)	трясти	[tris'ti]
to shave (vi)	бриться	['britsə]
to shine (vi)	светиться	[swi'titsə]
to shoot (vi)	стрелять	[stri'ʎatʲ]
to shout (vi)	кричать	[kri'tʃatʲ]
to show (to display)	показывать	[pa'kazɪvatʲ]
to shudder (vi)	вздрагивать	['vzdragivatʲ]
to sigh (vi)	вздохнуть	[vzdah'nʊtʲ]
to sign (document)	подписывать	[pat'pisɪvatʲ]
to signify (mean)	означать	[azna'tʃatʲ]
to simplify (vt)	упрощать	[upra'ɕatʲ]
to sin (vi)	грешить	[gri'ʃitʲ]
to sit (be seated)	сидеть	[si'detʲ]
to smash (~ a bug)	раздавить	[razda'witʲ]
to smell (have odor)	пахнуть	['pahnʊtʲ]
to smell (sniff at)	нюхать	['nyhatʲ]
to smile (vi)	улыбаться	[ulɪ'batsə]
to solve (problem)	решить	[ri'ʃitʲ]
to sow (seed, crop)	сеять	['seitʲ]

to spill (liquid)	пролить	[pra'lit']
to spill out (vi, flour etc.)	просыпаться	[pra'sɪpatsə]
to spit (vi)	плевать	[pli'vat']

| to stand (toothache, cold) | терпеть | [tir'pet'] |
| to start (begin) | начинать | [natʃi'nat'] |

to steal (money, property)	красть	[krast']
to stop (cease)	прекращать	[prikra'ɕat']
to stop (for pause etc.)	останавливаться	[asta'navlivatsə]
to stop talking	замолчать	[zamal'tʃat']

to stroke (caress)	гладить	['gladit']
to study (vt)	изучать	[izu'tʃat']
to suffer (feel pain)	страдать	[stra'dat']

to support (cause, idea)	поддержать	[padder'ʒat']
to suppose (assume)	предполагать	[pritpala'gat']
to surface (ab. submarine)	всплывать	[fspli'vat']
to surprise (amaze)	удивлять	[udiv'ʎat']
to suspect (of wrongdoing)	подозревать	[padazre'vat']
to swim (vi)	плавать	['plavat']
to switch on (vt)	включать	[fkly'tʃat']

256. Verbs T-W

to take (get hold of)	брать	[brat']
to take a bath	мыться	['mɪtsə]
to take a rest	отдыхать	[addi'hat']
to take a seat	сесть	[sest']
to take aim (at the target)	целиться	['tselitsə]

to take away	уносить	[una'sit']
to take off (airplane)	взлетать	[vzle'tat']
to take off (remove)	снимать	[sni'mat']
to take pictures	фотографировать	[fatagra'firavat']

to talk to ...	говорить с ...	[gava'rit' s]
to teach (give lessons)	обучать	[abu'tʃat']
to tear off (vt)	оторвать	[atar'vat']
to tell (story, joke)	рассказывать	[ras'kazivat']

to thank (vt)	благодарить	[blagada'rit']
to think (believe)	считать	[ɕi'tat']
to think (vi, vt)	думать	['dumat']
to threaten (vt)	угрожать	[ugra'ʒat']
to throw (stone)	бросать	[bra'sat']

| to tie (~ sb to a tree) | привязывать | [pri'v'azivat'] |
| to tie up (prisoner) | связывать | ['sv'azivat'] |

to tire (exhaust)	**утомлять**	[utəm'ʎat']
to touch (one's arm etc.)	**касаться**	[ka'satsə]
to tower (over ...)	**возвышаться**	[vəzvɪ'ʃʌtsə]
to train (animals)	**дрессировать**	[drisira'vat']
to train (vi)	**тренироваться**	[trinira'vatsə]
to train sb	**тренировать**	[trinira'vat']
to transform (vt)	**трансформировать**	[transfar'mirəvat']
to translate (word, text)	**переводить**	[pireva'dit']
to treat (patient, illness)	**лечить**	[li'tʃit']
to tremble (with cold)	**дрожать**	[dra'ʒat']
to trust (vt)	**доверять**	[dawe'rʲat']
to try (attempt)	**пытаться**	[pɪ'tatsə]
to turn (change direction)	**поворачивать**	[pava'ratʃivat']
to turn away (vi)	**отворачиваться**	[atva'ratʃivatsə]
to turn off (the light)	**тушить**	[tʊ'ʃit']
to turn over (stone etc.)	**перевернуть**	[pirewer'nʊt']
to underestimate (vt)	**недооценивать**	[nidaa'tsenivat']
to underline (vt)	**подчеркнуть**	[patʃerk'nʊt']
to understand (vi, vt)	**понимать**	[pani'mat']
to undertake (vt)	**предпринимать**	[pritprini'mat']
to unite (join)	**объединять**	[abʰedi'ɲat']
to untie (vt)	**отвязывать**	[at'vʲazɪvat']
to use (phrase, word)	**употребить**	[upatre'bit']
to vaccinate (vt)	**делать прививки**	['delatʲ pri'wifki]
to vote (vi)	**голосовать**	[galasa'vat']
to wait (vi, vt)	**ждать**	[ʒdat']
to wake sb (vt)	**будить**	[bʊ'dit']
to want (wish, desire)	**хотеть**	[ha'tet']
to warn (of the danger)	**предупреждать**	[pridʊpreʒ'dat']
to wash (clean)	**мыть**	[mɪt']
to water (plants)	**поливать**	[pali'vat']
to wave (the hand)	**махать**	[ma'hat']
to weigh (have weight)	**весить**	['wesit']
to work (vi)	**работать**	[ra'botat']
to worry (make anxious)	**беспокоить**	[bispa'koit']
to worry (vi)	**волноваться**	[valna'vatsə]
to wrap (goods, parcel)	**заворачивать**	[zava'ratʃivat']
to wrestle (sport)	**бороться**	[ba'rotsə]
to write (letter etc.)	**писать**	[pi'sat']
to write down	**записывать**	[za'pisivat']

2803517R00144

Printed in Great Britain
by Amazon.co.uk, Ltd.,
Marston Gate.